LOST CITIES

FROM THE ANCIENT WORLD

WHITE STAR
PUBLISHERS

EDITED BY

MARIA TERESA GUAITOLI AND SIMONE RAMBALDI

Texts by

MARCO CERESA

ANTONELLA CORALINI

DAVIDE DOMENICI

MARIA TERESA GUAITOLI

ANTONELLA MEZZOLANI

CINZIA PIERUCCINI

MARCO PODINI

SIMONE RAMBALDI

RICCARDO VILLICICH

MARCO ZECCHI

Editorial project
VALERIA MANFERTO DE FABIANIS

Graphic design
CLARA ZANOTTI

Editorial coordination
LAURA ACCOMAZZO
LARA GIORCELLI

Graphic realization
MARIA CUCCHI

Translation
RICHARD PIERCE

© 2002 White Star S.r.l.
Via Candido Sassone, 22/24
13100 Vercelli, Italy
www.whitestar.it

ISBN 88-8095-827-5

Reprints:
1 2 3 4 5 6   06 05 04 03 02

Printed in Italy by G. Canale & C., Turin
Color separation by Chiaroscuro, Turin

CONTENTS

1 top Fresco from the House of the Vettii, Pompeii.

1 bottom Marble medallion from the Basilica of Septimius Severus, Leptis Magna.

2 Fresco from the House of the Vettii, Pompeii.

3 Fresco of a garden in House VI, 17-42, Pompeii.

4-5 The Forum in Rome.

6-7 The Temple of Karnak, Luxor.

8 top Dying Gaul, Rome.

8 bottom Statue of Artemis Ephesia, Sabratha.

9 Relief from the Temple of Angkor Wat.

CONTENTS

PREFACE
by Maria Teresa Guaitoli   PAGE 10

INTRODUCTION
by Maria Teresa Guaitoli and Simone Rambaldi   PAGE 20

EUROPE *INTRODUCTION*
by Marco Podini   PAGE 24
- KNOSSOS
  by Marco Podini   PAGE 28
- MYCENAE
  by Marco Podini   PAGE 40
- ATHENS
  by Marco Podini   PAGE 48
- ROME
  by Marco Podini   PAGE 62
- POMPEII
  by Antonella Coralini   PAGE 82

AFRICA *INTRODUCTION*
by Simone Rambaldi and Marco Zecchi   PAGE 98
- THEBES
  by Marco Zecchi   PAGE 102
- LEPTIS MAGNA
  by Simone Rambaldi   PAGE 112
- SABRATHA
  by Simone Rambaldi   PAGE 120
- THUGGA
  by Simone Rambaldi   PAGE 130
- VOLUBILIS
  by Simone Rambaldi   PAGE 138

MIDDLE EAST *INTRODUCTION*
by Antonella Mezzolani and Riccardo Villicich   PAGE 144
- UR
  by Antonella Mezzolani   PAGE 148
- NINEVEH
  by Antonella Mezzolani   PAGE 156
- BABYLON
  by Antonella Mezzolani   PAGE 164
- PERSEPOLIS
  by Antonella Mezzolani   PAGE 170
- EPHESUS
  by Riccardo Villicich   PAGE 182
- GERASA
  by Riccardo Villicich   PAGE 190

- PALMYRA
  by Riccardo Villicich   PAGE 196
- BAALBEK
  by Riccardo Villicich   PAGE 204

FAR EAST *INTRODUCTION*
by Marco Ceresa   PAGE 210
- HAMPI
  by Cinzia Pieruccini   PAGE 214
- ANGKOR
  by Marco Ceresa   PAGE 220
- PAGAN
  by Marco Ceresa   PAGE 232
- AYUTTHAYA
  by Marco Ceresa   PAGE 240

THE AMERICAS
INTRODUCTION
by Davide Domenici   PAGE 246
- TEOTIHUACÁN   PAGE 252
- PALENQUE   PAGE 262
- TIKAL   PAGE 274
- CHICHÉN ITZÁ   PAGE 282
- TIAHUANACO   PAGE 294
- CHAN CHAN   PAGE 300
- MACHU PICCHU   PAGE 306

INDEX   PAGE 314

BIBLIOGRAPHY   PAGE 317

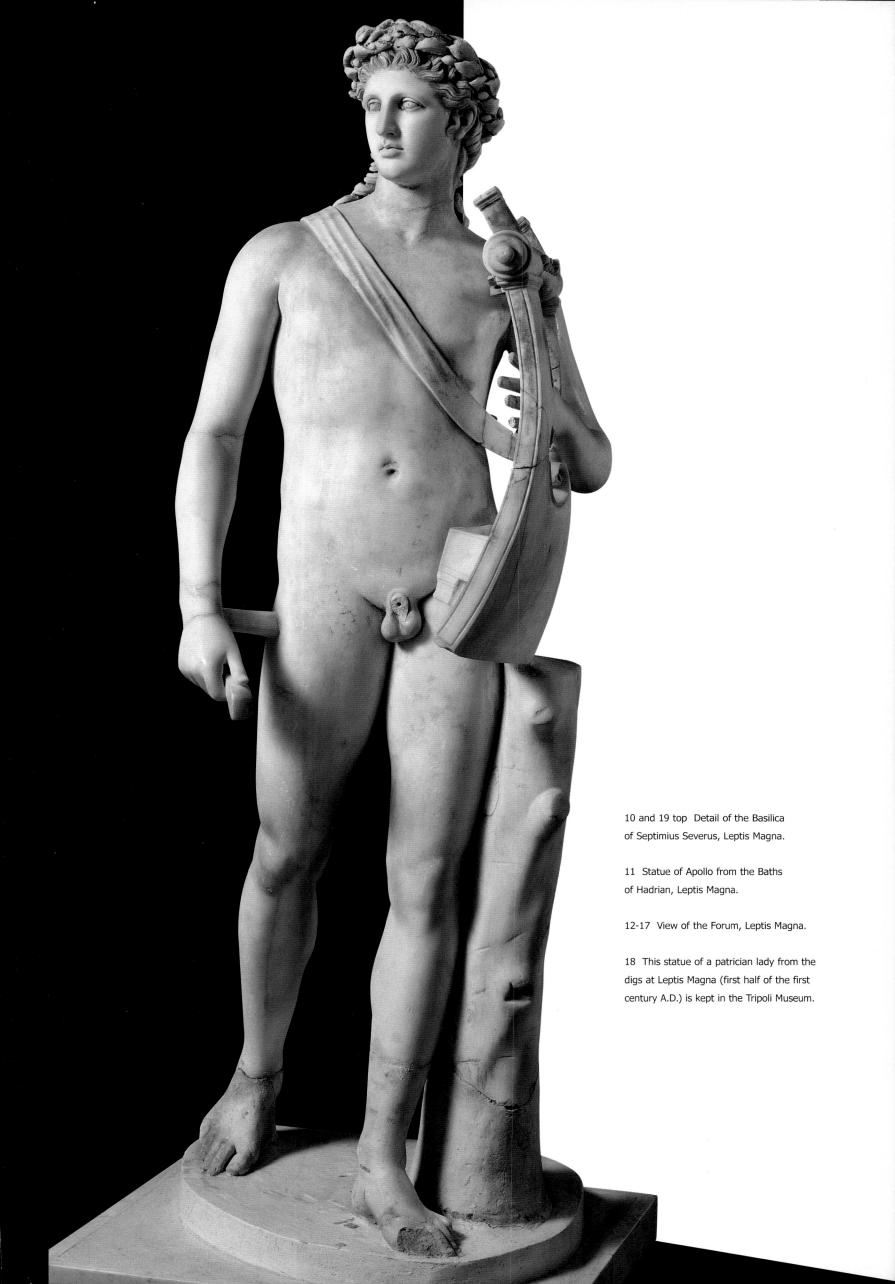

10 and 19 top Detail of the Basilica
of Septimius Severus, Leptis Magna.

11 Statue of Apollo from the Baths
of Hadrian, Leptis Magna.

12-17 View of the Forum, Leptis Magna.

18 This statue of a patrician lady from the
digs at Leptis Magna (first half of the first
century A.D.) is kept in the Tripoli Museum.

PREFACE

Both in the ancient and modern world, cities understood as urban communities have always been the characteristic feature of the societies that have produced them, an expression of the essence of their culture, ideology, and activities. Furthermore, despite the enormous and infinite variety of the phenomena known as cities, the fact that they have been inhabited (and often rebuilt) for such long periods, and the attempt to preserve their ancient ruins, manifest the desire to create a bond between past and present in order to perpetuate the heritage left by the great civilizations of antiquity. Thus, by means of an itinerary of what could be called the urban marvels of the ancient world, one can "visit" the urban fabric of the principal ancient metropolises and witness the historic processes that made them come alive.

This itinerary encompasses the main periods in both Western and Eastern civilization. In Europe this journey ranges from the centers of the Minoan and Mycenaean civilizations, Knossos and Mycenae – which automatically make us think of epic and heroic feats but which at the same time are the symbols of a certain type of pioneering archaeological research – to what are considered the two great "capitals" of antiquity: Athens, the mother of democracy and the prototype of ambitious town planning, and Rome, which perpetuated the Greek heritage (albeit with an original Latin spirit), promoting and spreading its culture throughout the ancient world. The Roman cities in North Africa, the Near East, and the Middle East complete the topic of urban development, which began in the more ancient cities of Mesopotamia and Egypt (magnificent Ur,

TEXT BY

MARIA TERESA GUAITOLI

Babylonia, Persepolis, Nineveh, and Thebes). Further on, a section is dedicated to the remains of the more distant civilizations of the Far East and the Americas, which generated complex cultures quite different from the Western ones yet likewise expressed their vision of the world through cities.

This itinerary is a combination of realities from different periods and areas that nonetheless have a common denominator: the monumentality of their urban configuration, which generally has been well preserved or is at least easily interpretable. In fact, the possibility to interpret the monuments and urban fabric was the criterion used in choosing these ancient cities instead of others that are equally famous but have left few traces of their former splendor, or which have been obliterated by contemporary developments. Furthermore, in the case of ancient Egypt the choice fell on only one city, Thebes, simply because there are few ruins of true cities available in Egypt, whereas this civilization has left behind an abundance of mortuary and religious architecture.

For that matter, the Greek historian Pausanias, already in the second century A.D., stated that in order for a settlement to be considered an urban community it had to have structures that manifested its civic function such as a theater, agora, and public buildings that bear witness to its political and judicial activities.

This book is divided into continental areas, each of which is represented by sites that were the characteristic hub of the political and social life of their respective periods and which, obviously, are cornerstones of human history.

INTRODUCTION

TEXT BY

MARIA TERESA GUAITOLI
AND SIMONE RAMBALDI

The phenomenon of urbanization is part and parcel of the modern world. The very concept grew out of the study of cities and their structure that followed on the heels of the population growth produced by the Industrial Revolution. This led to the idea of the city in the modern sense of the word: a metropolis or megalopolis linked to the needs of a new model of society. But leaving aside differences of an ideological nature, another revolution had generated an analogous phenomenon, the "urban revolution," which in eastern Mesopotamia between the fourth and fifth millennia B.C. marked the birth of the city and its spread throughout the ancient world, resulting in the formation of urban communities that met the changing economic and social needs of a cultural climate. The city is therefore to be understood as the hub and connective tissue of all the primary and secondary activities connected to it, which were re-elaborated and articulated there.

This functionalization of roles and necessities is often connected to the need to erect monumental centers and therefore to the birth of the true city. In fact, although differing according to the topographical and climatic conditions, the driving force behind the city is always a monumental complex (be it a sanctuary, as in the case of Thebes, or the palace in the Minoan and then the Mycenaean world) that is often sacred and that acts as the catalyst for the various activities that revolve around it. Around this cell, understood as the center of religious or political power, are the nuclei of those activities that help to foster the characteristic features of the city, including houses, workshops, storehouses, and necropoli. It is precisely the distribution, articulation, and functionalization of space that lends order to a stratified society that expresses itself from an architectural/urbanistic standpoint in the building programs that have

helped to immortalize the memory of certain ancient cities such as Athens and Rome and to confirm the continuity of residence that persists to this day.

However, in ancient times the city was also an indispensable tool for control of the territory under its dominion. It is for this reason, for example, that many cities were founded by Alexander the Great during his conquest of the known world. This phenomenon was most clearly manifested in the Roman world, where the city was always the key link between Rome and the regions it dominated. This had already become true in the Republican Age with the rise of the colonial system.

The cities that Rome had relations with could have been true cities in their own right with a long history and a fully developed urban layout that, once diplomatic relations were established, became *civitates foederatae* upon forging an alliance (*foedus*) with Rome that normally entailed providing military contingents. In exchange for this alliance, the Roman Republic intervened if these cities were in danger. However, they were free to maintain their own institutions and religions.

These pre-existing cities could also become colonies: either *coloniae Latinae*, basically independent cities whose citizens enjoyed certain privileges such as the right to trade and to marry Roman citizens, or *coloniae Romanae*, which were nuclei for full-fledged Roman citizens who settled in unstable or dangerous areas where a stronger military force was necessary. The latter were cities – located even in areas quite far from the mother country – that had Roman institutions and traditions. A separate category consisted of the *municipia*, cities that Rome had annexed, granting Roman citizenship to the inhabitants while leaving them a certain degree of autonomy. In fact, the *municipia* were governed by magistrates elected from among the local notables who

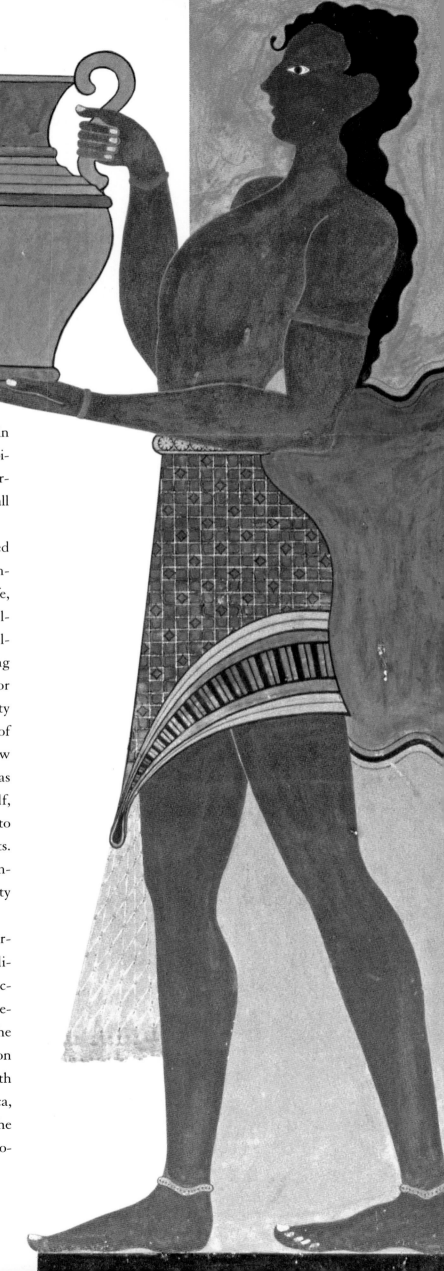

20 top Detail of the Basilica of Septimius Severus, Leptis Magna.

21 Figure of a bearer in the Palace of Knossos.

22-23 Relief showing bearers with offerings, Persepolis.

managed all aspects of city life except for judiciarl activity and, naturally, foreign policy, which remained the prerogative of the central power. When in A.D. 212 Caracalla granted full citizenship to all the inhabitants of the Roman Empire, the above-mentioned differences in local status and statutes were superseded because all the cities automatically became *municipia*.

However, Roman urbanism must not be interpreted solely as a political phenomenon. The need to superimpose a new culture and style of public and private life, even its most everyday aspects, certainly required a well-planned organization of urban space. However, this almost never entailed the destruction of already existing urban structures, but rather the central government (or the local authorities, who could finance building activity with loyalist or patronage aims) enhanced the potential of the city and in a certain sense "modernized" it. The new civic and religious structures were not justified only as places where the political authority could establish itself, but were also considered of fundamental importance to the pursuit of public life in a Roman city in all respects. Not only temples and *curias*, but baths, theaters, amphitheaters, and circuses became an integral part of city life during the Imperial Age.

Therefore, the phenomena of urbanization are differentiated in relationship to the gamut of territorial, climatic, and strategic conditions of the individual sites, factors that also influenced the individual town planning decisions as well as the building techniques utilized for the different projects. But despite the fact that urbanization occurs in worlds that are distant from one another both spatially and culturally, from the Eurasian bloc to Africa, the Americas, and the Far East, it always reflects the needs that crop up every time there is a change in the social fabric.

EUROPE

ROME●
POMPEII●

ATHENS
●
MYCENAE

KNOSSOS

THE CITIES OF ANCIENT EUROPE: DIFFERENCES BETWEEN THE WESTERN AND EASTERN MEDITERRANEAN

TEXT BY

MARCO PODINI

Any discussion of present-day Europe, especially considering the recent establishment of a common European currency, only serves to underscore the contrast that arises between what we now mean by and perceive as "Europe" and the chaotic political, social, and cultural history of the first civilizations on this continent. This is a question of important differences that persisted even during the Roman Empire, so much so that the constant opposition between East and West obstructed total cultural cohesion in Europe.

The first European civilization, the Minoan, rose up in Crete after populations from northwestern Anatolia moved there more or less at the beginning of the Bronze Age (2800 B.C.). The Cretans' most important cultural and commercial relations were with Egypt and Syria, and the same was true of the Mycenaeans, who around the mid-fifteenth century B.C. "replaced" the Minoan civilization, extending trade relations to include the coasts of Sicily, Sardinia, and North Africa. Thus, there were close cultural affinities between Greece and the East, even after the long period of economic crisis that struck the Mediterranean basin from the twelfth to the eighth century B.C. But it is also in this context that, from the eighth to the seventh century B.C., the political and social

EUROPE

foundations were laid for the spread of Greek colonies both eastward, embracing the Chalcidian peninsula and the Black Sea, and to the west, toward the coasts of Sicily and southern Italy and as far as Gaul (with the city of Massalia, present-day Marseille, founded by the Phocaeans) and Spain (the port of Emporion). This colonial phenomenon was based on the creation of self-sufficient urban communities that were not part of a policy of conquest of the territories involved, which is the reason why these cities rarely came into conflict with the indigenous civilizations. The Greek colonies were founded only on the coastlines and the immediate hinterland: the process of expansion therefore stopped wherever the local populations occupied vast territories, as in the case of the Etruscans, Latins, Osci, Messapians, Siculi, Sicani, etc. In a later period, the colonies were gradually absorbed by the indigenous civilizations, not without important consequences, especially with regard to the spread of a new urban culture. However, the cultural difference between the Greeks from the central Mediterranean and the indigenous peoples of the West was (and remained) considerable, even between the most evolved populations.

For example, despite the fact that the Etruscans had very close relations with the Eastern world during an earlier stage (from the end of the eighth century and through the entire seventh century B.C., in the so-called orientalizing period) and with the Greek world later on (during the archaic and classical periods), they followed their own path, maintaining substantial religious, political, and social differences.

Likewise, the Romans reacted in an autonomous manner to the "European" cultural scene, continuing with their own traditions but also receptive to new customs from the East, in an ongoing dialectical relationship between respect for their own customs and the assimilation of Greek-Hellenistic life styles and urban models, the latter stance arousing a strong reaction on the part of the more conservative sections of Roman society. It was this continuous relationship between consideration for one's own past and receptiveness to new, attractive stimuli that produced the most original contributions in the field of architecture and town planning in the Latin world, first and foremost the whole-hearted adoption of Hippodamus' geometric layout of new cities and its "reproduction" in the field of agriculture by means of centuriation.

However, the configuration of the Roman Empire was an acknowledgment of the contrasts and differences between the Eastern and Western worlds, which was manifested lin-

27 top Mosaic depicting a Circus
charioteer (Museo delle Terme,
Rome).

guistically as well: the language spoken in Greece and the lands formerly occupied by Hellenistic rulers was Greek, while Latin was the official language in the West. Rome was well aware that in the East it had to contend with a reality that was culturally superior (or at least equal), while in the West it dealt mostly with people who, leaving aside their potential, were markedly inferior. Therefore, the Western world was the ideal place to establish and impose predetermined urban models in order to create solid political, social, and cultural unity.

The aim of this section given over to Europe is, obviously, not to provide a complete description of the civilizations that occupied this continent in ancient times (which is an absurd objective, to say the least), but rather to offer an idea of how heterogeneous and variegated were the cultures and populations that interacted, on different levels, in Europe. The cases under consideration in this book are significant examples of the major cultural realities in certain chronological periods. As stated, the first European civilization was the Minoan, whose most representative city was without doubt Knossos. And, it was no coincidence that Knossos was chosen as the capital of Crete after the rise of the Mycenaeans – a Greek-speaking population of Indo-European origin whose name derives from the city that best expressed their power and character, Mycenae. Athens was also founded in the context of Mycenaean culture and tradition, and this great city did not fail to assert its Achaean origins as an expression of its "Greekness." It dominated the political and commercial scene of the central Mediterranean until the fourth century B.C., and until the late Roman age remained a cultural landmark and beacon.

It was then the Roman empire that embraced a complex of heterogeneous elements and became the leading cultural center in the West. The urbanization of the Western world, which still lacked an urban culture, was the most significant contribution of Roman rule to these regions. Naturally, this does not apply to the numerous cities that had already come into contact with Greek culture. The Oscan city of Pompeii, partly thanks to its extraordinarily fine state of preservation, is an extremely evident manifestation of the link with the Hellenic-Hellenistic world that became closer and closer from the second century B.C. on. Whereas the case of Italica, the Roman colony in Spain in its two-fold role as ancient and new city, is an important example of the transmission/imposition of an urban model that was also subject to the direct intervention of the emperor, in accordance with specific ideological and representational needs.

28 TOP IN THIS PHOTOGRAPH TAKEN AROUND 1905 ONE CAN RECOGNIZE DOLL, ONE OF THE MEMBERS OF SIR ARTHUR EVANS' MISSION, SUPERVISING THE PLACEMENT OF A HEAVY BLOCK OF STONE FROM THE GREAT STAIRCASE.

28 BOTTOM THE POLYCHROME MOTIF OF SQUATTING GRIFFONS AMONG LILIES IS REPEATED OVER THE ENTIRE PERIMETER OF THE THRONE ROOM, LENDING BOTH MAJESTY AND DYNAMIC MOVEMENT TO THE TOTAL EFFECT.

29 TOP LEFT THE THRONE ROOM SEEN FROM THE WEST, IN A PHOTOGRAPH TAKEN IN 1900. FRAGMENTS OF THE ORIGINAL FRESCOES WERE STILL PRESENT ON EITHER SIDE OF THE THRONE. AT RIGHT, ABOVE, ONE CAN MAKE OUT THE PROFILE OF SIR ARTHUR EVANS.

KNOSSOS

29 TOP RIGHT THE RESTORATION WORK EFFECTED BY EVANS SHOWS THAT THE ONLY ELEMENT THAT REMAINED TOTALLY INTACT WAS THE THRONE ITSELF, WHILE THE REST HAD COLLAPSED. THE PICTURE ALSO SHOWS THAT THE RESTORATION WAS RATHER HEAVY-HANDED.

29 BOTTOM SIR ARTHUR EVANS (LEFT) WITH HIS ASSISTANTS, THE ARCHITECT THEODORE FYFE (MIDDLE) AND DUNCAN MACKENZIE (RIGHT). CONSIDERING THAT ARCHAEOLOGY WAS A NEW SCIENCE AT THE TIME, THE WORK DONE BY EVANS' TEAM WAS A NOTEWORTHY CONTRIBUTION TO THE EXCAVATION OF THE COMPLEX.

Text by MARCO PODINI

The ruins of ancient Knossos are the most significant manifestation of the development of town planning, architecture, and art in the first European civilization, which Sir Arthur Evans called Minoan, after the legendary king Minos. The origins of this city are inextricably connected to the legend of this king, the son of Zeus who according to literary tradition civilized the inhabitants of Crete, whom he ruled wisely and justly, establishing laws and laying the foundations for Cretan naval supremacy in the Aegean by building its first fleet. Minos is associated with the legend of the Minotaur, the

KNOSSOS

monster born of the unnatural passion of the king's wife Pasiphae for a bull. The king, ashamed of this creature with a human body and bull's head, ordered Daedalus to build a huge palace (the famous labyrinth) where the monster could be confined. Every year (or perhaps every three or nine years) seven youths and seven maidens from Athens were sacrificed to the Minotaur as an offer-

ing, since that city had been responsible for the death of one of Minos' sons. Theseus managed to kill the Minotaur and, with Adriane's help, to make his way out of the labyrinth.

The geographical position of Crete, a crossroad of major trade routes between Europe, Asia, and Africa, led to the rise, in the late third millennium B.C., of strong economic and political centers which thanks to commerce and trade prospered and became true cities in which power was wielded from impressive, luxurious palaces. Among these, Knossos played a leading role.

There had been human settlements on the island since 6500 B.C., but only in the late Neolithic Period (4750-3000 B.C.) did it become demographically and cul-

30 left The portico-veranda of the Palace at Knossos lies at the north entrance. Inside, on the wall behind the colonnade, is a fresco of a bull.

30 center This fresco, which decorated the *propylaea* of the Palace of Knossos, portrays a cupbearer. Two Dutch painters who worked with Evans did the restoration. However, their work has been criticized, above all because it seems to have been strongly influenced by the Art Nouveau style that prevailed in that period.

30 right In this sacred precinct, the so-called Pillared Crypts, the Serpent Goddess was worshipped.

30-31 The cement elements, the repainting of the original frescoes, the rebuilding and raising of the structures, which is quite evident in the palace *propylaea*, manifest the rather forced nature of the restoration work done by Sir Arthur Evans in the 1920s.

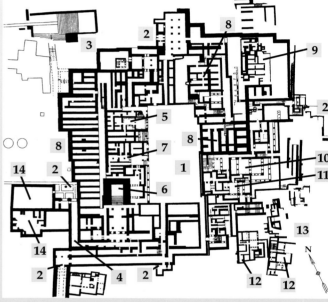

1) LARGE CENTRAL COURTYARD
2) ENTRANCES AND ATRIA
3) STAIRWAY AND THEATER AREA
4) PROCESSION CORRIDOR
5) THRONE ROOM
6) GREAT STAIRCASE
7) CRYPTS AND PILLARS
8) STOREROOMS
9) ARTISANS' QUARTER
10) HALL OF THE DOUBLE AXES
11) QUEEN'S MEGARON
12) HOUSES CONTEMPORARY WITH PALACE
13) STRUCTURES BUILT BEFORE PALACE
14) STRUCTURES BUILT AFTER PALACE

32-33 This axonometric projection shows what the Palace of Knossos must have looked like around 400 B.C.

33 The libation vase in the shape of a bull's head is one of the most famous artefacts found at Knossos.

KNOSSOS

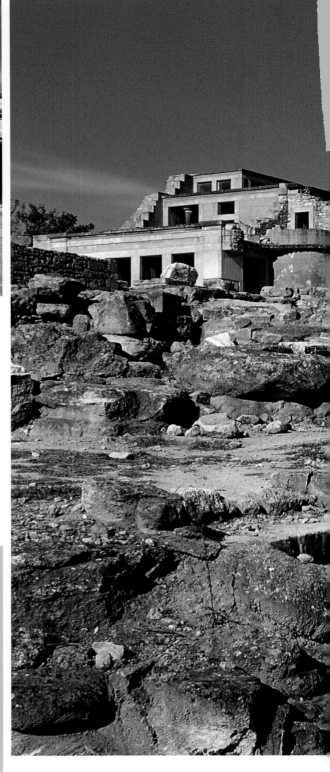

34 top left In the east wing of the Palace is the vestibule of the Hall of the Double Axes, here seen from the outside.

34 top right This partial reconstruction illustrates–inside the Palace–a shaft of light between the South Propylaeum and the Procession Corridor.

34 bottom This lively naturalistic fresco dates from the early fourteenth century B.C. and depicts a marine scene with fish and dolphins. It decorates the upper wall of the Queen's Megaron, in the southeast sector of the Palace.

34-35 View of the northern area of the palace complex near the north entrance. In the distance, the portico-veranda can be seen to the east; at right are the remains of the large Hypostyle Hall that lent monumentality to the complex.

KNOSSOS

turally uniform. However, the people scholars recognize as true Minoans belonged to populations that in the early Bronze Age (2800 B.C.) arrived in Crete from the coasts of northwestern Anatolia and merged with the pre-existent Neolithic Cretan civilization. The arrival of the new immigrants led to major transformations that drastically changed the social, cultural, and economic order of the power centers. The development of agriculture, concentrated in the region around Knossos, was so efficient that it produced much more than the islanders needed. Consequently the products of the land were

traded for raw materials that were lacking in Crete. Such trade was carried out mostly with the populations on the Syrian-Palestinian and Egyptian coasts, with Crete often serving as an intermediary between these civilizations. Through the importation of metal, the Minoans learned metallurgy and stone cutting, which led to the development of totally self-sufficient local handicrafts characterized by a highly original creativity. These changes went hand in hand with a considerable growth in population, which in turn led to an enlargement of Knossos and the other major cities, the founding of new cities, and a new,

complex, and stratified society.

This phenomenon was due to the emergence of charismatic individuals, the descendants of those who first ventured into commercial activity, becoming wealthy and indispensable members of the community who thereby enjoyed a higher social status. These new rulers were inclined to enjoy their power in impressive palaces. Thus, at Knossos in the latter part of the third millennium B.C., large architectural structures with different economic, religious, political, and administrative functions (residential and civic quarters, warehouses, and sacred areas) were merged into a single entity under the supervision of the prince. The plan of the first palace of this kind is relative-

ly unknown. Only a few structures and a couple of rooms, as well as the present west façade of the palace (built in the twentieth century B.C.), can be connected to it with any certainty. However, it seems plausible that the layout of the architectural nuclei, at first separate and later incorporated into a single complex around a large central courtyard, dates from the "proto-palace" period. The reconstruction of the first palace is also problematic because of the frequent restoration and remodeling projects carried out in three different centuries up to 1700 B.C. when a violent earthquake razed the whole edifice to the ground (it also destroyed other towns such as Mallia, Phaistos, and Zakro).

36-37 The Throne Room is in the northwest wing of the Palace. The frescoes inside, dating from the fifteenth-fourteenth century B.C., represent griffons that alternate with plant motifs. In the middle is the throne after which this chamber was named.

KNOSSOS

37 top The loggias in the west wing, seen here from the north, give access to the Throne Room, while a broad stairway in the back leads to the upper floors.

37 center The architectural structure in the middle of this courtyard of the royal palace has a light shaft that highlights the colors of the frescoes on the sides of the court.

37 bottom left This fresco depicts the so-called Ladies in Blue, three women watching a ceremony, and dates from the second half of the fifteenth century B.C. Leaving aside the rather showy elements of the modern restoration, mention must be made of the attention paid to the ornamental details (such as the hairstyle, the jewels, and the embroidery work).

37 bottom right This fresco known as the Prince of Lilies dates from the fifteenth century B.C. and probably portrays a priestess during a sacred rite. Like the other wall paintings found at Knossos, this work is now in the Archaeological Museum of Heraklion.

These palaces were immediately rebuilt after the cataclysm, so that there was no break between the end of the proto-palace and "neo-palace" periods. The Egyptians' conquest of the entire Syrian coast further consolidated the role of the Minoans as intermediaries between Egypt and the populations of that coastline.

The prosperity enjoyed in this period allowed for the construction of an immense palace at Knossos, whose impressive ruins were brought to light from 1900 on by the English archaeologist Evans. It had been built on a low hill, the various levels of which were exploited so that the edifice was articulated on several floors (at least two in the west wing and four along the east one), around a large central courtyard on an almost perfect North-South axis. The complexity of the inner plan seems to echo the legend of the labyrinth. The palace had several entrances, all of which converged toward the central courtyard by way of monumental corridors. The western one still has a frescoed portion depicting a series of gift bearers in two superposed rows (the so-called Procession Corridor). The northern entrance led to a road which, further west, intersected with a stepped complex that was perhaps used for theater performances. Although it is still unclear what many halls and rooms were used for, archaeologists have plausible theories concerning the function of some sections of the palace. The western wing in particular is distinguished by its reception rooms (the "Throne Room," the large corridors, and the monumental staircases that led to the main floors, which no longer exist) and its sanctuaries (the complex of small rooms known as "Pillared Crypts," where the Serpent Goddess was worshipped). Thus this section of the palace clearly had a public and religious function. Again in this wing, along a corridor on a North-South axis, there were the storerooms, also found in the northeastern part of the palace together with a large handicrafts zone. These two sections were therefore used for production and storage (as demonstrated by the presence of large jars used for foodstuffs). The residential quarters

lay in the southeastern wing of the palace. A large staircase, flanked by a light well, descended for four flights to the private apartments. For their layout, painting decoration, and building technique, the most interesting of the chambers are the "Hall of the Double Axes," which may have been a private chapel, and the "Queen's Megaron," a luxurious apartment with baths and a water drain.

The inhabited area of Knossos has yielded few ruins; in fact, it has not yet been determined whether it was a sin-

gle city or a conglomeration of villages. Most of the houses found date from the "neo-palace" period. Their different sizes suggest a complex social stratification. The smallest ones must have belonged to the lower middle and middle classes. Others, larger and more elaborate, have been interpreted as annexes of the palace, which may have served as residences for court officials. It has been estimated that, at its peak the city, including the port and prince's residence, boasted a population of 100,000.

In 1450 B.C., when the Minoans were going through a crucial period, Greek-speaking populations from the Mycenae conquered Crete and destroyed the palaces. However, the island's role remained the same even under Mycenean domination. The city of Knossos became the new king's seat, but it was then destroyed in 1370 B.C. by the Myceneans themselves from the Peloponnesus. This date marked the definitive disappearance of the legendary city of Knossos from the Mediterranean scene.

38-39 top This painting (fifteenth century B.C.) depicts a *taurokathapsia* in the Palace of Knossus. The bull, a sacred animal in Minoan civilization, played a part in this spectacular sport in which acrobats grasped its horns and executed extraordinary somersaults.

38-39 bottom A fragment of a reconstructed fresco that is part of the decoration of the so-called Caravanserai Pavilion in the Palace of Minos. It represents a series of birds, including partridges and hoopoes, which are rendered with an obvious preference for colors combined with fresh, lively realism.

40 TOP THE LION GATE IN A PHOTOGRAPH TAKEN DURING THE FIRST EXCAVATIONS AT MYCENAE.

40-41 TOP INSIDE THE GRAVE CIRCLE A AREA ARCHAEOLOGISTS FOUND THE TOMBS OF THREE KINGS WHO HAD LIVED IN THE FIRST PALACE.

40-41 BOTTOM THIS DECORATIVE ELEMENT DECORATED THE BLADE OF A BRONZE KNIFE WITH DAMASCENED GOLD.

41 TOP AND CENTER THE TWO DRAWINGS SHOW THE ACROPOLIS, IN SCHLIEMANN'S EXCAVATION PLAN (ABOVE) AND IN A TOPOGRAPHICAL VIEW OF THE TOMBS IN THE AGORA (BELOW).

41 BOTTOM HEINRICH SCHLIEMANN, ALREADY FAMOUS FOR HIS EXCAVATION CAMPAIGNS AT TROY, ALSO FOUND SPLENDID TREASURES AT MYCENAE. THE MOST NOTEWORTHY ASPECT OF HIS DISCOVERIES WAS THAT HE DOCUMENTED THE EXISTENCE OF THE PRE-HELLENIC CIVILIZATION.

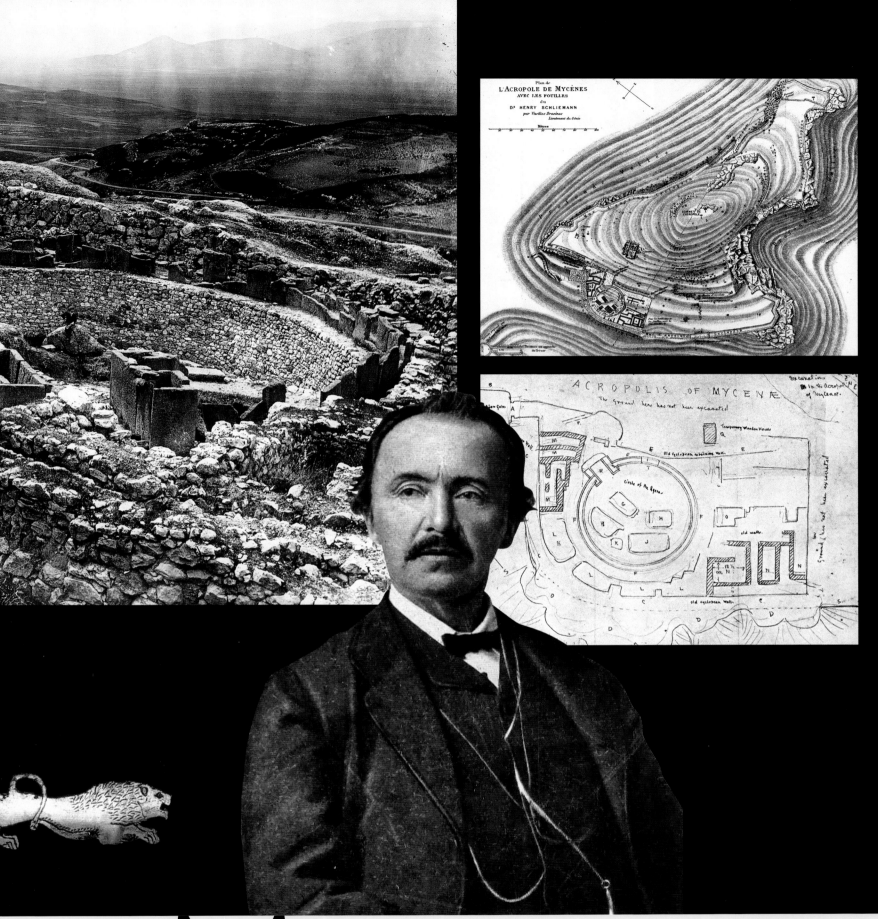

MYCENAE

MYCENAE

Text by MARCO PODINI

In marking out an itinerary from Corinth to Argos, Pausanias, in his *Description of Greece*, describes the ruins of Mycenae as a complex of structures – including the walls built by Cyclops, heroes' tombs, and underground caves – with treasures that can be seen once travelers descend from the Treto Pass toward the Argive Plain. Still recognizable, thanks to this ancient Greek geographer whose aim was to keep alive the memory of the heritage of "Greek" culture as bequeathed to him by his ancestors, these impressive ruins bear witness to the important role once played by this city. It was no accident that it is linked with the epic deeds and to the felicitous excavations of Schliemann who, after his sensational discovery of Troy, continued to follow Pausanias' descrip-

42-43 The Citadel of Mycenae stretches along the slopes of Haghios Elias Hill. Below are the massive city walls with polygonal and square blocks of stone, while the Palace is featured above.

43 top This large stairway, which has a well at the bottom, gave access to the walkway along the walls.

43 bottom left The structural similarity between the Lion Gate, the exterior of which is seen here, and the access to the so-called Treasury of Atreas has led scholars to believe that both works were built by the same dynasty. The gate, consisting of four huge blocks, probably had two wings and still supports the famous relief described by Pausanias. The threshold has furrows for the chariots' wheels as well as two grooves for draft animals.

tion to find Mycenae and Tiryns where they once lay in the wake of Agamemnon and Menalaus' return voyage from Troy. Although archaeological documentation has provided proof of human settlements from the Neolithic Era, the site was permanently occupied only from the Ancient Helladic period (3000-2100 B.C.) on. Between the late sixteenth and early fifteenth centuries B.C., Mycenae began to emerge as a political and economic power (Mycenaean pottery has been found on the coasts of Sicily, Sardinia, North Africa, and Syria). This transformation, which necessarily also modified the economic and social status of the city, must be considered the basis of its urban development, which reached its apex in the Late Helladic IIIA-IIIB Period (1400-1200 B.C.). Despite the catastrophes that struck the palatial structures in the

thirteenth century B.C., the political and commercial decline of Mycenae (marked by significant episodes of destruction) became definitive only in the following century. The long period of crisis and economic recession that lasted from 1200 to 800 B.C. involved most of the Mediterranean, but did not lead to the abandonment of the city, which actually continued to be inhabited up to the Roman age. Important structures dating from various periods from the Archaic to the Hellenistic are proof

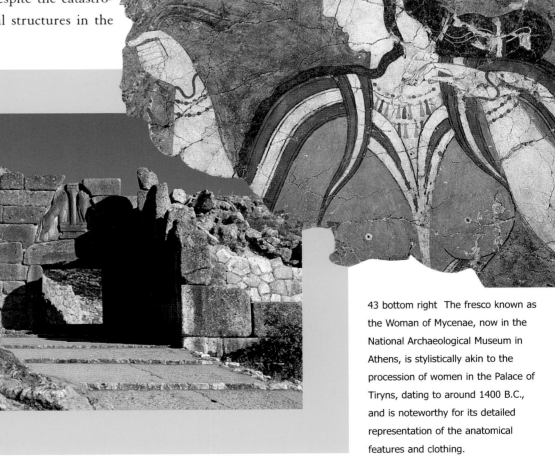

43 bottom right The fresco known as the Woman of Mycenae, now in the National Archaeological Museum in Athens, is stylistically akin to the procession of women in the Palace of Tiryns, dating to around 1400 B.C., and is noteworthy for its detailed representation of the anatomical features and clothing.

of this continuity, as are the few existing references in literary sources.

Mycenae was built on the top of a small rocky ridge with a massive wall that is still in a good state of preservation, with the exception of the southern side. The fortification system was made more efficient by the presence of steep rises both north and south of the city. Archaeological finds discovered near the wall have brought to light three building stages from the mid-fourteenth to the late thirteenth century B.C. Around 1250 B.C. the most important fortification works were carried out, including the southeastern tower, the monumental northern access way, and the famous gate "surmounted by lions" as Pausanias calls it, known as the Lion Gate, with the two sculpted animals in a heraldic pose on either side of a thin column, on a triangular slab placed directly

over the architrave. These structures are so impressive that ancient literary tradition attributed them to the Cyclops.

By carefully looking at a map of the city one will note the "bipolar" nature of its town plan. On the one hand, around the wall from the inner side, are different structures with various functions: residential, productive, commercial, and religious. On the other side, in the middle of the acropolis, the imposing palace stands out for its size and architectural complexity. This structure had two building phases, the first of which (about which almost nothing is known) must have been the residence of the monarchs buried in Grave Circle A, a large funerary area enclosed for religious reasons in a circular wall where, according to Pausanias, the tombs of Agamemnon and Cassandra lay. The second phase led to the demolition of the

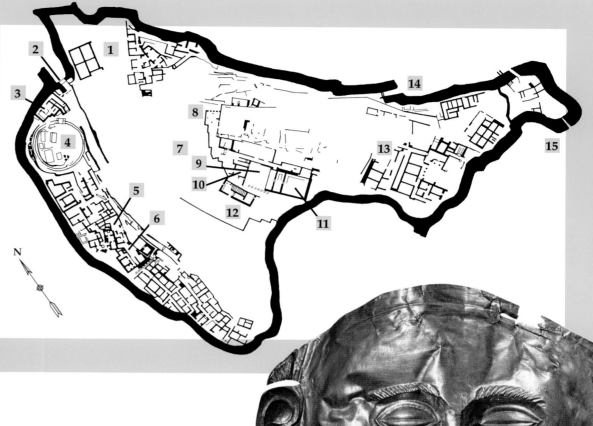

1) WAREHOUSES IN THE
   NORTHWEST SECTOR
2) LION GATE
3) GRANARY
4) GRAVE CIRCLE A
5) HOUSE OF THE CITADEL
6) TSOUNTAS HOUSE
7) PALACE
8) NORTHWEST ENTRANCE
9) GREAT COURT
10) GUESTS' APARTMENT
11) MEGARON
12) GREAT STAIRWAY
13) ARTISANS' WORKSHOP
14) MONUMENTAL NORTH
    ACCESS WAY
15) SOUTH TOWER

44-45 In Grave Circle A, seen here from inside the city, Schliemann found five of the six pit tombs, which yielded important Mycenean art objects and handicraft work such as gold masks, swords, knives, stelae, and other items.

45 top The so-called Mask of Agamemnon is one of the gold casts that covered the face of one of the Mycenaean rulers buried in Tomb V of Grave Circle A.

45 bottom left The Tholos of Aegisthus is, along with the Treasury of Atreus, one of the nine examples of monumental *tholos* tombs with a *dromos* and an inner chamber with a false vault.

45 bottom right The *tholos* tomb, or as Schliemann called it, the Treasury of Atreus, is a large burial chamber with an ogival dome and false vault, the entrance of which is preceded by a monumental passage, or *dromos*.

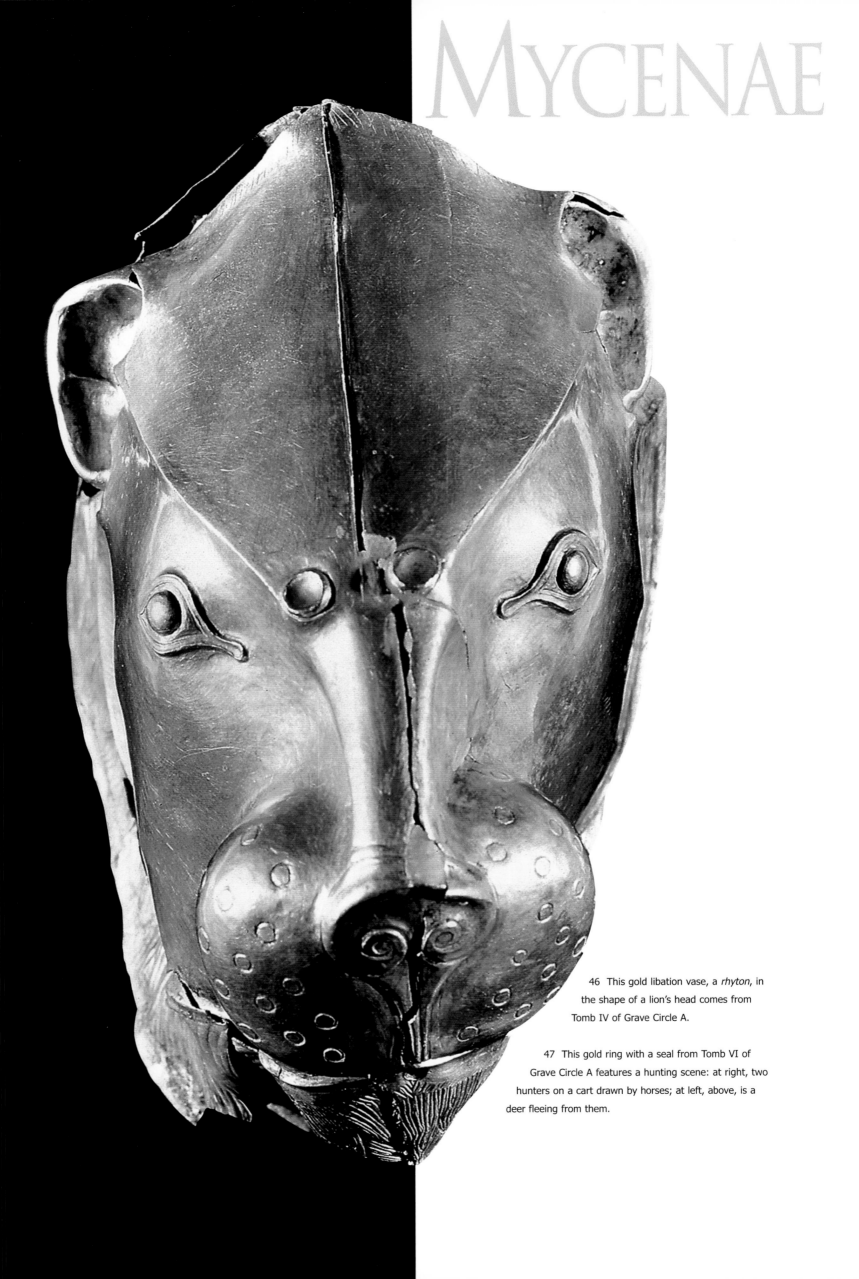

46 This gold libation vase, a *rhyton*, in the shape of a lion's head comes from Tomb IV of Grave Circle A.

47 This gold ring with a seal from Tomb VI of Grave Circle A features a hunting scene: at right, two hunters on a cart drawn by horses; at left, above, is a deer fleeing from them.

preceding palace and a noteworthy leveling of the terrain. Divided into several living quarters on various levels, the new palace has a complex inner layout. The original entrance was at the northwestern corner and afforded access, through corridors, to the Great Court. At the sides of this, arranged symmetrically, were the two main living quarters: the *megaron* (the original living quarter around which revolved the entire Mycenae palace structure) and the so-called Guests' Apartment. Agricultural and livestock products from the lands of the kingdom, which was divided into provinces, districts, and villages, were channeled through the palace (which in turn functioned as handicrafts center), where they were sorted out, stored, and then distributed.

The rest of the city lay around the walls, basically concentrated in three sectors – eastern, northwestern, and southwestern – in each of which archaeologists have found dwellings laid out in a rather homogeneous manner. Some of the houses, which were divided into rooms and had upper floors and sunken storehouses made possible by the various levels, were probably the homes of palace officials. However, besides the residential nature of these sectors, each of them seems to have a distinctive feature. The eastern one, for example, is characterized by a large edifice, the so-called Artisans' Workshop, which was probably closely linked to the Mycenae palace. The discovery in this area of a great deal of working materials such as fragments of pottery, bronze, ivory, gold, and precious stones has led scholars to consider this the productive sector of the city. On the other hand, the northwestern zone of ancient Mycenae revolved around commerce

and storage. Here digs have brought to light a series of rooms most probably used for storage, together with the impressive Granary built behind the Lion Gate. Lastly, the southwestern sector of the city, surely the most urbanized one, has recently yielded finds that provide new interpretations of the function of some buildings. The area of the so-called House of the Citadel and the Tsountas House in particular seems to have been a religious precinct with a ceremonial passage leading to a courtyard with a round external altar. Each sector, though different in character, interacted at different levels with the others with which they shared a common residential function. This gave the city self-sufficiency and social compactness that was embodied, both symbolically and architecturally, in the impressive palace.

The funerary area, together with other important houses, lies mostly outside the city walls. The most ancient burial areas are Grave Circle B, with tombs of the princes and nobles (which is the reason why they have a ring-shaped wall structure) and the Prehistoric Cemetery reserved for commoners. Circle A dates from the sixteenth century B.C., and yielded a great many gold objects, including the famous funerary mask of Agamemnon, while from 1510 B.C. on the impressive *tholos* tombs, circular "beehive" chambers with an ogival dome and a false vault, were adopted. Outstanding examples are the so-called Treasury of Atreus, the Tomb of Aegistus, and the Tomb of Clytemnestra. It therefore seems evident that funerary architecture was quite varied, not only chronologically, but also in terms of types and ideology.

48-49 AND 49 TOP THIS RECONSTRUCTION OF THE ACROPOLIS SEEN FROM THE WEST SIDE SHOWS THE MULTICOLORED RELIEFS OF THE DECORATION OF THE MAIN TEMPLES, IN PARTICULAR THE WEST PEDIMENT OF THE PARTHENON. FOR THOSE ENTERING THE ACROPOLIS FROM THE PROPYLAEA, THE VIEW OF THE GREAT STATUE OF ATHENA PROMACHOS MUST HAVE BEEN AWESOME. AT THE LOWER RIGHT IS PERICLES' ODEION WITH A POINTED ROOF MUCH LIKE A PERSIAN TENT.

49 BOTTOM THE *MOSCHOPHOROS* (CALF BEARER) IS ONE OF THE MOST FAMOUS EXAMPLES OF ARCHAIC GREEK SCULPTURE. IT WAS FOUND IN THE "PERSIAN FILL" DURING THE EXCAVATION OF THE ACROPOLIS IN 1865 AND IS STRIKING FOR THE POSITION OF THE ARMS OF THE MAN (RHOMBOS) AND THE CALF'S LEGS.

ATHENS

ATHENS

Text by MARCO PODINI

Athens is best known for the fifth century B.C. Periclean monuments, but the city's birth as an urban community dates back to the Mycenaean age. The remains of the original citadel lie precisely in the heart of classical Athens, the Acropolis. The Mycenaean palace, built around 1300-1200 B.C., was located between the future Erechtheion and the Parthenon. The site was advantageous because of its difficult accessibility and was further protected by the addition of a massive enclosure wall (the *Pelargikón*). From the outset the site was closely connected to the cult of the "protective goddess of the *polis*," Athena Polias, in whose honor a sanctuary was erected. Three constructions dedicated to

this goddess are known. The first archaic Temple of Athena, built during the time of Peisostratis around 529-520 B.C., was destroyed by fire during the Persian Wars (480-479 B.C.). The second temple, the ancestor of the Parthenon, was the *Hekatompedon*, dedicated in 566 B.C. and made of soft limestone (*poros*) decorated with marble reliefs. It was torn down in 488 to make room for the *Früh-Parthenon*, which was destroyed by fire in 480-479 B.C. Lastly, the Parthenon, an innovative and anomalous religious edifice designed by Ikitinos and Callicrates, was built between 447 and 438 B.C., while the decoration was completed in 432.

The general layout of the Parthenon is the work of the

genius of Phidias. Two basic themes are intertwined in the decoration: the Panathenaic procession and the struggle between barbarism and civilization. This struggle is represented by the battle of the gods and giants (east side), the battles of the Lapiths and centaurs and of the Greeks and Trojans at Troy, or *Ilioupersis* (north and south sides), and that of the Greeks against the Amazons (west side). The frieze on the *cella* portrays two distinct processions: the great Panathenaic procession and the parade of the contests celebrated in the presence of the gods of Olympia and the eponymous heroes of the city. The pediment reliefs celebrate the greatness of Athens with the scene, on the east pediment, of the birth of Athena from the head of Zeus, while the west pediment shows the victory of Athens over

50 top left The portico of the Caryatids (409-407 B.C.) stood above the tomb of the mythical King Cecrops and presents an interesting architectural novelty: the usual columns were replaced by statues of women from Caryae, executed by the workshop of the sculptor Alcamenes, a contemporary of Phidias.

50 bottom left One of the many inscriptions facing the east side of the Parthenon mentions the archon Basileus and the demos of Athens.

50 right Kore 680 is one of the prototypes of archaic female statues. The apparent static quality of the statue is animated by the gesture of the outstretched hand holding fruit.

51 This view of the northwest side of the Acropolis highlights the sanctuary complex, which dominates the city from the high citadel that had already been occupied by a Mycenaean palace. Past the Propylaea is the majestic Parthenon, while in the background is the Erechtheion.

52 bottom This detail of the 525-foot frieze that decorated the *cella* of the Parthenon, executed by Phidias and his workshop, belongs to the west side with the procession of horsemen.

52-53 The west side of the Parthenon is decorated with the cycle of metopes illustrating the battle between the gods and giants, which symbolizes the triumph of civilization over barbarism, while the birth of Athena from Zeus' head stands out on the pediment.

53 bottom On the east frieze of the Parthenon *cella* is the triad of seated gods: Poseidon, Apollo, and Artemis.

Poseidon for possession of Attica. The color used on the sculpture attracted pilgrims visiting the Acropolis, greeting those who entered on foot from the Propylaea. This work, along with the Athena Lemnia and the Athena Parthenos, inside the Parthenon *cella,* composed the triad of statues dedicated to Athena. Phidias' masterpiece, the Parthenos, the armed goddess made of gold and ivory, was undoubtedly the major attraction. The 33-foot-high statue was famous for the sheer quantity of material used in its execution and for its high cost, which gave rise to bitter disputes in Athens. The decoration on the shield, sandals, and base of the Parthenos once again employs myth to narrate the victory and supremacy of civilization over barbarism.

The monumental entrance, the Propylaea, was designed

N

1) PROPYLAEUM AND SMALL TEMPLE OF *ATHENA NIKE*
2) PARTHENON
3) ERECHTHEION
4) TEMPLE OF ROME AND AUGUSTUS
5) THEATER OF DIONYSUS
6) *ODEION* OF PERICLES
7) *ODEION* OF HERODES ATTICUS
8) HADRIAN'S ARCH
9) *OLYMPIEION*
10) MONUMENT OF PHILOPAPPOS
11) TOWER OF THE WINDS (ANDRONICUS' WATER-CLOCK)

12) HADRIAN'S LIBRARY
13) ROMAN *AGORA*
14) HADRIAN'S NYMPHAEUM
15) LIBRARY OF *PANTANIOS*
16) *ODEION* OF AGRIPPA
17) BASILICA OF HADRIAN
18) TEMPLE OF ARES
19) *HEPHAISTEION*
20) GATE OF DIPYLON
21) STADIUM
22) *BOULEUTERION*
23) *STOA* OF ATTALOS

by the architect Mnesikles in 437-432 B.C. This magnificent portal consisted of two side foreparts, however only one hall on the north side, the Painting Gallery, was finished. On the southern side, in front of the entrance, was another small Ionic temple dedicated to Athena (Athena Nike) with only one chamber. This edifice has the famous marble balustrade depicting a series of Nikai (winged victories), the work of the sculptor Callimachus (ca. 410 B.C.). Three more major monuments were built in places already occupied by older sacred edifices. One was the Erechtheion, built on the site of the first temple dedicated to Athena, dedicated to Athena Polias and Poseidon. Distinguished by its atypical plan and for the famous portico of the Caryatids, it was built over the tomb of the mythical King Cecrops. The second monument is a quadrangular edifice with a

ATHENS

54-55 In this reconstruction of the Acropolis and its southern side, the monuments of classical Athens are flanked by Roman ones built during the Imperial Age.

55 The Hadrianic copy of the statue of Athena Parthenos shows what this ivory and gold masterpiece by Phidias must have looked like, but naturally cannot imitate the extraordinary richness of the original.

pointed roof that imitates a Persian tent, the Odeion of Pericles. Constructed on the southeastern slopes of the Acropolis, it hosted music, poetry, and theater contests. The third monument is the Theater of Dionysus Eleuthereus, rebuilt by Lycurgus in a later period. The fifth-century layout of the Acropolis remained essentially unaltered in the following century. During the Hellenistic age, there was the addition of the so-called Pergamun donation, a gift of Attalus (ca. 159-138 B.C.), which bore the usual mythical battles accompanying the historic representations.

Pericles' reorganization program involved another major public area, the Agora, used for religious, judicial, and political assemblies. The new layout was realized in a large area on the east slopes of the Kolonos Agoraios Hill, formerly used as a burial site. Various streets converged here, especially the one that went toward the Acropolis, and was

56 top This view of the west façade of the Parthenon shows traces of centuries of spoliation of the decoration on the entablature and pediment. The metopes that alternate with triglyphs, and the tympanum, have all deteriorated, while the best pieces, known as the Elgin Marbles, are in the British Museum.

56 bottom The entrance to the Acropolis, with the Propylaea and the small Temple of Athena Nike, the work of the architect Kallikrates, reflects Pericles' ambitious urbanization program.

56-57 The view of the west façade of the Erechtheion shows the variety of this structure with respect to classical canons, a difference that was perhaps due to the various cults associated with this edifice and also by the need to adapt it to the different levels of the terrain.

therefore a hub of the Panathenaic Procession.

The first monuments in the Agora are known to us thanks to the comparison made between literary sources (Pausanias' *Description of Greece*) and the result of systematic digs carried out by American archaeologists. The arrangement of the monuments did not follow a logical order and it was only in the mid-sixth century that a more organic layout was planned. The apogee of this urbanizing operation was completed in the fifth century with a series of porticoes that ran around the north and south sides of the square and the Stoa of Zeus. The style of these colonnades corresponds to Phidias' conception of the Parthenon, which advocated the Doric order on the exterior and the Ionic order in the interior and created a sort of border to unify the

various monuments. Archaic buildings include the original Bouleuterion, or Council House, and two small sanctuaries dedicated to Apollo and perhaps to Zeus, as well as the first *stoa*, the Stoa Basileios, which was the seat of the king-archon and housed the ancient Athenian law codes. The Pisistratids added a public fountain that supplied water for the nuptial bath, the famous Enneakrounos, and the Altar of the Twelve Gods (522-521 B.C.), destroyed during the Persian invasion and later rebuilt. The Agora also underwent a massive program of monumental construction after the Persian invasion of 479. This began around 460 B.C. with the erection of the Tholos, a round building that was the residence of the Prytaneis, and the Painted Stoa (Poikile), famous for the paintings representing both historic

and mythical subjects. Other important artists did sculpture pieces for the Agora. The foremost of these was Alcamenes, who executed the bronze statues of Athena and Hephaestus displayed in the large temple known as the Hephaisteion, construction of which began in 440 B.C. A new Bouleuterion was built behind the old one, functioning as both an archive and the temple of the mother of the gods, the Metroon. Other works carried out in the fifth century mainly involved the addition of new *stoas* to close off the Agora square and the introduction of many honorific statues.

The Agora remained essentially the same for the entire fourth century, apart from the construction of a new fountain house to meet the city's growing need for water. The generosity of the ruler of Pergamun, Attalus II, made possi-

ble the construction in the second century B.C. of the famous Stoa of Attalus, now the Agora Museum. It was a two-story building with a wide double colonnade, as if modeled after the Phidias' Parthenon, the rooms of which were used as shops. The Roman period in Athens began with the sack of the city by Sulla's troops in 86 B.C. The Agora was badly damaged, numerous public and private buildings were destroyed, and many statues were either torn down or plundered. The first signs of a revival of building activity came later in the first century B.C. with the construction of the Tower of the Winds, the elegant, octagonal edifice that housed the water clock of Andronicus. However, Athens was fortunate to represent the traditional center of culture in

the eyes of the Roman aristocracy. This "sentiment of respect" led Augustus to finance the reconstruction of the city, albeit in the context of the imperial regime's ideological principles. The first interventions in the Augustan period concerned the Acropolis. The round Temple of Rome and Augustus was built on a large podium opposite the east façade of the Parthenon sometime after 27 B.C. The decorative scheme of this temple was modeled after the Erechtheion, integrating a specific artistic "style," that of fifth- and fourth-century B.C. Athens. Augustus also turned his attention to the Agora. From eleven to nine B.C. the final additions were put on the "Roman Agora," designed by Caesar in 47 B.C. This impressive marketplace had three entrances and numerous shops behind the colonnades. The statuary decoration served the aims of the cult of the imperial dynasty. However, the most innovative and emblematic edifice of the Augustan age was built in the

58-59 The Odeion of Herodes Atticus lies at the foot of the Acropolis: the stage area is rectilinear, with Roman-style niches and arched windows

58 bottom The Temple of Olympian Zeus was begun during Pisistratus' time and finished under the emperor Hadrian, becoming the seat of the Pan-Hellenic imperial cult.

59 top The Monument of Philopappos, built toward the end of Trajan's reign (A.D. 114-116), is the celebration of C. Julius Antiochus.

59 bottom The Theater of Dionysus viewed from the Acropolis. The structure we see today is Roman in origin.

ATHENS

center of the old Agora square: the famous Odeion of Agrippa (15 B.C.), the impressive concert hall covered by a rectangular structure with two superposed orders. The interior marble orders, strongly influenced by classical architecture, were brightly colored. This edifice combined Neo-Attic and Italic-Hellenistic decorative tastes. Thus, the Odeion was an explicit assertion that public architecture in Athens was the exclusive prerogative of Rome. The first century A.D. was a period of stagnation for construction. During the reigns of Claudius and Nero few additions were made to the city, while the first signs of renewed building activity emerged during Trajan's rule.

This period was characterized by two major monuments: the Library of Pantanios (named after the donor), built in A.D. 100 and consisting of a colonnade about 230 feet long with shops behind it; and the Monument of Philopappos (A.D. 114-116), both an honorary and mortuary edifice. The period of the emperors Hadrian and Antoninus Pius witnessed a surge of building activity.

ATHENS

60 top Hadrian's Library is the largest construction commissioned by this emperor and has particularly rich decoration. It had 100 columns, made of Phyrgian marble, and a multicolored inlay floor.

60 bottom left The Tower of the Winds, also known as Andronicus' water-clock, dates from the first century B.C.

60 bottom right The Gate of Hadrian was part of this emperor's town planning program, which set out to create a "city of Hadrian" as opposed to the "city of Theseus," the ideal passageway of which was this arch. It was 59 feet high and consisted of a Roman arch surmounted by an open, Corinthian style attic.

60-61 This view of the Old Agora shows, in the background, the temple known as the Hephaisteion (or pseudo-Theseion) which, though influenced by the Parthenon workshop, remained faithful to the traditional Doric order and housed the statues of Athena and Hephaestus. In the foreground are the remains of the Altar of Zeus Agoraios.

During the reign of the latter the Theater of Dionysus was transformed into a Roman theater, while after A.D. 164 Herodes Atticus built the grand Odeion on the southern side of the Acropolis.

Hadrian decided to invest large amounts of money to plan a new city east of Old Athens. In A.D. 132 the Temple of Olympian Zeus was completed and transformed into a sanctuary of the imperial cult that identified Hadrian with Jupiter. The main entrance to this temple had a monumental arch (the Gate of Hadrian) characterized by a unique design. Herodes Atticus later financed the construction of an enormous stadium on the left bank of the Ilissos and a bridge to link the two quarters. Hadrian's most impressive construction was his famous Library, north of the Roman

Agora. A large quadriporticus with rectangular and semicircular *exedrae* on its north and south sides, the library proper with reading rooms was located behind the east colonnade. A semicircular *nymphaeum* and the great basilica were built in the Agora. Hadrian's aim was arguably to lend Athens a monumental aspect worthy of the most important cities in the Roman Empire. The invasion of the Heruli in 267 marked a blow from which Athens would never recover. The Acropolis again served as a defensive bulwark, sustaining serious and often permanent damage. (The damage was further aggravated many centuries later, during the Turkish occupation, when the Parthenon itself was turned into a munitions depot.) The Slavic invasion of 582-583 marked the end of the ancient city.

ROME

Text by MARCO PODINI

I f it is true that the history of any great metropolis must be interpreted not as a continuous flux but rather as a series of moments connected to one another that should be evaluated in relation to the economic, political, and cultural changes of the society, this is all the more true in the case of Rome.

The first permanent settlement of the hills of Rome dates from the last period of the Bronze Age, attested to by the floors of some huts on the Palatine. Since it was a marshy area, the central part of the Forum could not be settled permanently, at least in the first period. The fusion of these villages coincides in a significant manner with the traditional date of the city's foundation, set at 753-754 B.C., a date that in turn coincides with the rise of the first king of Rome, Romulus.

62 bottom left The Colosseum, built by Vespasian in A.D. 79 in place of the artificial lake in the Domus Aurea, is the largest amphitheater in the Roman Empire. The travertine structure consists of three floors of arches with columns of different orders crowned by an attic with Corinthian pilasters.

62 right The statue of Augustus from the Villa di Prima Porta. The emperor is depicted in the act of asking for silence before beginning a speech. This statue is characteristic for the decoration of the armor, which has ideological contents: in the middle of a cosmic setting is the episode of the restitution of Crassus' insignia on the part of the Parthian king.

62-63 View of the Roman Forum. In the background, the arches of the north nave of the Basilica of Maxentius; in the middle, part of the Sacred Way; at left is the Arch of Titus and, in the distance, the Colosseum.

63 top The Capitoline She-wolf is a significant example of archaic sculpture that can be dated approximately to the first decades of the fifth century B.C.

64 bottom right The Temple of Saturn, last restored sometime after A.D. 283, was built in the fifth century B.C. The symbol of the foundation of the Republic, this building housed the public Treasury. Further north, Septimius Severus built an impressive three-opening arch to commemorate the victory over the Parthians in the two campaigns of A.D. 195-198.

64-65 The Roman Forum, originally a marshy hollow, during the monarchy had already become the site of monumental buildings.

64 bottom left The west section of the Roman Forum. Below, the House of the Vestal Virgins and ruins of the Temple of the Vestal Virgins; above right is the Temple of Antoninus Pius and Faustina; in the middle are the remains of the Temple of the Divine Caesar; in the back, left, is the Arch of Septimius Severus and the Curia.

ROME

65 top The House of the Vestal Virgins was laid out around a peristyle courtyard with fountains in the middle. It was the home of the priestesses of the cult of Vesta, whose temple stood next to this residential complex, which had several rooms with different functions (oven and mill rooms, kitchen, and reception rooms, as well as the rooms of the Vestal Virgins on the upper floor).

65 bottom The Forum of Caesar viewed from the north-east. Planned in 54 B.C. and inaugurated in 46 B.C., this complex comprised a large colonnaded square, southwest of which was a series of shops with irregular plans. To the north-west was the Corinthian hexastyle Temple of Venus Genetrix, which housed precious art works. The Forum of Caesar was important because it was the model for later forums.

Around the mid-eighth century B.C., the increase in population led the rulers to modify a town plan that was no longer compatible with the needs of a growing society.

The following period witnessed the rise of a new dynasty of monarchs of Etruscan origin: Tarquinius Priscus, Servius Tullius, and Tarquinius Superbus (Tarquin the Proud). The building activity promoted by the first Etruscan king met several needs: civil, such as the drainage system in the valley of the Roman Forum (Cloaca Maximus), collective (Circus Maximus), and religious (Temple of Jupiter Maximus on the Capitoline). His successor, Servius Tullius, is traditionally attributed with the construction of large city walls, called the Servian walls. Archaeological finds dating from the mid-sixth century B.C. reveal a remarkable development of commerce, while literary sources emphasize the enterprising spirit of the Servian economic policy.

ROME

67 left Below, the section of the Forum of Augustus now visible, in which the ruins of the Temple of Mars Ultors can be seen between the two *exedrae*. Above right is Trajan's Market complex, and to the left is a part of the Basilica Ulpia, behind which is Trajan's Column.

67 right Lying against the impressive hemicycle, above which was a street lined with shops, is the large Trajan's Market complex.

66 The frieze around Trajan's Column consists of about 2,500 figures, and the emperor himself is depicted about 60 times. Battle scenes alternate with works of peace and sacrifices to the gods to ensure victory.

Up to this time the Republican aristocracy had managed to prevent members of the inner circle of the Roman oligarchy from distinguishing themselves from the others by promoting self-aggrandizing building activity. But the rapid conquest of the Italian peninsula, which ended in the early decades of the third century B.C., drastically changed the political and economic scene in Rome, determining the rise of different kinds of public figures.

The conquest of the eastern ancient world, which began after the Punic Wars, paved the way for the assimilation of Hellenistic culture and a period of prosperity that traditionally has been negatively interpreted as *luxuria asiatica*. Prestigious building was concentrated in the area comprising the Circus Flaminius (in the Campus Martius), the Forum Olitorium, and the Forum Boarium. Significant monuments dating from the beginning of the second century B.C. included the arches along the triumphal ways and the Porticus Aemilia, Galbana, and Lolliana warehouses along the Tiber, which together formed a massive emporium.

In 184 B.C. the first basilica was erected by Cato the Younger. This was destined to become a basic feature of Roman architecture. Functionally, the basilica replaced the atria built in the preceding century, while from an architec-

tural standpoint it was inspired by a totally new model of Hellenistic-Alexandrian origin. The Basilica of Portius was followed by the Basilica Fulvia-Emilia and the Basilica Sempronia. The construction of religious edifices also developed considerably in this period. In the late second century B.C. Minucius Rufus had the Largo Argentina sacred precinct enclosed by the huge Porticus Minucia. Marble was introduced in Rome with the construction of the Temple of Jupiter Stator, designed by the architect Ermodorus of Salamis. The round temple of the Forum Boarium was also made of marble; it was dedicated to Hercules Victorious by a rich merchant from Tivoli. The first century B.C. was marked by the emergence of persons with strong personalities and great ambition. The appearance of Sulla on the political scene determined further aggrandizement of personal charisma. The most ambitious project in town planning during Sulla's time was the leveling of the west slopes of the Capitoline hill for an impressive and showy architectural work, the Tabularium, the state archive.

The third quarter of the first century B.C. marked the definitive decline of the senatorial aristocracy, which was crushed by Pompey and Caesar. The conflict between these two figures not only influenced the politics and military policies of Rome, but its architecture as well. Pompey had the first permanent theater in Rome built in the Campus Martius, incorporating porticoes and civic, residential, and religious edifices into the complex. His aim was to realize a magnificent precinct comparable to the royal palace of a Hellenistic dynasty. After defeating his arch-rival, Caesar decided to concentrate on the Forum, the traditional seat of political power in Rome. Here he dismantled and rebuilt the Basilica Sempronia, which he renamed Julia, and also rebuilt the Curia, changing its axis and turning it into a passageway between the Forum area, the symbol of republican Rome, and the new Forum of Caesar, the expression of the new political power. Other colossal projects were brought to an abrupt end by his death. The Imperial Age was characterized by the marks that each emperor made on the urban development of Rome. While Caesar had signaled the beginning of a new political period, Augustus (31 B.C.-A.D.14) legitimized the emperor's power from an ideological standpoint. The addition to the Campus Martius area of buildings with strong ideological overtones underscored the dynastic nature of Rome's new architecture.

68 top The Arch of Constantine, built in A.D. 315, is decorated with the most important episodes of this emperor's reign.

68 bottom The imperial Palace of Domitian, designed by the architect Rabirius, was built on the Palatine. This complex occupied almost the entire hill and comprised a state reception sector (the Domus Flavia) and a private wing (the Domus Augustana), to which was added a garden in the shape of a stadium.

68-69 The structure of the Flavian Amphitheater (Colosseum) is clearly illustrated here: the huge oval cavea was divided into sectors of tiers that were reserved for the different sectors of the social hierarchy.

69 right The wall paintings in the House of Augustus on the Palatine (ca. 30 B.C.) reveal the development of a new decorative style for interiors that coincided with the transition from the Second to the Third Style: uniform surfaces dominated by large panels in the middle of which were single elements or scenes.

But the most representative manifestation of the new imperial institution was the construction of the Forum of Augustus. An emblematic reply to the Forum of Caesar, the new forum was conceived, both in its decorative scheme and its use, as a legitimization of the new regime. The sculptural decoration of the temple, square, and porticoes became a systematic ideological journey through the history of Rome, which ended with Augustus.

The building activity of the Claudian emperors (14-54 A.D.) basically modified Rome as it was during Augustus' time. It resulted in public works, large-scale restoration of monuments, and the promotion of commemorative and religious structures. Nero (A.D. 54-68) effected a clear-cut break with the Augustan building program. The great fire of A.D. 64 gave this emperor the pretext to build, by means of the illegal expropriation of land, a new imperial residence and to lay out new residential quarters. The unified arrangement of streets and squares harked back to the Hellenistic model of the city, which revolved around the dynastic palace, the Domus Aurea. Surrounded by greenery the new imperial residence actually consisted of numerous pavilions. The first architectural works promoted in the Flavian age were demagogic: the monuments erected during Nero's reign were largely demolished and land illegally confiscated was symbolically "given back" to the people.

ROME

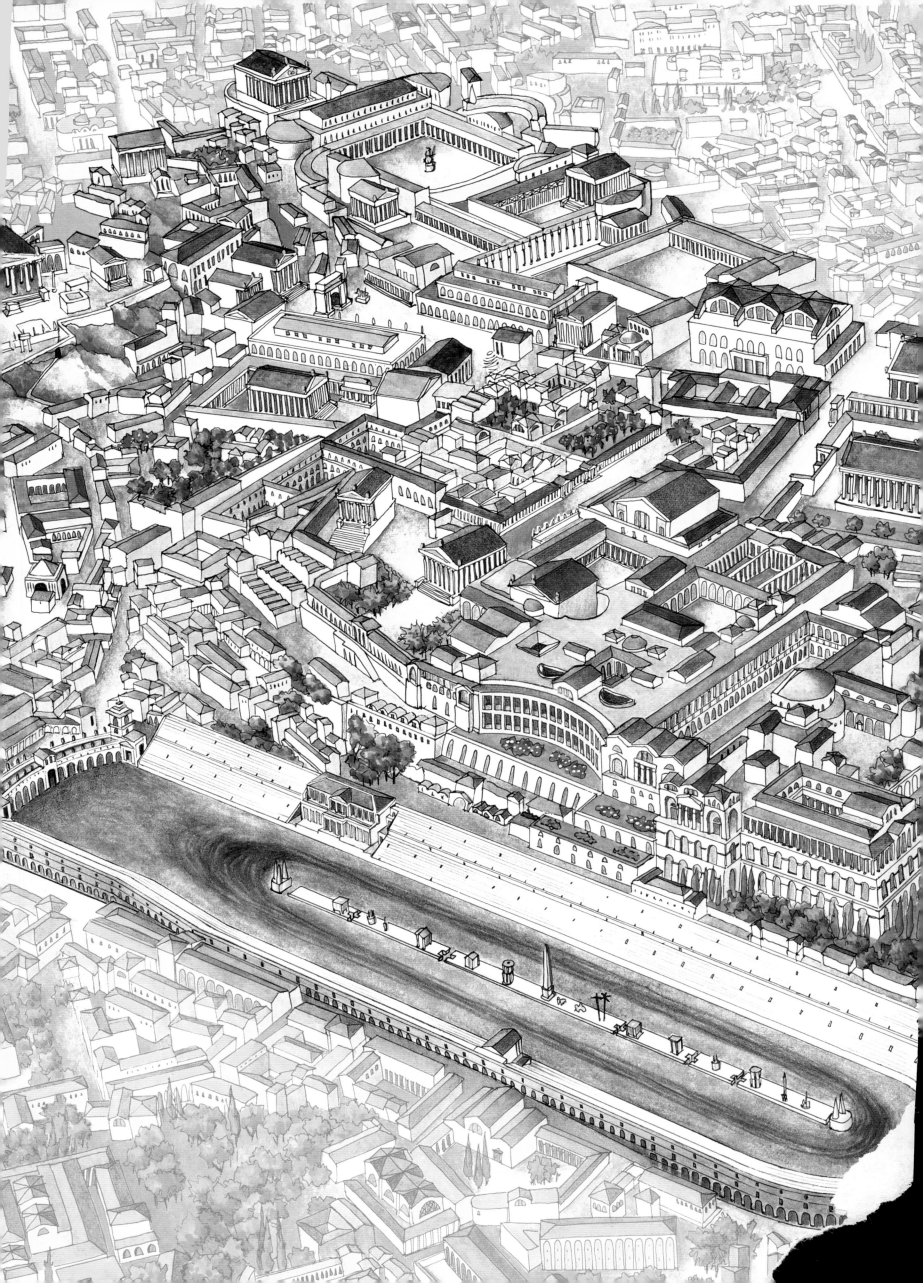

1) ROMAN FORUM
2) TEMPLE OF JUPITER CAPITOLINUS
3) CIRCUS MAXIMUS
4) FORUM BOARIUM
5) FORUM OLITORIUM
6) CAMPUS MARTIUS
7) LARGO ARGENTINA SACRED PRECINCT
8) CIRCUS FLAMINIUS
9) PORTICUS AEMILIA
10) GALBANA WAREHOUSE
11) PORTICUS METELLI (PORTICUS OCTAVIAE)
12) TABULARIUM
13) THEATER OF POMPEY
14) FORUM OF CAESAR
15) BATHS OF AGRIPPA
16) PANTHEON
17) AUGUSTUS' SUN-DIAL
18) ARA PACIS OF AUGUSTUS
19) MAUSOLEUM OF AUGUSTUS
20) FORUM OF AUGUSTUS
21) BATHS OF TRAJAN
22) COLOSSEUM
23) TEMPLUM PACIS
24) ARCH OF TITUS
25) STADIUM OF DOMITIAN
26) ODEUM
27) FORUM TRANSITORIUM
28) DOMUS AUGUSTANA AND DOMUS FLAVIA
29) FORUM OF TRAJAN
30) MAUSOLEUM OF HADRIAN
31) TEMPLE OF VENUS AND ROMA
32) ARCH OF SEPTIMIUS SEVERUS
33) SEPTIZODIUM
34) BATHS OF CARACALLA
35) AURELIAN WALLS
36) TEMPLE OF THE SUN
37) BATHS OF DIOCLETIAN
38) BASILICA OF MAXENTIUS

In particular, new markets and trade areas were promoted (the Forum Olitorium and the Forum Boarium). In fact, two symbolic edifices were built in this period, including the king's Royal Palace and the Comitia, the seat of political activity. According to tradition, the Etruscan dynasty was overthrown and a republican government was instituted at the end of the sixth century B.C. The consequence of these events was the confiscation of a large Tarquin property northeast of the Forum, the Campus Martius, which would be the focal point of prestigious construction from the mid-fourth century B.C. on. After a period of intense construction activity resulting in the Temple of Saturn and the Temple of Castor and Pollux, the early Republican Age was distinguished by a long economic recession that was largely responsible for the conflict between the patricians and the plebs. Signs of recovery appeared in 367 B.C. when it was established that the plebs were to have equal rights.

71-74 The color plate on the preceding pages drew inspiration from the model made in the 1930s by Italo Gismondi. This bird's eye view is a rather accurate reproduction of the heart of Rome with the Forum area between the Capitol and the Colosseum as it appeared during the reign of Constantine.

75 In the late Roman Empire, many mosaics depicted the feats of the charioteers, who were very popular and generally became very rich.

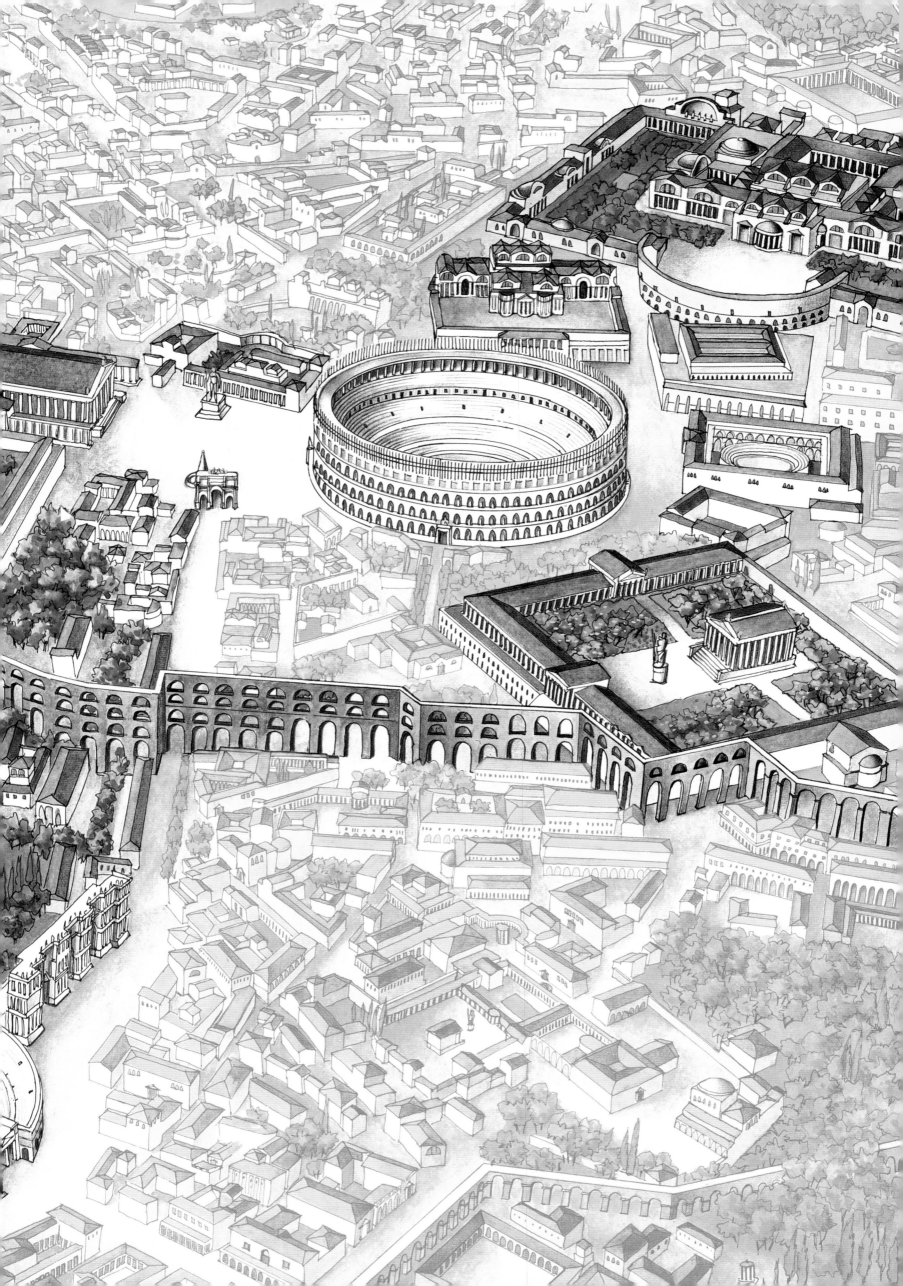

76-77 The Pantheon of Agrippa, built in 27 B.C., was damaged by fire in the second century A.D. The edifice we see today was completely rebuilt by Hadrian in A.D. 118-128.

76 top The interior of Hadrian's Pantheon is illuminated from above by the large oculus, which has a diameter of 30 feet.

76 center The Ara Pacis is the monumental symbol of Augustus' reign. This altar lies in a marble area decorated with mythological scenes and processions portraying the imperial family.

76 bottom The Column of Marcus Aurelius was finished in A.D. 193, a short time after the death of the emperor. Its reliefs narrate the Germanic wars waged by the emperor 171-175.

77 bottom Augustus built his Mausoleum in 32-28 B.C. This edifice, 285 feet wide and almost 130 feet high, was crowned by a colossal statue of the emperor.

Vespasian (A.D. 69-79) and Titus (79-81) had the Domus Aurea torn down. They replaced the artificial lake with the first permanent amphitheater in Rome, and the largest in the Roman Empire. The colossal statue of Nero in the vestibule of the Domus Aurea, over 115 feet high, depicting the emperor as a god, was redone to portray the god Helios, and the new Flavian amphitheater was called the Colosseum because this sculpture was placed next to it. Southeast of the Forum of Augustus, Vespasian built the Templum Pacis, a large colonnaded area that comprised the Temple of Peace, gardens, libraries, and halls for displaying works of art. Here there were also the most important depictions of the Roman triumph in Judaea, immortalized in the inner panels of the Arch of Titus on the Sacred Way. Domitian's reign (81-96) was also characterized by intense building activity. Besides the construction in the Campus Martius of a stadium and the Odeum, this emperor intervened in the Templum Pacis, which he connected to the Forum of Augustus by building another imperial forum called the *Transitorium* since it con-

nected this area with the city's residential quarters. Domitian also built the imperial residence on the Palatine, which was divided into two sectors, the private area (Domus Augustana), and the public one (Domus Flavia). This became the formal residence of the Roman emperors.

After Nerva's brief reign (96-98), the emperor Trajan (98-117) realized the vastest town planning program ever seen in Rome with the creation of a continuous monumental area between the Forums and the Campus Martius. Made possible by eliminating the saddle connected the Capitol and the Quirinal. The Forum of Trajan, financed by booty, was the manifestation of this continuity.

Recent excavations there seem to have demonstrated that the entrance was to the north and that it led into a large peristyle where the famous Trajan Column and the two libraries (Greek and Latin) were located. This court in turn gave access to the Basilica Ulpia, which was followed by a huge porticoed square in the middle of which was the equestrian statue of Trajan. The decorative scheme, and perhaps the plan of the Forum itself (modeled after the rectangular layout of the *castrum*), were an explicit glorification of the emperor's warlike inclinations.

The emperor Hadrian (117-138) abandoned his predecessor's expansionist policy and set out to hark back to the great Augustan tradition through public works that, although less spectacular, were equally effective on an ideological and propagandistic level. Particularly important

78-79 The Aemilian Bridge, commonly known as the Broken Bridge, was built in the second century B.C. The arch we see today, however, dates from the mid 1500s.

were the Mausoleum (now Castel Sant'Angelo) and the total rebuilding of the Pantheon of Agrippa, which was drastically changed with the erection of a huge dome that is still perfectly intact. The pro-Hellenic propensities of Hadrian are manifested in the Temple of Venus and Roma, which was directly inspired by Greek models. The period after Hadrian's rule up to A.D. 193 produced the Temple of Antoninus Pius and Faustina in the Roman Forum and some major works in the Campus Martius such as the Temple of Hadrian. The first concern of the emperors from 193 (Severus) to 235 (Alexander Severus) was to legitimize the continuity of their dynasty. Septimius Severus (193-211) did this by having an arch built on the slopes of the Capitol at a fork in the Sacred Way that led to the two tops of the hill, which was one of the major passages in the triumphal procession. The emperors of the Severus line also enlarged Domitian's Domus, flanking it with a sort of monumental *nymphaeum*.

79 top right The Temple of Portunus has four Ionic columns on its façade and a travertine cella lined with stucco. The edifice we see today is the result of restoration effected in the first century B.C.

79 bottom The Mausoleum of Hadrian, now Castel Sant'Angelo, was inaugurated after the death of the emperor, in A.D. 138. The cylindrical structure lies on a square base.

78 bottom The Fabrician Bridge (Pons Fabricius) was built in 62 B.C. Two hundred and three feet long, its two great arches are still standing on the central pier, which was divided in two in order to better support the pressure of the water.

79 top left The Theater of Marcellus was named after Augustus' grandson, who died at an early age. It is one of the best preserved entertainment venues in Rome.

The building programs of the succeeding emperors was marked by the construction of monumental works; Caracalla (211-217) was responsible for the massive Baths of Caracalla at the southeastern end of the city. The absolutist policy of these rulers, which degenerated during the reign of Heliogabalus (218-222), was abandoned to some degree by Alexander Severus (222-235), who attempted to mediate between the oligarchy and the plebs. His building policy aimed at restoring the infrastructure and at seeing to the immediate needs of the city. After the death of Alexander Severus there was a long period of military anarchy in which twenty emperors succeeded from 235 to 284. Signs of revival began to appear only in the second half of the third century with the rise of Aurelian, who initiated a process of putting the power back in the hands of the emperor, which can be seen in the construction of massive defensive walls (the Aurelian Walls).

The reform effected by Diocletian (284-305), whereby the empire was divided into four parts, led to a brief period of stability. But the new administrative system soon broke down, and in A.D. 305 began the struggle among the claimants to the imperial throne, which led to the conflict between Maxentius and Constantine, the latter winning in 312 in the battle of the Milvian Bridge. Thus began a period in which Rome and the Western Empire tended to become less important. The final attempts to revive the prestige of the capital can be noted in Maxentius's building activity, the most noteworthy works of which are the Basilica of Maxentius in the Roman Forum and the imperial residence on the Appian Way.

80 left The erection of the monumental Aurelian Walls (built in A.D. 272-279 and still in a fine state of preservation) marked the beginning of renewed building activity after the third-century crisis.

80 right The Laocoön, which decorated the Palace of Titus, was executed by the sculptors Hagesandrus, Athenodorus, and Polydorus.

80-81 The Baths of Caracalla are one of the most impressive and significant examples of Severan architecture in Rome. Built in A.D. 212-216, it revolutionized the previous plan used for *thermae* by separating the baths proper (baths, dressing rooms, and other service rooms) from the rest of the complex (libraries, nymphaea, and resting and conversation rooms).

81 bottom left The stretch of the Appian Way outside the city walls began at the Porta San Sebastiano gate. Here various types of sepulchers and monumental tombs were built.

81 bottom right On the Appian Way are two of the most impressive examples of
Roman architecture, constructed in different periods: the large cylindrical Mausoleum
of Caecilia Metella (built around the mid-first century B.C.) and, a short distance
further north, the imperial residence of Maxentius, consisting of the palace, the
mausoleum, and circus grounds (built in the first decade of the third century A.D.).

82-83 TOP A PLATE BY ARCHITECT L. JAUSSELY (1910), PART OF A HYPOTHETICAL RECONSTRUCTION OF THE FORUM. FROM LEFT TO RIGHT ARE THE TEMPLE OF APOLLO, THE CAPITOLIUM, THE DOUBLE COLONNADE, AND THE BUILDING OF EUMACHIA.

82-83 CENTER THIS WATERCOLOR BY THE ARCHITECT J.-L. CHIFFLOT (1903) SHOWS A SUPPLEMENTAL RESTORATION OF THE HOUSE OF THE CENTENNIAL: THE LONGITUDINAL SECTION IS REPRODUCED, FROM THE LARGE ATRIUM TO THE *NYMPHAEUM*.

83 FROM THE LATE NINETEENTH TO THE EARLY TWENTIETH CENTURY, EXCAVATIONS WERE CARRIED OUT FROM HOUSE TO HOUSE. ONCE THE DIGGERS REACHED THE FLOOR OF ONE ROOM, THEY PROCEEDED TO EXCAVATE THE OTHER ROOMS. THE STRUCTURES BROUGHT TO LIGHT WERE IMMEDIATELY RESTORED BY REINFORCING THE WALLS AND REPLACING THE WOODEN BEAMS.

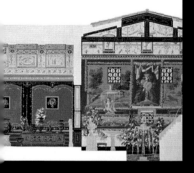

POMPEII

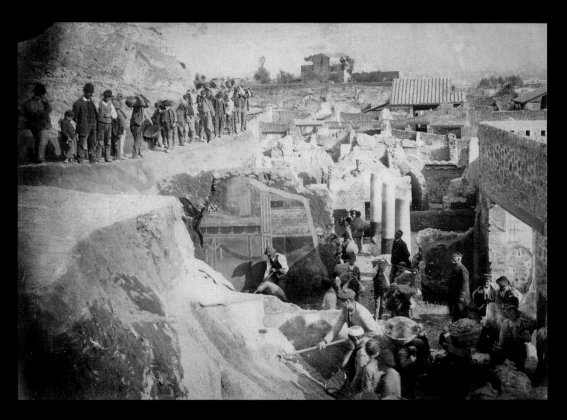

POMPEII

Text by ANTONELLA CORALINI

B etween the end of the seventh century and first half of the sixth century B.C., the city of Pompeii rose up on a spur about 98 feet above sea level that dominated the mouth of the Sarno River. From the beginning, the new city had a defensive wall made of local tuff. It covered a vast area of over 150 acres, almost equal to the size of the city in A.D. 79 when Vesuvius erupted.

The result of the merger of indigenous peoples (the Aurunci) with Etruscans and Greeks, Pompeii was from the outset characterized by a "mixed" culture that is most noticeable in its two main sanctuaries, built in the second half of the sixth century. Centrally located in the higher area of the city is the Temple of Apollo (VII 7, 32), which was totally renovated in the second century B.C. combining Italic elements (the tall podium with a stairway on the

84 top In Pompeiian wall painting an important role is played by portraits in medallions, and often the stereotyped motif of the poetess was used for women.

84 bottom left In the *lararium* of the House of the Centennial, the decorative painting also included an unusual image of Bacchus next to Mount Vesuvius covered with grapevines.

84 bottom right This statuette–a cupid in the guise of Dionysus with a theater mask–was part of the sculpture in the garden of the House of D. Octavius Quartius, where it probably decorated a fountain.

84-85 This aerial view clearly shows the East-West axis, starting from present-day Porta Marina, skirting the Temple of Venus and the Basilica, until reaching the Forum, then proceeding along Via dell'Abbondanza.

front) and Greek ones (the colonnade around the *cella*). To the south-east, in a more marginal position on the cliffs of the hill overlooking the river, is the Doric Temple (VIII 7, 30-34), which was perhaps originally dedicated to Athena and Heracles and then remodeled several times until it was finally abandoned after the A.D. 62 earthquake.

The original town plan of Pompeii was laid in the fifth and fourth centuries B.C., when the city was ruled by the Samnites. This was also the period when the second city wall, made of limestone, was built, faithfully following (and reinforcing) the more ancient one. This later wall was in turn replaced by a new, thicker version in limestone when Pompeii came under the Roman sphere of influence.

By the end of the fourth century the town plan was perfected. Its main features can be seen in the A.D. 79 urban layout. In the second century B.C. several monuments were built in the public areas such as the Forum (on the north side of which the Temple of Jupiter was

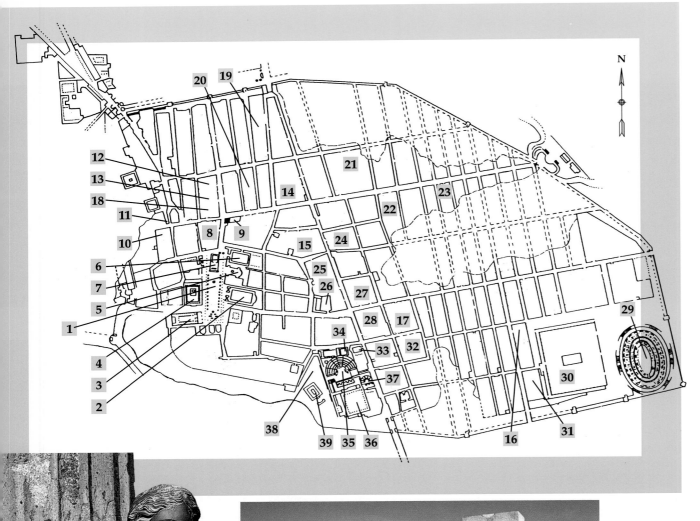

1) FORUM
2) BUILDING OF EUMACHIA
3) BASILICA
4) TEMPLE OF APOLLO
5) SANCTUARY OF THE PUBLIC LARES
6) *MACELLUM*
7) TEMPLE OF JUPITER
8) BATHS OF THE FORUM
9) TEMPLE OF FORTUNA AUGUSTA
10) HOUSE OF M. FABIUS RUFUS
11) HOUSE OF THE GOLDEN BRACELET
12) HOUSE OF THE SMALL FOUNTAIN
13) HOUSE OF THE LARGE FOUNTAIN
14) HOUSE OF THE SCIENTISTS
15) HOUSE OF THE BEAR
16) HOUSE OF THE OUTDOOR TRICLINIUM
17) HOUSE OF THE CEII
18) HOUSE OF ADONIS
19) HOUSE OF THE VETTII
20) HOUSE OF THE FAUN
21) HOUSE OF THE SILVER WEDDING
22) HOUSE OF THE CENTENNIAL
23) HOUSE OF OBELIUS FIRMUS
24) HOUSE OF M. LUCRETIUS
25) HOUSE OF SIRICUS
26) STABIAN BATHS
27) HOUSE OF M. EPIDIUS RUFUS
28) HOUSE OF THE LYRE PLAYER
29) AMPHITHEATER
30) LARGE PALAESTRA
31) HOUSE OF HERCULES' GARDEN
32) HOUSE OF MENANDER
33) TEMPLE OF JUPITER MEILICHIUS
34) TEMPLE OF ISIS
35) LARGE THEATER
36) QUADRIPORTICUS OF THE THEATERS
37) ODEUM
38) TRIANGULAR FORUM
39) DORIC TEMPLE

built) and the south section of the city, where the theater was erected.

During the Social War (90-89 B.C.) Pompeii was a faithful ally of Rome, however it later opposed Sulla who laid siege to the city and conquered it. In 80 B.C. it became a Roman colony with the name of Cornelia Veneria Pompeianorum. The foundation of the colony marked the beginning of a particularly prosperous period, which resulted in the construction of new public buildings and the increasing luxury of private homes.

One of the first public buildings was the Temple of Venus (VII 1, 3), constructed in honor of the protective goddess of Lucius Cornelius Sulla, who was identified with the patron of the city, Venus Physica. This temple, which stood on the southeast spur in a dominating position overlooking the sea and the Sarno river, must have

86 left The sculptural decoration of the Temple of Apollo probably included a bronze group depicting the massacre of Niobe's children, of which the statue of Apollo was a part.

86 right View of the interior of the Basilica. In the background one can make out the Tribunal.

87 The "Terrace of the Theaters," in the lower part of this aerial view, includes the Large Theater built in the second century B.C., the small roofed theater or Odeum, and the Quadriporticus, which was built soon after Sulla founded the colony (80 B.C.).

been the most striking and sumptuous religious edifice in Pompeii, but its poor state of preservation – only a tuff podium surrounded by a portico remains – gives us little idea of its original appearance.

The Temple of Jupiter (VII 8, 1), on the northern side of the Forum, became the Capitolium, or Capitol Temple, dedicated to the cult of the Capitoline Triad, which included Jupiter, Juno, and Minerva. Adjacent to the theater was the Odeum, or Little Theater (VII 7, 17-20), with a roof that provided excellent acoustics and a large area porticoed on all four sides known as the "Quadriporticus of the Theaters," (VIII 7, 16-17) which was used for activities related to theatrical performances and may have been transformed into a barracks for gladiators after the A.D. 62 earthquake.

The new Forum Baths complex was added to public baths built during the Samnite period, the Stabian Baths.

Urban development flourished thanks to the important contributions made by benefactors. An example of this is the amphitheater, the construction of which in 70 B.C. was paid for by the first two quinquevirs of the colony, C. Quinctius Valgus and M. Porcius. Built in the southeastern part of the city, it was used for gladiatorial combats and could seat more than 20,000 spectators. In A.D. 59 it was the site of the famous riot between the citizens of Pompeii and Nucera, which led to the imperial disciplinary measure whereby the amphitheater was closed for ten years, an act that was annulled after the A.D. 62 earthquake.

During the Augustan age there began a systematic renovation of the public areas of the city, which was completed in the Tiberian age.

The most important stage of this work concerned the Forum complex, where the changes made represented a veritable "urban revolution" in the heart of Pompeii.

The large-scale use of marble dressing, the enlargement of the arcades, and the addition of many statues and inscriptions were flanked by the construction of sanctuaries of the cult of the emperor, which also modified the orientation of the public square. The Forum was no longer

on a longitudinal North-South axis that afforded a view of the Capitolium, but now pointed eastward affording views of buildings connected in varying degrees with the imperial cult.

In A.D. 79 this string of edifices began in the north with the Macellum (VII 9, 7-8), the city's main marketplace, which dates from the second century B.C. In the Augustan age a *sacellum* dedicated to the cult of the emperor was placed in the back end of the peristyle courtyard. The second building was presumedly the Sanctu-

ary of the Public Lares (VII 9, 3), which was also probably built during the Augustan age (and not, as some scholars maintain, after the A.D. 62 quake as public expiation to placate the gods' supposed hostility toward the city).

There followed the Temple of Vespasian (or Aedes Genii Augusti, VII 9, 2), a small temple on a podium with a statue of the emperor in the back of a roofless courtyard. This may have been built during Augustus' time and in A.D. 79 was certainly dedicated to the cult of the Genius of the Emperor Vespasian. The se-

POMPEII

88-89 In the southeastern sector of the city was the amphitheater, built around 70 B.C., which in the Augustan age was flanked by the large porticoed structure now known as the Large Palaestra, which was perhaps used for young people's gymnastics.

89 top After the earthquake in A.D. 62, the Temple of Isis was rebuilt, the expenses being paid by a wealthy private citizen, N. Popidius Ampliatus. It was in the form of a temple on a podium in the middle of a peristyle courtyard, with rich pictorial and sculptural decoration, which also included a statuette of Venus Anadyomene (photo right).

89 bottom Almost all the public baths in Pompeii, with the exception of the Central Baths, had separate sections reserved for men and women. This was also the case of the Baths of the Forum, of which the *calidarium* in the male section is seen in this photograph.

90 top A double colonnade ran along the long sides of the Forum square. It had honorific statues, the pedestals of which have survived. In the background is the Temple of the Divine Vespasian.

90 center The Via di Mercurio seen from the north. In the foreground is a pedestrian crossing; in the background is the Arch of Mercury, an honorary arch that may have been built by the emperor Caligula.

90 bottom The Temple of the Divine Vespasian, dedicated to the cult of the emperor, was at the time of the eruption in A.D. 79 a small temple set on a podium in the back end of an outdoor courtyard and preceded by an altar (seen in the middle of this photograph).

90-91 Via dell'Abbondanza, seen here from the Forum, was along with Via di Nocera part of the southern quarter of Pompeii, an urban area that has now been restored and gives us an idea of the splendor and vitality of the city.

POMPEII

quence of buildings ended to the south, on the Via dell'Abbondanza, with the Building of Eumachia, a large porticoed complex built in the Tiberian age by Eumachia, the *sacredos publica Veneris* (public priestess of Venus) and protectress of the *fullones* (cloth-makers' guild).

The renovation and beautification of the city initiated in Augustus' time continued during the reign of Tiberius: changes were made in the Capitolium, two commemorative arches were erected at either side of this same building, and honorific statues were placed throughout the Forum. The general theme imitated Rome, as demonstrated, for example, by the *elogia*, or eulogies, of Aeneas and Romulus, clearly modeled after the inscriptions in the Forum of Augustus.

Examples of domestic architecture can be found in the northwestern part of the city, which seems to have been the most residential one, delimited to the south by the *decumanus maximus* (Via della Fortuna) and to the east by the upper part of the *cardo maximus*, now called Via di Stabia. In this area (which corresponds to the present-day Regio VI) lay the greatest concentration of prestigious, luxurious *domus*, or residences. The most outstanding of these is the "house-museum" now known as House of the Faun *(VII 12, 2)*, which in A.D. 79 still displayed most of the mosaics exhibited today, including the great one de-

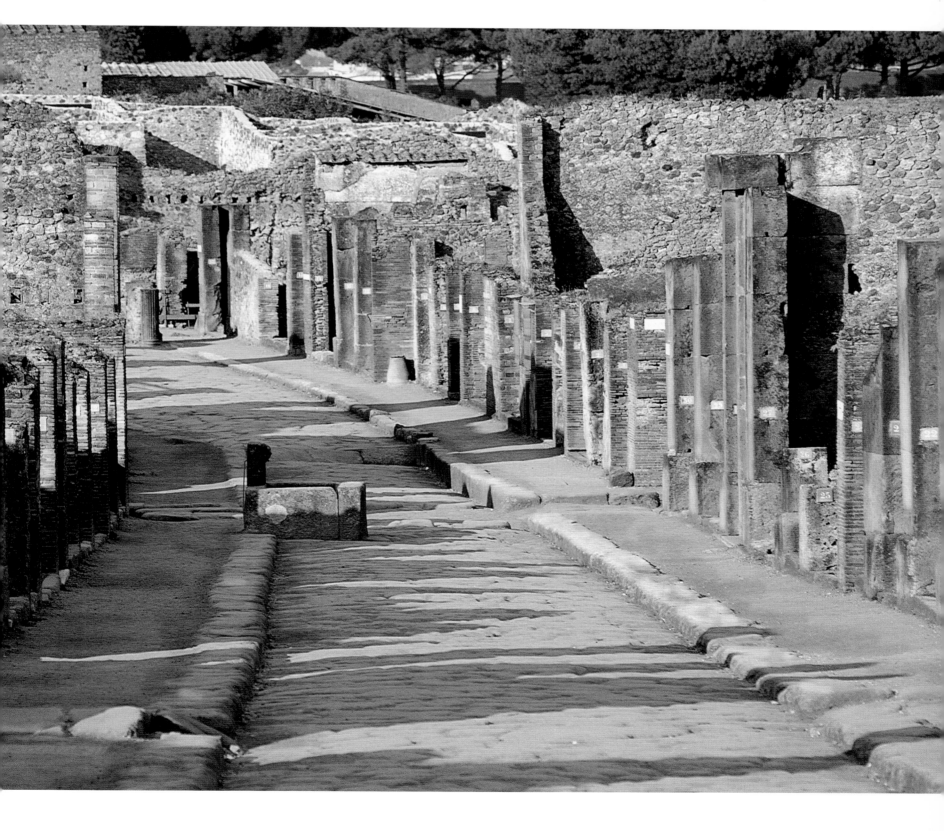

92 top In the main reception room of the House of the Faun, the exedra in the middle of the back of the first peristyle court boasted the large mosaic in *opus vermiculatum* with the famous *Battle of Issus* between Alexander the Great and Darius (333 B.C.), which was a copy of a famous Greek painting.

92 center At the time of the eruption of Vesuvius, the House of the Faun still had its original decoration, installed 150 years earlier. The luxuriousness of this mansion was evident from the entrance, in the elegant *opus sectile impluvium* and in the small bronze Faun.

picting Alexander at the Battle of Issus.

The House of the Faun belonged to the small group of *domus* with a double atrium, and more infrequently, as in this case, with a double peristyle as well.

In its final building stage it was further beautified with a *viridarium*, or garden, that featured paintings of a garden, a *paradeisos*, and marine fauna, and with a stepped *nymphaeum*. Furthermore, in the *lararium* (located in the service quarters) was a unique painting of Bacchus wearing a bunch of grapes next to a mountain whose slopes are covered with vineyards, probably a representation of Vesuvius before the terrible eruption.

Even in those houses where the lack of space preclud-

92-93 The decoration in the House of the Faun is famous for the rich, elegant *opus vermiculatum* mosaics. The threshold between the *fauces* (passageway) and the atrium, with theater masks in a plant festoon, was also made using this masonry technique.

93 top The decoration of the gardens in the houses of Pompeii after the A.D. 62 earthquake was often enhanced by large wall paintings with mythical figures (such as Venus in a shell) or by reproductions of gardens and fights between wild beasts.

ed a peristyle or a sufficiently large and rich garden, the decoration was still quite striking. In the House of the Ceii (I 3, 25), the walls of the small courtyard that delimited the building to the north were entirely covered with paintings of a garden and the representation of a *paradeisos*. The same is true of the House of the Bear (VII 2, 44). A similar pattern was adopted in a small pseudo-peristyle (a peristyle with columns on only one or two sides) in three *domus* on the Via di Mercurio: the House of Adonis (I 7, 1), the House of the Large Fountain (I 8, 22), and the House of the Small Garden (I 8, 23). The focal point of these painted gardens was often a *nymphaeum* dressed in multicolored mosaics, a characteristic feature in the houses of Pompeii in its last phase. *Nymphaea* with mosaic casing are to be found in at least fifteen houses in the city, which vary quite a lot in size. Besides the houses of the Large Fountain and Small Fountain, the Ceii, and the Bear, there are the House of the Centennial, the House of the Golden

Bracelet (VI 17, 42), the House of the Scientists (VI 14, 43) and, in a unique version with two opposite-facing, outdoor *nymphaea*, the House of the Triclinium.

The patrician mansions, with their architecture and decoration, also served as models and sources of inspiration for middle class citizens who imitated them in their own houses, which were understandably often of inferior quality, given the people's limited economic resources. Types of houses that were perhaps common among the middle class were the so-called terrace or unit houses, named after the scholar who first recognized this type (the "Quadrati-Hoffmann"). They were characterized by a simple layout: a narrow entrance vestibule flanked by two cubicles, a central open courtyard with two or more rooms at the sides, and at the end, a garden with a small portico. The small houses often had large gardens (as in the House of Hercules' Garden, II 8, 6) and were concentrated in the southeastern sector of the city, northwest of the amphithe-

ater. There are also many ruins of the lower class houses often represented by workshops with living quarters or with *pergulae*, or mezzanines, and rented rooms.

In A.D. 79, when Vesuvius erupted and buried the city under 20 feet of ashes and cinders, Pompeii covered a surface area of about 173 acres, only 109 of which have been brought to light. Archeological digs, which have continued from 1748 to the present, have restored the image of this Roman city during the early Imperial Age caught by surprise and "frozen" by the eruption in a particular mo-

ment of its daily life. The buildings not only bear traces of the destructive action of the eruption, but in many cases lack the decoration (paintings, sculpture, and furnishings) that one would expect to find in a city whose life had stopped dead on August 24, A.D. 79, just a normal day. Because of the almost total lack of sculptural decoration, the public areas and private houses without their usual marble dressing, the many unfinished wall paintings, and the numerous edifices with stacks of building materials in one or more rooms, most scholars have come to the con-

clusion that at the time of the eruption the city was still in a flurry of construction work, and that the series of quakes that had followed the tremendous one in A.D. 62 had made restoration work extremely difficult.

In the case of private houses, the dynamic real estate market most probably had contributed to that impression of "work in progress." In fact, remodeling and re-decoration was quite common, as was the transfer of property, both within the same family and from one family to an-

94-95 The wall decoration in the House of the Vettii is the most complete surviving example of Fourth Style painting. In this period (A.D. 54-79) the Eros motif was quite common, as can be seen in the frieze that ran between the base and central zone, filled with Cupids and Psyches engaged in various activities, in the atrium (wine merchants, perfume vendors, etc.). Mythological scenes were in the predelle.

94 bottom and 95 top The peristyle of the House of the Vettii was lined with the most important reception halls. The Fourth Style decorative scheme in each one had uniform motifs: on the three walls of the colonnaded "Theban" hall were three episodes of the Theban myth (clockwise: the young Hercules strangling the snakes; Pentheus' torment; Dirce's death).

other, partly due to what we would now call a "turnover" in the dominating class of Pompeii in the late Republican and early Imperial Age.

As for the civic buildings, the "work in progress" phenomenon has been more frequently explained by a delay in restoration work. Building activity was probably concentrated on edifices used for public gatherings such as the amphitheater and on the public baths, in other words, the new focal points of the Pompeiian community. In A.D. 79 the city's baths were the Stabian Baths (the most ancient in the city), the Baths of the Forum, and the Suburban Baths, while the new Central Baths were still being built. The amphitheater, the theater (whose stage and skene, dressed in marble and adorned with statues, had been restored after the A.D. 62 quake), and the Odeum were also operative. The Macellum and Temple of Venus were partially restored. On the other hand, the Forum and the Capitolium and its annexes, which had been part-

96 and 97 The villas in the suburbs of Pompeii stood out for their rich architecture and decoration. The Villa of the Mysteries, which dominated the landscape with its impressive base consisting of large niches, is famous above all for the large painting after which it was named. The large pictorial frieze with its life-size figures decorated the walls of the most important hall in the villa. The origin and subject of this exceptional work have been written about countless times. According to the theory most widely accepted today, the frieze is not a Roman copy of a Greek work as was believed for many years, but rather an original Roman work created in the first century B.C. that represents the mystery (Dionysian) rites connected with the initiation of a young woman.

ly or totally destroyed (as can be seen in the reliefs decorating the *lararium* in the House of Caecilius Iucundus, an *argentarius*, or banker), do not seem to have been included in the list of urgent restoration work.

Lastly, by A.D. 79 restoration work had been completed on the Temple of Isis, built in the Augustan Age and restored to its original form (a temple on a podium in the middle of a peristyle courtyard) after the A.D. 62 quake with rich Fourth Style painting decoration. The work had been carried out at the expense of a freedman, N. Popidius Ampliatus, who had emphatically attributed the work to his son, N. Popidius Celsinus, who was only six years old at the time, probably to pave the way for a po-

litical career when he became an adult.

However, recent studies have stressed the importance of the role played by spoliation, both ancient and modern, in creating this impression of an "unfinished" city. Considering this, the state of "abandon" in such a large area of Pompeii should not be attributed only to the delay in restoration work due to many factors such as the series of earthquakes and the priority given to other buildings. Furthermore, plundering was presumedly systematically organized by the powers that be after the eruption. According to this theory, the fact that the Temple of Isis was in such a good state of preservation is due to the fact that its painted wall dressing was considered of little value.

98 top The face of Ramesses II, from the Temple of Luxor.

98 bottom Roman statue from Leptis Magna, now in the Tripoli Museum.

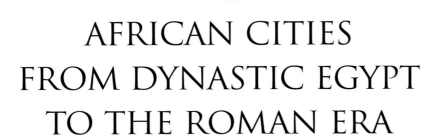

AFRICAN CITIES FROM DYNASTIC EGYPT TO THE ROMAN ERA

TEXT BY

SIMONE RAMBALDI - MARCO ZECCHI

Before the Roman conquest, which united the northern regions of the African continent from Suez to the Atlantic Ocean, cities spread in various ways according to the historic context that had determined the patterns of settlement and to influential cultural traditions. In fact, some of these territories, which are now part of present-day Egypt, Libya, Tunisia, Algeria, and Morocco, witnessed the rise of great civilizations with important urban development, while in other areas the form of settlement remained in a less evolved stage. Ancient Egypt was dotted with cities and villages, some of which had originated in primitive hut settlements. There were many farmers' villages and agglomerates of houses made mostly of lime from the Nile River. Besides these communities, the country had hundreds of cities as well. Apart from the great capitals that were founded during the various dynasties, such as Memphis and Thebes, some of these cities were important because they were either provincial capitals or religious sites of national prominence. The characteristic feature of other cities was their geographic position and the economic activity centered around their temple. For example, Said in the Delta was known as a major textile production center, and Sile was a garrison site.

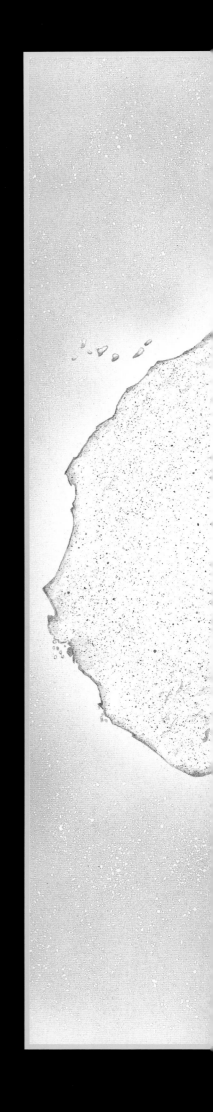

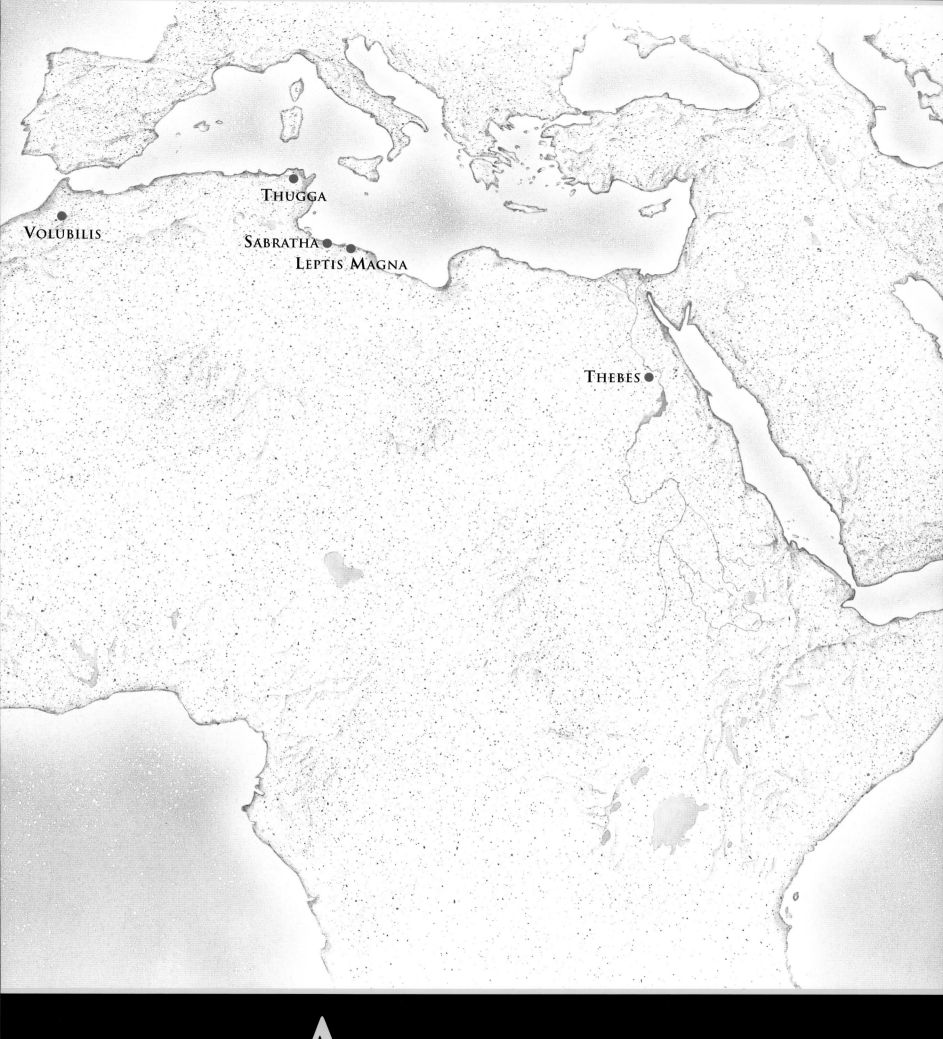

VOLUBILIS

THUGGA

SABRATHA
LEPTIS MAGNA

THEBES

AFRICA

AFRICA

INTRODUCTION

The traditional towns lay in a rather confined space, both to make available as much land as possible for cultivation and because of the annual Nile floods. Egypt's particular geographic position must be taken into account: the cultivable land was limited to a thin strip that ran along the Nile, as well as the Delta and oases. Beyond the periodically irrigated zones lay the desert. The Egyptians were virtually obliged to found their villages and cities either in desert areas at the boundary of their farmland, in elevated positions along the river, or on the low hills in the Delta in order to be safe from the floods.

New houses made completely of bricks were continuously being built, often over the ruins of older, demolished houses. Neither the large urban communities nor the smaller ones had any particular town plan or building regulations. However, some that were founded anew and have survived reveal a precise construction program, with streets intersecting at right angles and regular blocks with houses built according to almost identical specifications. These were the so-called cities such as Kahun in the Fayyum, Deir el-Medina at Thebes, and Amarna in Middle Egypt, which were conceived as towns for the workmen and artisans (and their families) who built the tombs in the various necropolises.

The Phoenicians undoubtedly began to arrive in the area west of the Nile Valley before 1000 B.C. They then founded commercial centers along the Mediterranean coast of Africa in places where harbors could be built and which were often connected to the trade routes that reached into the interior of the continent. The most important of these was Carthage, which dominated the other colonies, laying the foundation for an empire that extended its sphere of influence beyond the African coast to include Spain, Sardinia, and western Sicily. This empire, already weakened to some extent by the conflict with the Greek colony of Syracuse, ended up being defeated several times and then finally destroyed by the power of ancient Rome.

The conquest of Carthage, which occurred at the end of the Third Punic War (146 B.C.), marked the beginning of the Roman occupation of Africa. After establishing the province of Africa, whose capital was Utica in present-day Tunisia, the Romans asserted themselves more and more, conquering territories that had already begun to acquire elements of classical civilization. The usurpation of King Jugurtha and the war that ensued paved the way for more direct intervention on the part of Rome in the countries west of Carthaginian territory, where they dismembered the ancient kingdom of Numidia, which had been an important ally in the war against Hannibal. The western sector of Numidia had been granted to Bocchus, the king of the friendly state of Mauretania, while the eastern sector had been left to the indigenous

101 Detail of a mosaic from the House of Liber Pater, Sabratha.

royal house, which had abandoned all claims to wielding power. But the aid that Juba I gave to Pompey during the civil war with Caesar brought about the Numidian territory's definitive loss of freedom, as it became part of a provincial administration. In fact, the Romans established a new province, its name, Africa Nova, distinguishing it from the previous one, which was now called Vetus. But soon afterward the large province of Africa Proconsularis was founded. It included Tripolitania, the seat of the ancient Phoenician trade centers that had been under Roman dominion for some time. The new capital was Carthage, refounded as a colony by Augustus, in compliance with Caesar's wishes.

Juba II, the legitimate heir to the throne of Numidia, was made king of Mauretania, where Bocchus' dynasty had ended, as recompense for having lost his father's kingdom. The new sovereign gave a strong Hellenistic stamp to the country: he added the name Caesarea to his capital, Iol, and built many classical-style edifices throughout the land (such as the theater, which was clearly modeled after the Theater of Pompey in Rome), as well as copies of sculptures in keeping with the current fashion in the major cities of the Mediterranean world. This remarkable period of splendor in Mauretania came to an abrupt halt when Ptolemy, Juba II's son, was treacherously assassinated by Caligula while in Rome. This large territory was then divided by Claudius into two new provinces, Mauretania Tingitana, with Tingis (present-day Tangier) as its capital, and Mauretania Caesariensis, whose capital was Iol-Caesarea. The division of the African territory within the Roman Empire remained virtually unaltered (with the exception of the elimination of Numidia in the late second century A.D.) up to the age of Diocletian, when the continent was divided into an even greater number of provinces during the emperor's total reorganization of the Roman Empire.

When Rome acquired all these regions, it found it possessed urban communities including the colonies founded by the Phoenicians for particular commercial purposes but that had often developed into true cities, even if in territories with a small population like Tripolitania. This was the case with Leptis Magna and Sabratha. Then there were communities and colonies with quite different histories behind them such as fortresses like Thugga perched on top of steep hills, or towns like Volubilis that had prospered during the Hellenistic age. However, in many cases the Romans founded cities in places that had never really had a true urban configuration such as the site of Thamugadi (Timgad). Here, as in the other provinces of the Roman Empire, Roman civilization was manifested not only in the enlargement of the urban area (when there was one), but also through a considerable revamping and reinforcement of the edifices and areas used for community life.

102 TOP ENTRANCE TO THE TEMPLE OF LUXOR AS SEEN BY EUROPEAN TRAVELERS IN THE EARLY TWENTIETH CENTURY.

102 BOTTOM WORKMEN EXCAVATING BETWEEN THE THIRD AND FOURTH PYLONS OF THE TEMPLE OF KARNAK IN THE 1950S.

103 TOP RESTORATION WORK INSIDE THE HYPOSTYLE HALL OF THE TEMPLE OF KARNAK.

103 BOTTOM LEFT AN EARLY TWENTIETH-CENTURY PHOTOGRAPH SHOWS PART OF THE TEMPLE OF LUXOR COVERED BY RUBBLE.

103 BOTTOM RIGHT 1904: THE FIRST FINDS FROM THE CACHE AT KARNAK, A HUGE REPOSITORY OF STATUES.

THEBES

THEBES

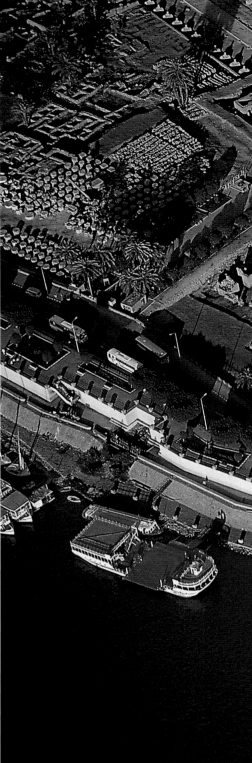

Text by MARCO ZECCHI

The city of Thebes, called Waset (the "scepter") in ancient Egyptian, was the capital of the IV *nome* (or province) of Upper Egypt. Its geographic position was crucial to its historic importance; the city was situated near Nubia and the Eastern Desert, rich in mineral resources. However, its centrality in Egyptian history is due to political and religious factors. Since the Middle Kingdom Thebes became increasingly important, as it was the birthplace of some Eleventh Dynasty pharaohs and of all the Eighteenth Dynasty ones. The golden age of the city coincided with this latter dynasty, when it became the capital of all Egypt. Its temples were the wealthiest and most important in the country, and its god Amon was recognized

as the "lord of the gods." Toward the end of the Eighteenth Dynasty and during the Nineteenth, the nation's capital was moved, but Thebes did not lose any of its prestige, as it still played a major role in the administration of the country and its temples continued to prosper, thanks to the intervention of many pharaohs. However, the power of the city was destined to end. Already in the Late Period the Egyptian Delta began to dominate the political and economic scene and Thebes lost most of its long-lived influence and prestige.

Little is known of the city, situated on the east bank of the Nile, because it lies under modern-day Luxor. The Middle Kingdom city, built around the central nucleus of

the Temple of Karnak, was razed to the ground to make room for a larger temple, while the city proper extended southward as far as the Temple of Luxor.

On the east bank of the Nile there are two groups of temples: to the south is Luxor and, two miles further north, Karnak. The Temple of Luxor, known as the "southern harem," was basically built by two pharaohs, Amenhotep III (Eighteenth Dynasty) and Ramesses II (Nineteenth Dynasty). Later, many other kings had the temple decorated with reliefs and inscriptions, added other minor edifices, and made some alterations. In front of the temple is the pylon of Ramesses II, the outer side of which has reliefs and inscriptions relating the famous

104 top left A relief from one of the chambers in the Temple of Luxor portraying Amenhotep III holding two vases during the "invocation of the funerary offering" ritual.

104 bottom left The entrance pylon and the obelisk of Ramesses II stand out to the north of the Temple of Luxor.

104 right Statue of Ramesses II wearing the *nemes* headdress; to the right is a detail of the obelisk, while in the background is one of the colossi of the pharaoh.

104-105 This aerial view shows the configuration of the Temple of Luxor complex along the banks of the Nile.

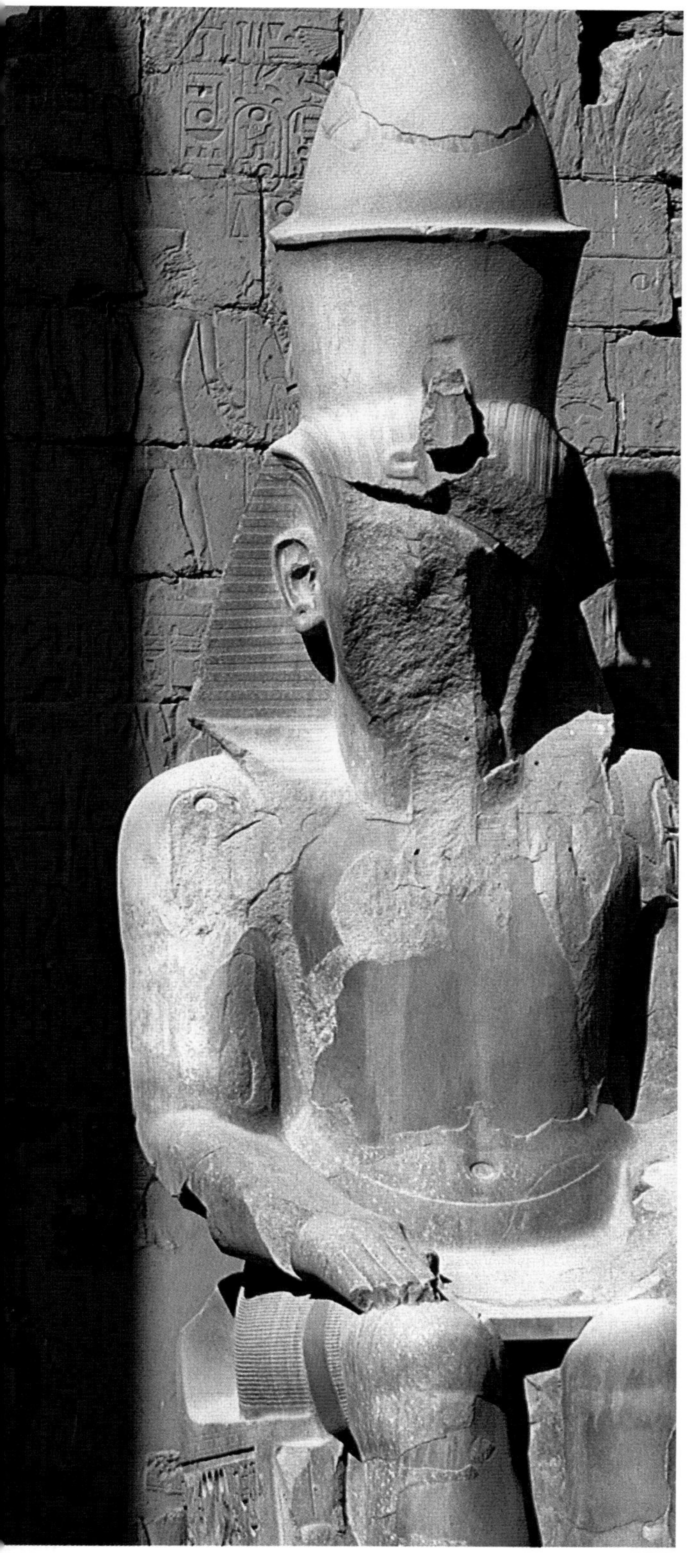

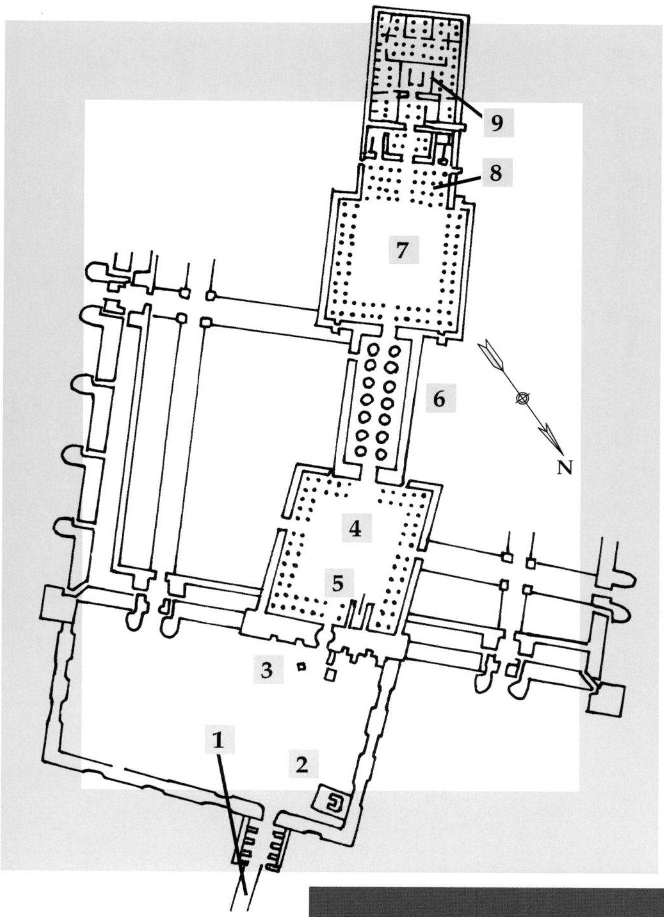

106-107 The two gigantic statues of the seated pharaoh and, in the foreground, the obelisk accentuate the monumentality of the entrance to the Temple of Luxor; in the interior is a third statue of the pharaoh Ramesses II.

106 bottom The entrance pylon at Luxor is the starting point for an avenue of human-headed sphinxes, the work of Nectanebo I (30th Dynasty), which linked this sanctuary with the sanctuary at Karnak, two miles away.

107 The courtyard of the temple was built by Ramesses II with a statue of the seated pharaoh placed just behind the entrance pylon, from which the processional colonnade of Amenhotep III began.

Temple of Luxor
1) Avenue of sphinxes
2) Chapel of Serapis
3) Pylon of Ramesses II
4) Courtyard of Ramesses II
5) Chapel of the Theban Triad
6) Colonnade of Amenhotep II
7) Front courtyard of Amenhotep III
8) Hypostyle atrium
9) Sanctuary

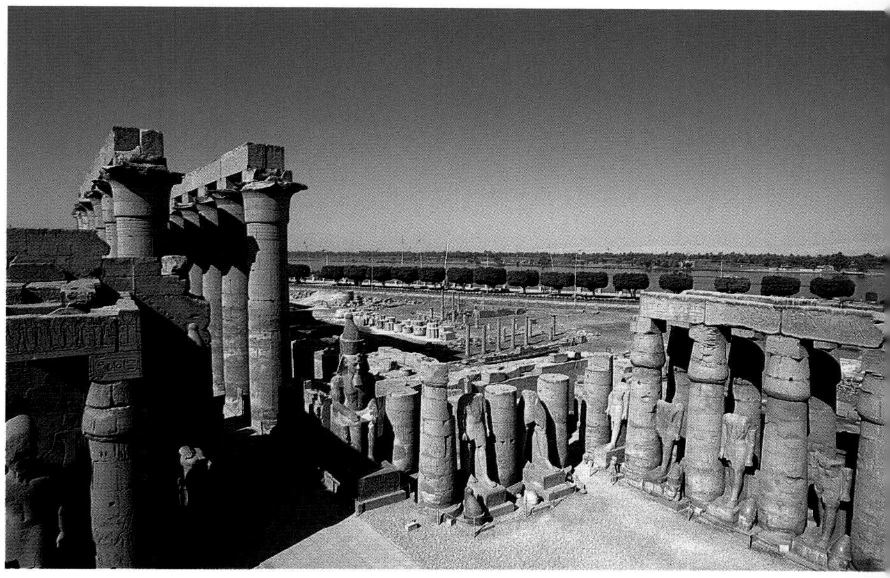

Battle of Kadesh against the Hittites. Two obelisks originally stood in front of the pylon but now only one remains, since the other one is now in Place de la Concorde in Paris. Some colossal statues of Ramesses II, two of which portray the pharaoh while seated, flank the entrance. Once past the gate of the pylon, one enters the first court, the work of Ramesses II, with 74 papyriform columns that bear relief scenes of the pharaoh in the presence of several deities. Proceeding along the axis of the temple, one comes to the second court, built by Amenhotep III. This has seven columns on either side and merges with the Hall of Columns, which is the first inner chamber of the temple and originally had a roof. From here one passes through four antechambers arranged one after the other and flanked by other side rooms. The innermost part of the temple is the so-called *sancta sanctorum,* or sanctuary, built by Amenhotep III. It consists of a 12-column vestibule that precedes three chapels, of which the central one had a tabernacle that housed a statue of the god Amon.

The Temple of Luxor was connected to the Temple of Karnak by means of an avenue flanked by human-headed sphinxes.

The name Karnak (*Ipet-isut* in ancient Egyptian) indicates a complex of temples and other religious edifices built in different periods. The archaeological site can be divided into three groups, each of which is bounded by the remains of brick walls. The largest wall, with a trapezoidal shape,

108 left In the back section of the Great Temple of Amon is a large obelisk built by Queen Hatshepsut.

108 top right The sphinxes on the avenue of Karnak have rams' heads; in Egyptian symbology this animal sacred to Amon was identified with fertility.

108 bottom right The first pylon in the Great Temple of Amon at Karnak is preceded by the avenue of ram-headed sphinxes. The pylon was probably built during the 30th Dynasty.

THEBES

was dedicated to Amon and enclosed the great temple of the god, a sacred lake, and some minor temples, including the one dedicated to the god Ptah of Memphis and another dedicated to the god Khonsu, the son of Amon and Mut. The Great Temple of Amon has a rather complex plan. There are six pylons, or large portals, and the temple is laid out on an East-West axis in keeping with the classic scheme: a monumental entranceway, a large court, a hall of columns, a hall of offerings, another hall for the sacred barque, and lastly, the sanctuary itself, or *sancta sanctorum*. However, the Temple of Amon has a particular feature: by means of four pylons, it extends along the North-South axis. Mention should also be made of the fact that the hall of columns in the temple, situated behind the second pylon, is the largest in the world. This part of the temple is without a doubt the most impressive in the entire edifice. The hall of columns is 338 feet wide and 171 feet long. The roof (which no longer exists) was supported by 134 columns covered with relief scenes and inscriptions. The reliefs decorating the hall date from the reigns of Seti I and Ramess-

108-109 This aerial view of the Karnak complex shows, in the foreground, the precinct of the goddess Mut, with the crescent-shaped sacred lake that was the starting point of the avenue of ram-headed sphinxes that led to the large precinct of the goddess' husband, Amon.

TEMPLE OF KARNAK

1) FIRST PYLON
2) FIRST COURTYARD
3) SECOND PYLON
4) HYPOSTYLE ATRIUM
5) THIRD PYLON
6) FOURTH PYLON
7) FIFTH PYLON
8) SIXTH PYLON
9) SANCTUARY
10) FESTIVAL TEMPLE OF
    TUTHMOSIS III
11) SACRED LAKE
12) SEVENTH PYLON
13) EIGHTH PYLON
14) NINTH PYLON
15) TEMPLE OF OPET
16) TEMPLE OF KHONS
17) TEMPLE OF RAMESSES II

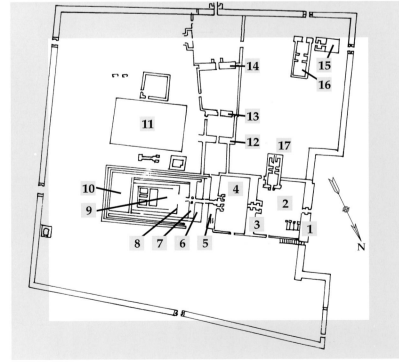

es II (Nineteenth Dynasty). Many pharaohs played a role in the construction of the temple, enlarging it by adding pylons and halls, or beautifying it with reliefs. Besides Seti I and Ramesses II, the Eighteenth Dynasty pharaohs—Tuthmosis I and III, Horemheb, Amenhotep II and III, and Queen Hatshepsut–should be mentioned in this regard. North of this sacred precinct of Amon is the one dedicated to Montu, the ancient god of Thebes generally depicted with a falcon's head. This complex, the smallest of all, includes the Temple of Montu, a sacred lake and other smaller temples. South of the Amon precinct is the sacred precinct of his wife Mut, a divinity often represented in the guise of a buzzard. This complex, which was connected to Amon's by a monumental way flanked by ram-headed sphinxes, houses the Temple of Mut, which is partly surrounded by a sacred lake in the shape of a half moon and other minor edifices.

Once a year Thebes hosted a great celebration during which the statue of Amon was borne in procession from the Temple of Karnak to the Temple of Luxor, where it remained for about three weeks.

On the west bank of the Nile, opposite Karnak and Luxor, are the Theban necropoli. Just beyond a small cultivated field lies the desert, and a short distance further are the hills of the Libyan plateau, the valleys of which were chosen by the New Kingdom pharaohs as their burial site (the Valley of the Kings). Other areas were used to house the tombs of the citizens of Thebes, while the southernmost part of the Theban necropolis contains the Valley of the Queens, where the pharaohs' consorts and children were buried. In the area between the cultivated fields and the hills lie the royal mortuary temples, whose main function was to keep alive the cult of the pharaohs buried in the Valley of the Kings.

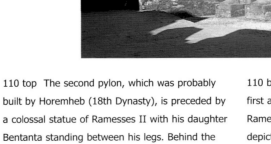

THEBES

110 top The second pylon, which was probably built by Horemheb (18th Dynasty), is preceded by a colossal statue of Ramesses II with his daughter Bentanta standing between his legs. Behind the pylon is Sethos I's colonnade.

110 bottom left A view of the Hall of Columns at Karnak, showing some of the 134 huge papyriform columns, which differ from the twelve central columns, which have open umbels.

110 bottom right View of the section between the first and second pylon of the small Temple of Ramesses III. Here we see the osiride pylons depicting the pharaoh in the guise of the mummified god Osiris.

111 From bottom to top: the first pylon, the first courtyard, the second pylon followed by the Hall of Columns.

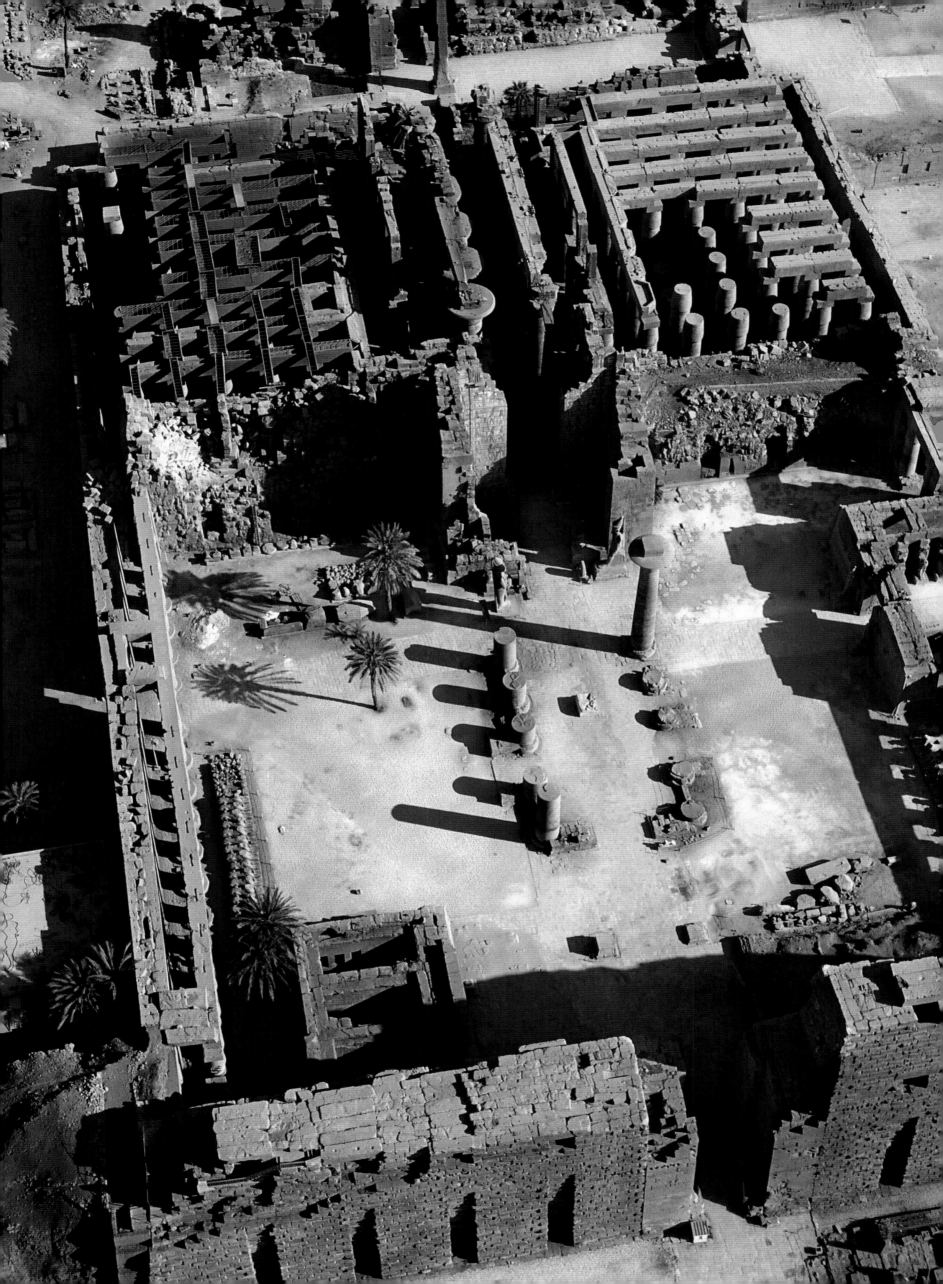

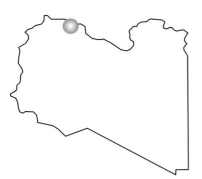

Text by SIMONE RAMBALDI

The Roman city of Leptis, later called Leptis Magna, rose up on a more ancient Phoenician city at an ideal spot for commercial activity, since some caravan routes linking the coast with the interior passed through. The original settlement, which later entered the Carthaginian sphere of influence, lay near the sea west of the Wadi Lebda, a torrent at the mouth of which the port later developed.

The city's first Roman monuments were built at the end of the first century B.C., after Tripolitania had been incorporated into the Roman province of Africa Proconsularis. In this period, some wealthy citizens financed the construction of important edifices that clearly demonstrated the desire to adapt to the tastes of

LEPTIS
MAGNA

112 bottom left The Forum built by Septimius Severus. At right are the partially rebuilt arches of the arcade on the south side of the square. In the background, past the shops, is the basilica wall.

the central power, despite the fact that the local culture had been Romanized only superficially and the common language was still Punic, as is attested to by official inscriptions. The names of these benefactors also clearly reveal their ethnic roots: Annobal Tapapius Rufus financed the building of the *macellum* (the city market) and the theater, while Iddibal Caphada Aemilius was responsible for the *chalcidicum* (most probably another commercial facility). A portrait of the latter patron is fundamental evidence not only of the quality of Tripolitanian sculpture but also of the degree to which the ruling class had assimilated Roman culture. Aemilius had himself represented in keeping with classical artistic canons, although his African features are easily recognizable.

The Augustan age also witnessed important works in the area of the Old Forum, which took on a wholly new monumental look. The Corinthian Temple of Rome and Augustus was built on the site of the preceding temple dedicated to Milk'ashtart on the northern side of the square, which was already a sacred quarter of the city's two protective goddesses. Next door, the other pre-existing Temple of Shadrapa was re-dedicated to his Roman

112 bottom right This was one of the medallions that decorated the arches of the Forum built by Septimius Severus. It has the portrait of the Oriental goddess Atargatis.

112-113 The ancient Severan basilica became a church in Justinian's time. The two Corinthian capitals seen in the foreground were used to build a pulpit. In the background is the west apse.

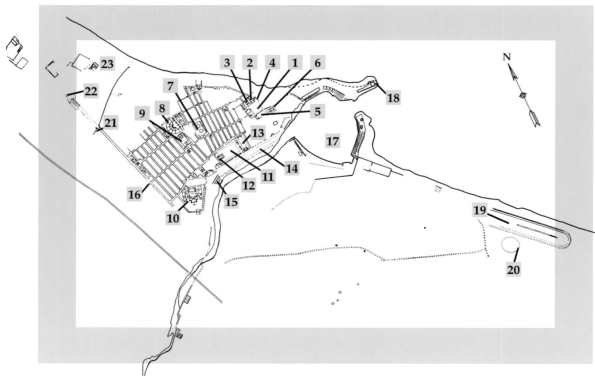

equivalent Liber Pater, or Bacchus. Milk'ashtart was also adapted to Roman criteria and the new Temple of Hercules was built for his cult at the northeastern corner of the square, which thus took on a trapezoidal shape. A basilica, whose main axis was perpendicular to that of the Forum, then occupied the entire opposite side, following a well-known Italic pattern. Rounding off the series of civic buildings, east of the basilica was the *curia*, the seat of the city magistrates, in the shape of a hexastyle temple on a podium enclosed by a colon-

nade. Both the town plan and the architecture used for these new edifices reveal a strong influence of Roman, or at least Italic, models. This is true not only of the religious and civic edifices but also for others such as the theater, whose *cavea* is crowned by a small temple dedicated to Ceres Augusta, a pattern very similar to the one in the Theater of Pompey, which was built in Rome in 55 B.C.

As for the town layout, an important clue to how it may have appeared over time is the position of the newer monuments. The *macellum*, for example, is not perfectly aligned with the surrounding street network,

114 top left Restoration work has revived the splendor of the four-façade Arch of Septimius Severus. The rich relief decoration on the attic on this side presents a scene of unity between the emperor and his family.

114 top right The large *palaestra* was one of the gems in the Baths of Hadrian, which provided Leptis Magna with a modern *thermae* in no way inferior to the great baths in Rome.

114-115 The interior of the theater seen from the tiers. Behind the remains of the *scenae frons* are the columns of a colonnaded area, which was a common feature of Roman theaters.

115 bottom The ruins of the Tetrapylon of Trajan at the junction of the *cardo maximus* and a side street that led to the theater. At right, behind the arch, are the remains of the Chalcidicum.

1) OLD FORUM
2) TEMPLE OF ROME AND AUGUSTUS
3) TEMPLE OF *LIBER PATER*
4) TEMPLE OF *HERCULES*
5) BASILICA
6) CURIA
7) *MACELLUM*
8) THEATER
9) *CHALCIDICUM*
10) BATHS OF HADRIAN
11) NEW FORUM
12) DYNASTIC TEMPLE
13) SEVERAN BASILICA
14) COLONNADED AVENUE
15) NYMPHAEUM
16) SEVERAN ARCH
17) HARBOR
18) LIGHTHOUSE
19) CIRCUS
20) AMPHITHEATER
21) ARCH OF ANTONINUS PIUS
22) ARCH OF MARCUS AURELIUS
23) HUNTING BATHS COMPLEX

while the orientation of the theater and the adjacent *chalcidicum* dovetails with the blocks that proceed to the southwest, which, however, we know were laid out definitively only a few decades later. Thus, these new monuments were originally placed in a sector of the city whose growth and development had already been planned but had not yet been regularized relative to the blocks and road network. In fact, the *cardo maximus* of the city, which passed east of these edifices, makes a considerable deviation at the point where an arch dedicated to Tiberius was erected.

During the second century A.D., besides the construction of other arches such as the four-façade Arch of Trajan on the *cardo* and the arches of Antoninus Pius and Marcus Aurelius on the *decumanus maximus*, the most impor-

tant architectural undertaking was certainly the construction of the large Baths of Hadrian a short distance from the Wadi Lebda. These baths also marked an important stage in the use of building material because, for the first time, marble was employed at Leptis, while before that time only the local limestone had been used. The orientation of the complex is completely different from that of the neighboring blocks. This was certainly due to the shape of the area at the architects' disposal, but another reason may have been the desire to have the baths in a position better exposed to sunlight, as was the case with the grandiose baths in Rome.

The emperor Septimius Severus was a native of Leptis, so it is not surprising that the city achieved its maximum splendor during the Severan age, between the end of the second century and the first decades of the third century A.D. During this period a new, large Forum was laid out in an area near the Wadi Lebda, with a colonnaded square with a grandiose dynastic temple standing on a tall podium in the middle of one of the short sides. In the opposite part of the area an enormous two-aisle basilica was constructed. The architectural decoration of the entire complex was particularly well planned. In the square, a row of marble medallions bearing heads, mostly of Gorgons, stood between one arch and the other one of the colonnade, while the temple was adorned with scenes of the Battle of the Gods and Giants in the column plinths. The interior of the basilica also contained elegant decoration, especially in the two semicircular apses at the short ends of the nave that were framed by pilasters with reliefs of maps and scenes of Hercules' labors on the east side, and Bacchanalian scenes on the west one. In this way, homage was paid to the two main divinities of Leptis while also serving as a tribute to the reigning dynasty, since the imperial propaganda identified Caracalla and Geta with Hercules and Liber Pater (Bacchus). There are other examples, even in Rome itself, of this connection between Septimius Severus' sons and the two divinities.

The project of the new Forum was also conditioned

116-117 In the foreground, one of the two *tholoi* that stood in the open space of the *macellum*. These were round pavilions surrounded by octagonal colonnades.

117 top left The entrance to the *macellum* seen from the *cardo maximus*. This complex, constructed during the feverish building activity that took place in the Augustan age, was an important commercial center for Leptis Magna.

by the previous town layout. The basilica is not exactly perpendicular with the main axis of the square, but makes an obtuse angle with it, and the square itself does the same with the adjacent blocks. The wedge-shaped areas thus created among these diverging spaces were occupied by rows of workshops of decreasing size, a very clever way to conceal the different axes. According to a theory proposed a few years ago, the Forum was supposed to have been doubled in size through the addition of another square on the other side of the basilica, but the project was never realized. Furthermore, a major colonnaded street was laid out along the axis consisting of the Wade Lebda torrent, beginning at the port and heading southward. After passing by the Severan Forum, it changed direction at the Baths of

117 bottom left The only remaining part of the second *tholos* in the Macellum is the perimetrical colonnade, the inner arches of which were not restored.

117 right This temple, now reduced to a few columns, was in the middle of the colonnaded area behind the theater. In the foreground, a tetrapylon that was added in a later period in order to support a group of statues of Septimius Severus' family.

Hadrian, opening onto an irregularly shaped square decorated with a magnificent *nymphaeum*. Further testimony of the wealth of decoration at Leptis is provided by the private homes, even though they are not as well documented as the public buildings. Mosaics such as the ones found in the so-called House of Orpheus and the Villa of the Nile clearly demonstrate the luxury common to certain residences.

In the same period major work was carried out to enlarge the port, which had already been enlarged during Nero's time, while the amphitheater was also built east of the city center. On the promontory that delimited the port harbor a lighthouse was built on the same axis of

118 top left A garden has been recreated in this seaside villa at Silin. This important find is testimony to the luxury of these residences, which were often built in splendid natural settings.

118 top right The Hunting Baths were also built in the Severan age, but far from the city center. The form of the concrete domes seems to prefigure Arab architecture.

the colonnaded street, thus creating a fascinating panoramic view.

Two more monuments dating from the Severan period and of a quite different nature are worthy of mention. The first is the four-faced arch that was almost certainly erected on the site where a previous one had stood, at the crossroads of the *cardo* and *decumanus*. This arch, which has been recently restored, was dressed with a wealth of reliefs that, besides providing essential examples of the sculpture of the time, reveal important moments in the public life of the Severan dynasty. Of particular significance is a scene showing Septimius Severus on a triumphal *quadriga* accompanied by his two sons in an atmosphere of harmony and concord that gives us no hint of the dramatic events that occurred after the death of the father, when Caracalla unscrupulously assassinated his brother in order to become the sole emperor. The second

monument is the Hunting Baths complex, named after a fresco of hunting scenes that still exists. These baths are quite fascinating because of the concrete domes, which inevitably remind modern visitors of Arab architecture.

After this period of great splendor, the city of Leptis Magna rapidly declined. It was invaded several times by the Austurians and the Vandals, and then, after a period of Byzantine dominion, the Arabs destroyed it. After remaining in oblivion for a long time, the city's history was recovered only at the beginning of the twentieth century, when excavations by Italian archaeologists brought the ruins to light.

118 bottom This mosaic from the Villa of Silin represents the punishment of Lycurgus, who was entrapped by vine branches and transformed into the nymph Ambrosia in order to regain his sanity.

119 Detail of the border of the pavement in the peristyle of the Villa of Silin, depicting a battle between a pigmy and a stork, a recurring motif in Greco-Roman art.

SABRATHA

Text by SIMONE RAMBALDI

Together with Leptis Magna and Oea, Sabratha was one of the three major cities in Tripolitania. Its history is much like those of the other two. At first a Phoenician emporium subsequently ruled by the Carthaginians, it was made part of the Roman province of Africa Proconsularis in 46 B.C. and became a *municipium* and then a colony during the Imperial Age. After its golden age during the Antonine and Severan periods, Sabratha began to decline rapidly in late antiquity because of the Austurian and Vandal invasions. After a partial revival under the Byzantine rulers, it was abandoned for good when the Arabs conquered the area.

Naturally, the hub of city life was the Forum, a rectangular colonnaded square surrounded by the buildings used for the main

120 left This polychrome mosaic is now in the Sabratha Museum.

120 right A colossal marble bust of Jupiter from the Sabratha Capitolium. Note the animated movement of the hair and beard, which creates a striking contrast to the flat surface of the face.

120-121 The theater, which dates from late second or early third century A.D. In the foreground are the tiers, and in the background, past the orchestra, is the *scenae frons* with three superposed rows of marble columns.

public activities. The complex we see today stands basically as it was in the second century A.D., when important renovation works were carried out after the restoration effected to repair the damage of an earthquake that occurred between A.D. 65 and 70. On the short western side stood the Capitolium, which faced the square with a large platform bordered by two side stairways. On the opposite side, in the middle of a courtyard with a peristyle on three sides, there was another temple whose dedication to Liber Pater on the part of the Romans served to maintain a connection with the ancient indigenous religion. The series of civic buildings was completed by two

structures behind the colonnade of the two long sides of the square: to the north was the *curia*, consisting of a rectangular hall connected to an open space, and to the south was the basilica. The plan of the latter, which had two aisles and a nave, included a room on the south side that probably housed the magistrate's tribunal, which may have also been used as a *sacellum* for the cult of the emperor. In late antiquity the basilica became a Christian church.

The colonnaded square serving as a sumptuous frame for a religious edifice was in keeping with a well-known pattern, which can be noted at Sabratha in the Temple of

1) Forum
2) Capitolium
3) Temple of Liber Pater
4) Curia
5) Basilica
6) Temple of Marcus Aurelius and Lucius Vero
7) Temple of an unknown deity
8) Temple of Serapis
9) Theater
10) Temple of Isis

122 left The atrium of the Curia near the Forum square. In the foreground is an arcade made from the Corinthian capitals of the colonnade.

122 right Although the elegantly sculpted capital and cornice are separated from buildings they once belonged to, they attest to the rich decoration in the public edifices of Sabratha.

122-123 A large area of ruins on the Mediterranean coast bears witness to the past sumptuousness of the ancient city.

SABRATHA

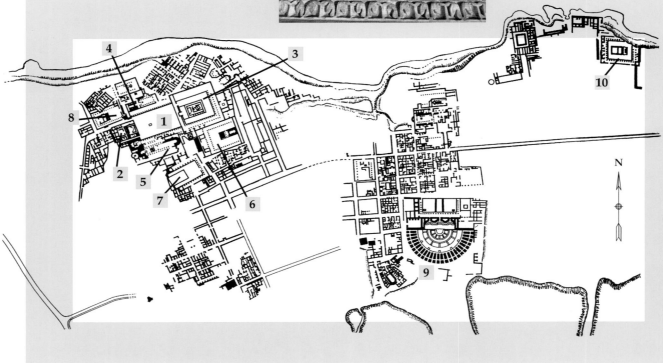

Liber Pater and other religious complexes, most of which were located near the Forum. East of the basilica was a small open area connected to two religious complexes, both dating from the Antonine age, that were built according to the above mentioned plan. One was dedicated to Marcus Aurelius and Lucius Verus, and the other to an unknown deity. At the northwest corner of the Forum, another temple, dedicated to Serapis, was also bordered by colonnades. Further away, on the seashore, in the middle of a peristyle, was the Temple of Isis, which was on a podium above the courtyard and thus had a stairway. Here archaeologists discovered a subterranean crypt where the mysteries of the goddess' cult were probably performed, as well as other chambers at the rear of the complex that may have been dedicated to minor deities.

Undoubtedly the most important monument in Sabratha was the theater, which was built in the late sec-

123 bottom View of the back of a Punic mausoleum, which can be dated to the first half of the second century B.C. Totally rebuilt, it reflects the prosperity of Sabratha before the Roman occupation.

ond century or perhaps the early third century A.D. This is certainly one of the most impressive examples of this type of edifice. The *cavea*, which had a double corridor at the base, was supported by three superposed rows of arches, with a portico crowning it. The magnificent *scaenae frons*, which was rebuilt by Italian archaelogists, still bears its sumptuous architectural decor which consists of three rows of marble columns in a staggered arrangement typical of the *skenai* of that time. The dressing of the walls behind the stage was also of marble, which no longer exists. Another very interesting feature of the theater is the *pulpitum,* or the front of the stage, which is animated by

protuberances and recesses that are alternatively rectangular and semicircular and decorated with a relief scenes. In the central niche is a scene of a sacrifice made by Septimius Severus, who is perhaps accompanied by his son Caracalla, before personifications of the cities of Rome and Sabartha, who are shaking hands. In the other two semicircular niches are the nine Muses (on the left) and a composition representing the Judgment of Paris, who stands with the Three Graces (on the right). The rectangular protuberances and niches are decorated with other figures that are not always easy to interpret but which in any case can be recognized as deities, theater masks, and

124-125 A row of columns barely conceals the enclosure wall of the theater whose arches, framed by semi-pilasters, lie on two partly preserved superposed rows of columns (there were originally three such rows).

125 top One of the dolphins sculpted at the two ends of the first row of seats in the cavea, reserved for leading citizens.

SABRATHA

125 center Detail of the sculptural decoration of the stage: the two theater masks are a specific reference to the function of this sumptuous edifice.

125 bottom left View of the exterior of the theater, which was once surrounded by a colonnade. Behind this is the façade of the stage, brought back to its original splendor thanks to the reconstruction by Italian archaeologists.

125 bottom right This semicircular niche in the middle of the stage shows Septimius Severus performing a sacrifice before personifications of Rome and Sabratha, and perhaps of his son Caracalla.

actors. The profile of each end of the enclosure that delimits the *proedria,* the area of the tiers reserved for local dignitaries, in the shape of a dolphin is another characteristic feature.

The amphitheater, which was probably constructed in the same period as the theater near the east end of the city, is one of the major attractions among the ruins of Sabratha. Partly cut out of the rock, this monument still contains remains of the tiers and the arches that surrounded it. The arena, which in ancient times was covered with wooden boarding with sand over it, is deeply traversed by two crossing corridors that were used as a passageway and storerooms by the personnel.

There are also many remains of domestic architecture in Sabratha, more than usually found in African cities. The houses, which often have porches that supported the upper floors, usually had a flat roof, as can be seen by the few roof tiles found here. At times archaeologists found underground rooms where the families took shelter from the torrid heat.

126 top In a public baths building quite near the beach is a fine polychrome mosaic floor divided into several panels decorated with different motifs separated by twisted fasciae.

126 bottom The amphitheater, at the east end of the Sabratha, was built in the depression formed by a stone quarry. The arena is traversed by two crossing galleries that were used for the spectacles.

126-127 Two rows of columns on the coastline mark the spot once occupied by the Temple of Isis, which stood inside an entirely porticoed court.

127 top left View of the ruins of the city, which are particularly evocative because they are washed by the Mediterranean Sea.

127 top right Little remains to show that these houses were once tall, but extensive portions of the mosaic floors that have been preserved testify to their luxuriousness.

128 top A panel of a mosaic floor in the House of Liber Pater with geometric decoration. In the middle is a flower surrounded by various types of cornices which in turn contain other decorative motifs.

128 bottom Detail of a mosaic from the Baths of Oceanus. This hexagonal panel, decorated by a braid motif, contains the beautiful head of the god Oceanus, who is bearded and has a crown of leaves and fruit on his head.

128-129 A mosaic from the House of Liber Pater. Of the three central tondos, the one on top represents the triumph of the god and Ariadne, standing on a chariot drawn by panthers, while the others have the heads of a panther and a lion.

SABRATHA

129 bottom left A polychrome mosaic panel decorated with a floral motif.

129 bottom right This mosaic is more simple than the preceding one because it has only one color and the leaves are stylized.

THUGGA

Text by SIMONE RAMBALDI

The original indigenous town of Thugga, present-day Dougga, in Tunisia, was founded on a hilltop. Remains of the pre-Roman period consist of traces of megalithic monuments, including the remains of walls and tombs, and the important Mausoleum of Ateban, dating to the second century B.C., the period when Thugga, after being in the Carthaginian sphere of influence, was part of the kingdom of Numidia. The Roman period began when Julius Caesar incorporated the city into the province of Africa Nova, which then became Africa Proconsularis under Augustus. During the Imperial Age it became a municipality and then a colony, after which it went into decline, a pattern common to all the North African cities.

The Roman city, which was not conditioned by the need for a defensive system but was basically oriented toward the exploitation of the neighboring farmland, extended to the foot of the hill where the previous city had stood. Its western and eastern "borders" were marked by two monumental arches during the Severan period. The Forum, planned at the beginning of the Imperial Age, was the junction between the two urban nuclei. The lack of available space was the cause of the particular configuration of the Forum complex, above all the irregular open area or square, which was in any case surrounded by three colonnades, and of the apparently

130-131 The Roman city of Thugga lies at the foot of the hill on which the earlier indigenous town was founded. The Capitolium dominates all the ruins.

131 top Through the finely wrought gate, which is difficult to interpret, one catches a glimpse of the Capitolium *pronaos*, which was a sort of monumental link between two different colonnaded precincts.

131 bottom left This statue near the Forum stands out for its rich drapery, which with its sinuous folds creates a charming play of shadows and light.

131 bottom right At the southern end of the city facing the countryside is the Mausoleum of Ateban, an impressive funerary monument several stories high that dates from the time when the site was part of the Numidian kingdom.

anomalous orientation of the Capitolium, which could not face the square but was built perpendicular to its major axis. This latter temple was built by a rich local family, the Marcii, during the rule of Marcus Aurelius. The scene sculpted on the pediment, with a human figure carried to the heavens by an eagle, can doubtless be interpreted as the apotheosis of Aurelius' predecessor, Antoninus Pius.

The generosity of the Marcii, who also paid for the construction of the theater, was part of a series of such acts of patronage that led to the construction of most of the monuments in Thugga. A few years later, another particularly important initiative in this regard was that of the Pacuvii, who financed a new public complex that enlarged the size of previous public areas to a considerable degree. East of the Capitolium, placed symmetrically with the Forum, a new colonnaded area was laid out. This is still known as the Wind Rose Square because of the round diagram carved into its pavement which in fact indicates the direction of the principal winds. On the southern side of this square is a market,

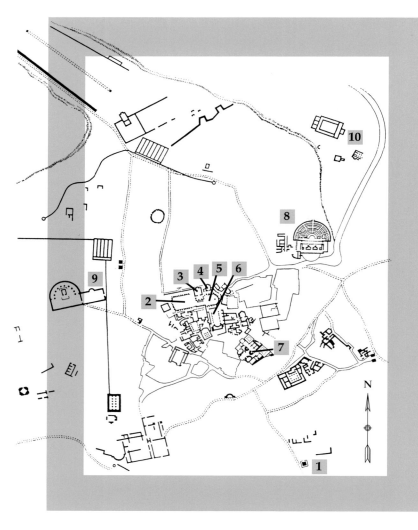

1) MAUSOLEUM OF ATEBAN
2) FORUM
3) CAPITOLIUM
4) TEMPLE OF MERCURY
5) WIND ROSE SQUARE
6) MARKET
7) LICINIAN BATHS
8) THEATER
9) TEMPLE OF CAELESTIS
10) TEMPLE OF SATURN

132 top The Arch of Emperor Alexander Severus marked the western border of the Roman city. It has one opening, flanked on both façades by four stepped Corinthian pilasters.

132 bottom The Temple of the Tellus was built in the second half of the third century A.D. next to the southwest corner of the market. It comprised an open area faced by three *cellae*.

133 The *pronaos* with four Corinthian columns stands on the access staircase. The tympanum had decoration that may have represented the apotheosis of Emperor Antoninus Pius.

which includes a colonnaded court along which the shops are lined and which ends in an apse (this layout is similar to the Market of Sertius at Thamugadi, but here there are no workshops in the apsidal section). The eastern side, the one opposite the Old Forum, is in the shape of a sort of semicircular *exedra*. On the northern side, beyond the colonnade and next to the Capitolium, is the Temple of Mercury, the layout of which is an interesting variation of the tripartite *cella* type of temple: the central *cella*, which is rectangular, is remarkably large, while the side chambers are mere semicircles that look more like *exedrae*.

Thugga has a fairly large number of religious buildings in a great variety of designs that probably reflect local traditions, as can be seen in the cults that were celebrated in them, perpetuating, within the new Roman context, the memory of the local deities. It was certainly the influence of the Punic religion, in which divine triads are recurrent, that determined the construction of a tripartite *cella* at the end of a colonnaded area in the Severan Temple of Saturn, which was built over the ancient Baal Hammon sanctuary. The sacred precinct of Caelestis, in which the Punic goddess Tanit continued to be worshipped, has on the other hand a peripteral temple. It stood on a podium with a single *cella* enclosed within a large semicircular colonnade and was originally crowned with statues. The shape of this sacred area was perhaps that of a crescent, an attribute of the goddess.

The *cavea* of the theater, surmounted by a colonnade, partly rested on the slope of the hill dominating the city. The structure was built thanks to the generosity of the same family responsible for the Capitolium, as previously mentioned. Several columns are still standing, which made it possible to reconstruct the profile of the niches that animated the *scaenae frons*, even though this structure could not be entirely rebuilt as it was at Sabratha.

During the Emperor Gallienus' reign, that is, after the mid-third century A.D., huge *thermae*, the so-called Licinian Baths, were built. This complex is aligned so that the *calidarium* and the other heated rooms connected with it were oriented south-west to have better exposure to the sun, while the *frigidarium* and the adjacent rooms are placed north-west, together with the *palaestra*, in a sheltered position against the slope of the hill, which had been cut for this purpose. These rooms were decorated with elegant mosaics and marble dressing.

As is characteristic of so many cities in North Africa, the domestic architecture at Thugga was a means to display wealth and luxury. But, perhaps the opulence and power of the leading families in the city are revealed in the most impressive way by the major role they played, on several occasions, in having monuments built for the city.

134-135 The interior of the theater viewed from the top of the cavea. The *scenae frons* was destroyed, but some columns on its lower register (as well as a small part of the upper one, at the far right) were restored.

135 left This Roman arch was built in the Thugga area with two Corinthian columns on its façade.

135 top right The House of the Trifolium, whose peristyle is seen here, was built in the third century A.D. and is the largest private house found at Thugga. Its name derives from one of the living rooms, the plan of which is in the shape of a *trifolium*, or clover.

THUGGA

135 bottom right In the foreground, the ruins of a private house; in the background, the massive walls of the Licinian Baths. In order to make room for the baths, the side of the hill had to be cut into.

136-137 This detail of a mosaic found at Thugga depicts Dionysus punishing the Tyrrhenian pirates who had tried to kidnap him by turning them into dolphins.

136 bottom This late fourth-century mosaic, which was found in a house near Thugga, shows the charioteer Eros, the victor in a circus race.

137 top This mosaic from Thugga, also dating from the third century A.D., depicts a mythological scene: Vulcan's busy workshop, inside a cave.

137 bottom Another mosaic from Thugga (third century A.D.) represents Ulysses tied to the mast of his ship as it approaches the Sirens so that he will not succumb to their lure.

THUGGA

VOLUBILIS

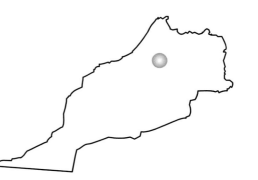

Text by SIMONE RAMBALDI

Volubilis corresponds to present-day Ksar Faraoun in Morocco and lies in the interior of west Mauretania. Originally an agricultural community of the local Mauri population, who were later joined by Phoenician colonists who founded a major emporium there, Volubilis became an important city during the reign of Juba II. It was made a municipality by the emperor Claudius, when it was included in the province of Mauretania Tingitana. During the fourth century A.D. the region was the site of bitter turmoil, some of it for religious reasons. The revolts of the Mauri chiefs Phirmus and Gildo paved the way for the Vandals' invasions in the following century. After the partial reconquest on the part of the Byzantines, the area was occupied by the Arabs.

138-139 The apsidal basilica with its colonnaded interior was connected to the Forum square by one of its long sides. Not far away, inside a porticoed area, stood the Capitolium.

139 left The floor and wall decoration of the House of the Columns peristyle no longer exists. Note the elegance of the two columns with their spiral volutes; one column seems to be intact.

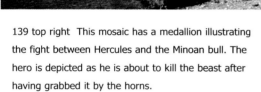

139 bottom right This gateway consists of a central arch flanked by two lower arches. In the background, at the opposite end of the *decumanus maximus*, is the Arch of Caracalla.

139 top right This mosaic has a medallion illustrating the fight between Hercules and the Minoan bull. The hero is depicted as he is about to kill the beast after having grabbed it by the horns.

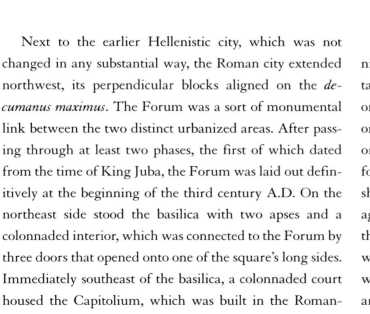

Next to the earlier Hellenistic city, which was not changed in any substantial way, the Roman city extended northwest, its perpendicular blocks aligned on the *decumanus maximus*. The Forum was a sort of monumental link between the two distinct urbanized areas. After passing through at least two phases, the first of which dated from the time of King Juba, the Forum was laid out definitively at the beginning of the third century A.D. On the northeast side stood the basilica with two apses and a colonnaded interior, which was connected to the Forum by three doors that opened onto one of the square's long sides. Immediately southeast of the basilica, a colonnaded court housed the Capitolium, which was built in the Roman-Italic style so typical of these temples in North Africa, with a tall podium and a broad access staircase. Of particular interest is the depth of the *pronaos*, which had two additional columns behind the side columns of the façade.

Isolated in the middle of another square at the beginning of the *decumanus maximus* is one of the most important monuments in the city, the Arch of Caracalla. It has only one opening, the springers forming two large piers, on each side of which are two gabled niches that were originally flanked by columns. Below these niches was a fountain, while above them were busts sculpted on round shields. Unfortunately, the sculpture work is badly damaged and it is not possible to establish the exact position of the trophies and victory scenes that belonged to the arch which were found in pieces. These figurative motifs, which are recurrent in the decoration of Roman arches, are however rather rare in the North African cities. The attic of the arch was surmounted by a bronze sculpture group representing Caracalla on a chariot drawn by six horses, as the inscription tells us.

In the northeastern quarter many houses were uncovered that provide valuable information on the daily life of a North African city in the Imperial Age. Their original designs seem to date for the most part to the Flavian period, but were later changed, particularly in the third century A.D. One of the most sumptuous houses in the city is the so-called House of the Procession of Venus, which boasts a peristyle, a common feature in the African regions, as can be seen in many such houses, in which the basic plan is re-elaborated upon with a great deal of imagination. The *domus* is laid out around the large central courtyard, access to which is afforded by an atrium that in turn is reached through a part of the front portico, which was incorporated into the house. This sumptuousness, which is to be found in other houses, is not surprising. It is proof of the power and influence that certain leading citizens could wield by taking over prop-

1) FORUM
2) BASILICA
3) CAPITOLIUM
4) ARCH OF CARACALLA
5) NORTHEASTERN QUARTER

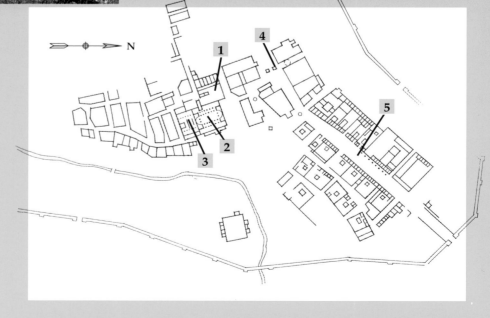

140 The short staircase on the exterior of the basilica has a row of arches framed by semi-arches that animate the surface of the edifice.

140-141 The Arch of Caracalla was erected with one opening and with niches on the front of each pier framed by two partly preserved columns. The sculptural decoration is also badly damaged.

141 View of the *triclinium* in the House of Dionysus and the Four Seasons. On the horizon, at the end of the stretch of ruins, one can make out the Arch of Caracalla.

erty that should have been reserved for civic purposes. An analogous, albeit less radical, desire to display one's wealth led some of the owners of these villas on the *decumanus maximus* – which was entirely colonnaded – to change the shape and arrangement of the columns in front of their houses, with the sole aim of showing their fellow citizens where they lived.

Going back to the House of the Procession of Venus, it must be pointed out that the axis of the entrance and peristyle is further emphasized by the position chosen for the *triclinium*, the main room of the living quarters, which opens out on the opposite side, next to a *nymphaeum*. The northwestern section of this villa is occupied by a bath that can be reached via the peristyle but also has an independent entrance on a side street. This residence, which is decorated with marvelous distinctive mosaics, yielded two bronze busts of different periods. One, probably dating from Nero's time, is a portrait of Cato of Utica, while the other is Hellenistic and is a probably a portrait of Juba II.

The so-called House of Hercules' Labors is also noteworthy. It is yet another example of the type of residence with a peristyle, around which are a large *oecus*, an elegant hall in the living quarter, and the other rooms. However, the entrance from the outside is not aligned with the peristyle, as in the villa described above, because the entire façade of the building where this *domus* is located is occupied by a row of totally independent workshops that face the *decumanus maximus*.

Here again there is a bath at the end of the *domus*, as well as rich mosaic decoration.

Nevertheless, the rooms used for productive or commercial activities were not always clearly separated from domestic areas. In the House of Dionysus and the House of the Four Seasons, for example, the living quarters, made up of various rooms, are connected by a corridor to a back wing with workshops and storerooms.

VOLUBILIS

143 center A pavement mosaic depicting, in the middle, the young Hylas, kidnapped by water nymphs who had fallen in love with him when they saw him drawing water from a spring.

143 bottom Mythological scenes are recurring motifs in almost all the mosaics at Volubilis. Here we see Diana bathing in a fountain with two nymphs, her weapons hanging on the branches of a tree.

142 This detail of a pavement mosaic depicts Dionysus, the Maenads, and the Seasons, separated by ornamental fasciae. The medallion contains a representation of Autumn with a crown of roses on its head.

143 top Another detail of the same mosaic. Here we see the central panel with the portrait of Dionysus crowned with vine leaves, leaning against a column.

MIDDLE EAST

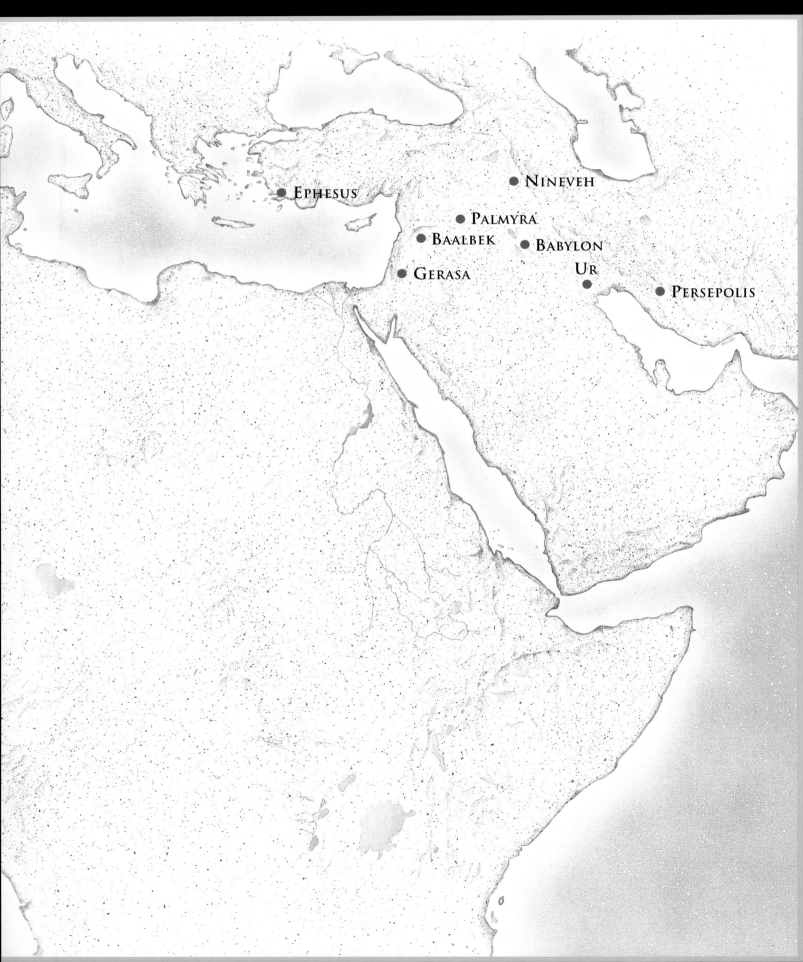

EPHESUS

NINEVEH

PALMYRA

BAALBEK

BABYLON

GERASA

UR

PERSEPOLIS

145 top Detail of a relief
decorating the Tripylon at
Persepolis.

145 bottom Detail of the
elegant architectural
decoration typical of Baalbek.

THE CITY IN ANCIENT MESOPOTAMIA AND IN THE CENTRAL-EASTERN MEDITERRANEAN

TEXTS BY

ANTONELLA MEZZOLANI - RICCARDO VILLICICH

In ancient Mesopotamia the development of cities was foreshadowed as early as the mid-fifth millennium B.C., when in the Obeid period there was a sudden surge of public building activity in the villages. Only in the middle of the following millennium, however, during the Uruk age, did what Gordon Childe called an "urban revolution" manifest itself on a global level as the result of the need for centralized economic, political, and territorial coordination.

In this changing context, the process of urbanization went hand in hand with the development of irrigation techniques and, therefore, of more efficacious exploitation of the land, the increase in specialized work, the production of surplus goods that could be traded, and above all, the development of a stratified society.

The evolution of urbanization not only involved lower and central Mesopotamia, but manifested itself in upper Mesopotamia as well, in Assyria at middle of the course of the Euphrates River with urban communities such as Habuba Kebira, which have been interpreted as true colonies of Uruk. This phenomenon also influenced more distant regions such as the upper Euphrates and western Persia.

In this period, the hub of the cities were the temple precincts, which not only served cultural and religious purposes, but also intervened actively in the social structure of the city by means of the direct management of the cultivated land and rigorously administered economic production. In the latest phase of this period the

MIDDLE EAST

palace seems to have made its appearance (for example, the public building in the Jamdat Nasr period), which seems to be a sign of the first "secular" political development.

In Phases II and III of the Protodynastic period (2750-2350 B.C.), characterized by a mixture of languages and ethnic groups, the evolution of urbanization was completed resulting in populated "islands" that seem to have had three levels (the capital, the intermediate towns with decentralized administrative functions, and the villages) and were surrounded by arid land that served as buffer zones between the various city states, which were similar in size and potential. The temple continued to carry out its religious and economic functions and was expressed architecturally by various types (tripartite structures, complex sanctuaries, oval temples, and temples on a tall podium or terrace), while the palace in this period became a crucial element in the cities, a complex organism in which groups of chambers were often laid out around central courtyards. A manifestation of communal activity was the construction of the city walls, which also marked the ideological difference between the city and what lay outside it. Lastly, although the growth of residential quarters was not the result of town planning but for the most part spontaneous as the road network clearly shows, their decoration and layout began to express social differences.

During the Akkadian period the center of political power shifted northwards while the distribution of settlements in the southern area remained the same. This period also witnessed a greater concentration of cultivable land in the hands of the royal family, a process that would continue in the successive Neo-Sumerian period during which the crisis in the minor communities led to greater power and larger populations in the cities. The building activity carried out by the Ur dynasties was for the most part limited to the capital, its most monumental expression being the ziggurat. While the cities manifested a strong attachment to tradition, there was no lack of experimentation, which produced cities founded with regular road systems and the planned distribution of the public buildings (especially in Haradum, in the middle Euphrates region).

The kings' urbanizing and building activity continued during the following Isin-Larsa phases and in the period when Mesopotamia was unified under Hammurabi, during which time the individual cities became provincial capitals and Babylonia played the role of the great capital. The attention the sovereigns paid to the development of the cities reached its height in the Neo-Assyrian period, when the foundation of new capitals was a propaganda tool for the royal ideology that set the cosmic order (the planned city) against chaos (non-urbanized territory). In reality, the activity in this regard was often more of an architectural nature (the enlargement or construction of palaces and the rebuilding of sacred precincts), but hydraulic engineering works were also realized.

A similar ideology seems to be at the base of the foundation and refoundation activity of the Achaemenids, whose architecture became the celebration of the royal house. An example of such building carried out in the Mesopotamian area, which was annexed to the Achaemenid empire in 539 B.C., was the construction of an *apadana*-type structure in Babylonia.

With the gradual decline of the major Mesopotamian cities, an increasingly important role was played by the cities in Asia Minor and the Middle East, founded by the Phoenicians and Greeks. In Asia Minor, Ionian and Aeolian colonization, which began around 1000 B.C., was of great im-

portance. In the seventh century B.C. the cities once founded by the Greeks subsequently founded new colonies. Miletus, for example, established many settlements along the coasts of the Mediterranean and Black Sea.

In the sixth century B.C. colossal architecture made its appearance in this region, with the planning and realization of ambitious sanctuaries such as the Didymaion, or Temple of Apollo, in Miletos and the Artemision, or Temple of Artemis, in Ephesus (which was considered one of the Seven Wonders of the Ancient World). Furthermore, Greek culture tended to merge with the culture of the ancient regions in the Anatolian peninsula such as Phrygia, Lydia, Lycia, and Caria.

In 546 B.C., when the kingdom of Lydia was conquered by Cyrus the Great, Anatolia passed under Persian dominion, which lasted until 334 B.C. when Alexander the Great passed over the Hellespont and dealt Darius' Persians one defeat after another, annexing all of Asia Minor into his short-lived empire. When this great Macedonian king died, his kingdom was split up into several minor states and his generals fought against one another to gain possession of them. From the ashes of Alexander the Great's dream of a universal kingdom there grew up a series of kingdoms ruled by dynasties of Hellenic culture and tradition—such as the Ptolemies in Egypt and the Seleucids in Syria—thanks to which the artistic style of the international Greek culture grew and spread.

During the Hellenistic age other cities became cultural centers, the prototypes of new models and grandiose monumental architecture: Pergamum, the capital of the Attalid kingdom, as well as Ephesus, Sardis, and Miletus. There were also the cities founded by the Seleucids, such as Antioch, Apamea, and Laodicea, and caravan cities like Petra, the capital of the Nabataean kingdom, Gerasa, and Palmyra, the ancient trade center whose origins go back to the early second millennium B.C.

When the regions in Asia Minor and the Near East became part of the Roman Empire, a long period of economic prosperity began that, while it meant the loss of political independence, guaranteed stability and a new civic pride that led to a great deal of building activity aimed at enhancing the monumental patrimony of the individual cities, which were often rivals. Thanks to the munificence of patrons or the intervention of the emperor, many new public monuments were built whose common denominator was "giantism," a veritable compendium of temples, theaters, broad colonnaded avenues, and city squares. However, in the third century A.D. the factors that had determined this favorable state of affairs began to disintegrate, partly because of such traumatic events. Examples of this are the destruction of Palmyra in 272, ordered by the emperor Aurelian in retaliation for Zenobia's expansionist policy; the continuous raids of local populations such as the Sassanid Persians that brought about the end of Dura Europos in 256; and the earthquake that struck Antioch around 526 and was followed by the Persian invasion in 540. Despite this, there was a continuity within Hellenistic-Roman culture, at least until the end of the fourth century. However, this common culture had already been somewhat undermined by the gradual assimilation of Byzantine culture and then Eastern culture, until the definitive predominance of the latter after the Arab conquest. This invasion ended the period of splendor of the Hellenistic-Roman urban culture in the eastern provinces of the Roman Empire.

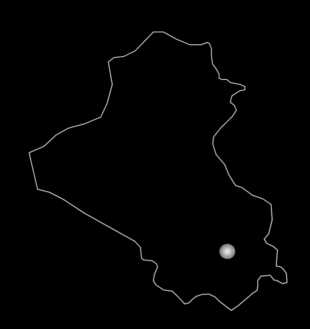

148 TOP C.L. WOOLLEY EXAMINING A LYRE DISCOVERED IN ONE OF THE PITS AND CHAMBER TOMBS IN THE ROYAL CEMETERY.

148-149 TOP WORKMEN AT THE EXCAVATION SITE OF THE ZIGGURAT, SEEN FROM THE NORTHEAST, WHERE THE MAIN ACCESS RAMP IS CLEARLY VISIBLE. DIGS AT THIS MONUMENT BEGAN IN 1923 AND TOOK SEVERAL SEASONS TO FINISH.

148-149 BOTTOM THE STANDARD OF UR, FROM TOMB PG 799 IN THE ROYAL CEMETERY, IS NOW IN THE BRITISH MUSEUM.

149 BOTTOM RECONSTRUCTION OF THE ZIGGURAT OF UR BY C.L. WOOLLEY SHOWS THREE STORIES OF DECREASING SIZE DECORATED WITH PILASTERS SUPPORTING A CULT CHAPEL REACHED VIA A FRONTAL RAMP.

Ur

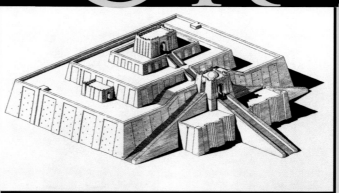

150 bottom A lyre from Tomb PG 800 of the Royal Cemetery, now in the British Museum. The wooden soundboard is decorated with the bust of a bull made of gold and lapis lazuli and shell and lapis lazuli inlay.

151 The ziggurat of Ur, with a core made of dried brick casing, was built by King Ur-Nammu, the founder of the third dynasty of Ur, who promoted large-scale construction on the ancient site.

150 top View of the ruins of Ur, at the site now called Tell el-Muqyyar, with the ziggurat in the background. The city was founded in the alluvial plain of Sumer on the banks of the Euphrates River.

UR

Text by ANTONELLA MEZZOLANI

The site of Tell el-Muqayyar, about nine miles west of the present course of the Euphrates River, was identified as Ur in 1854 by the British consul at Basra, J.E. Taylor, who was commissioned by the British Museum to carry out archaeological research in southern Mesopotamia. His discovery of cuneiform tablets led to our knowledge of the historical events and name of the city, which some scholars called "Ur of the Chaldeans" of biblical fame. After Taylor's initial inquiry, the site remained unexplored up to the late nineteenth century when a mission from the University of Pennsylvania began digs, the results of which were never published. After the First World War, R. Campbell Thompson began excavating at Ur, thus encouraging the British Museum to resume its exploration of this ancient site by sending a mission there, which was first headed by L. King and then by H.R. Hall.

Because of a lack of funds, the digs were again suspended until 1922 when the University of Pennsylvania Museum proposed a joint archaeological mission that was headed by Leonard Woolley, which for twelve years worked on rediscovering the site. After 1934, the work

undertaken by Iraqi archaeologists concentrated mostly on the restoration and preservation of the ziggurat.

The city of Ur was inhabited continuously from the el-Ubaid period (fifth millennium B.C.) to the fourth century B.C. Traces of the most ancient settlement were found under a thick alluvial stratum that Woolley interpreted as related to the biblical Deluge (now scholars think it was an local alluvial phenomenon). In fact, the area these discoveries were made in was called the "well of the Flood."

The influence of the Uruk period (3500-3000 B.C.) is

attested to at Ur by the characteristic pottery found in the oven layer located in the "well of the Flood." More substantial documentation concerning the Jamdat Nasr period (3000-2900 B.C.) was also found in the "well of the Flood" where archaeologists discovered levels with pottery and houses, while at the west corner of the ziggurat terrace they found a supporting wall that probably dates from the same period.

Material from the protodynastic period (2900-2350 B.C.), found in at least two excavation areas in what was a sacred quarter, proved to be even more abundant. In the temple sector, which was later incorporated into the ziggurat of Ur-Nammu, there must have been a tall terrace that had two court-like annexes that have been interpreted to be the temple kitchens, while the area of the so-called Royal Cemetery contained the most ancient tombs. The "cemetery" housed at least 2,000 tombs that covered a time span ranging from the protodynastic IIIa (2600-2450 B.C.) to the Ur III period (2100-200 B.C.). The name is derived from the sixteen tombs that are considered sepulchers of high-ranking persons that date from the most ancient period.

The type of tomb that seems to distinguish this series

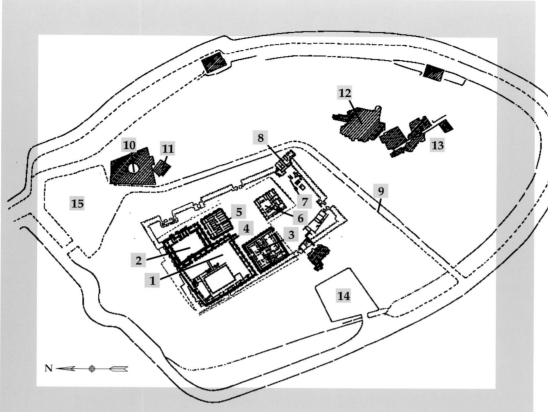

1) THE ZIGGURAT AREA
2) COURTYARD OF NANNA
3) GIPA
4) E-DUB-BLA-MAKH
5) E-NUNN-MAKH
6) E-KHUR-SAG OR PALACE OF UR-NAMMU
7) ROYAL CEMETERY
8) THIRD DYNASTY MAUSOLEUMS
9) NEO-BABYLONIAN PRECINCT
10) PALACE OF THE PRIESTESSES -EN
11) PORT TEMPLE
12) ISIN-LARSA RESIDENTIAL QUARTER
13) NEO-BABYLONIAN RESIDENTIAL QUARTER
14) WEST HARBOR
15) NORTH HARBOR

152-153 Panoramic view of the ruins of Ur, with the ziggurat in the background.

152 bottom The ziggurat was reconstructed in modern times by the Iraqi Department of Antiquities, which restored the first terrace in 1960-70.

153 bottom Seen from the south corner, the ziggurat is massive and seems impregnable.

UR

has a ramp giving access to a burial pit with a small brick or stone chamber, in front of which the funeral procession stopped. What most probably struck the imagination of the public most was that ritual, because these sepulchers seem to reveal sacrificial rites in which both the deceased's animals and retinue (which could consist of as many as 70 persons) found their death. The furnishings in these tombs were truly astonishing. An outstanding example is the so-called Standard of Ur, a wooden panel with a figurative decoration inlay of shells and lapis lazuli against a bitumen background, elegantly decorated musical instruments, and an extraordinary profusion of jewels made of precious metals and stones imported from distant coun-

tries. Other tombs, which do not seem to be royal because of the difference in type and ritual, have also yielded an extremely large amount of funerary objects.

With the III Dynasty of Ur (2112-2004 B.C.) the city became the true capital of a vast and powerful empire that was the result of a gradual policy of expansion and centralization on the part of the monarchs. The founder of this dynasty, Ur-Nammu, and his son Shulgi promoted much building activity, which was a source of pride and exaltation for the king, as can be seen in the Stele of Ur-Nammu, which clearly depicts construction work being carried out under the aegis of the gods. Ur-Nammu is to be credited with the construction of the ziggurat in the

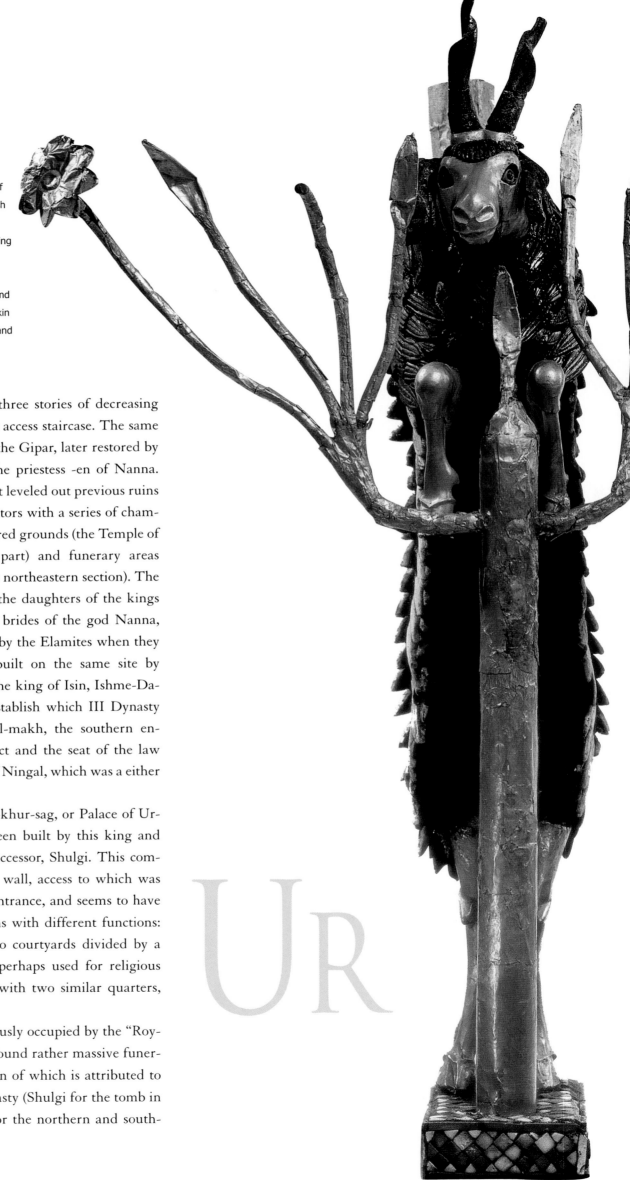

154 An object found in Tomb PG 1237 of the Royal Cemetery and now in the British Museum: on a base made of silver and colored stone inlay is a kind of goat leaning against a tree of rosettes made of wood and gold leaf. The animal has a wooden core, its stomach is covered with silver and the head and legs with gold, while the skin and other parts are made of lapis lazuli and shell inlay.

sanctuary of Nanna with its three stories of decreasing size, inclining walls and triple access staircase. The same king was also responsible for the Gipar, later restored by Amar-Sin, the residence of the priestess -en of Nanna. This was built on a terrace that leveled out previous ruins and was articulated in two sectors with a series of chambers, among which are the sacred grounds (the Temple of Ningal in the southeastern part) and funerary areas (tombs of the priestesses in the northeastern section). The Gig-par-ku, the residence of the daughters of the kings who were consecrated as the brides of the god Nanna, was most probably destroyed by the Elamites when they sacked the city and was rebuilt on the same site by Enanatuna, the daughter of the king of Isin, Ishme-Dagan. It is more difficult to establish which III Dynasty sovereign built the E-dub-lal-makh, the southern entrance of the ziggurat precinct and the seat of the law court, and the E-nun-makh of Ningal, which was a either a warehouse or the treasury.

The same is true of the E-khur-sag, or Palace of Ur-Nammu, which may have been built by this king and probably completed by his successor, Shulgi. This complex was inserted into a side wall, access to which was given by a single "bayonet" entrance, and seems to have been divided into two sections with different functions: one was centered around two courtyards divided by a monumental wing and was perhaps used for religious purposes whereas the other, with two similar quarters, was used as apartments.

Lastly, in the sector previously occupied by the "Royal Cemetery" archaeologists found rather massive funerary structures the construction of which is attributed to the first rulers of the III Dynasty (Shulgi for the tomb in the middle, and Amar-Sin for the northern and south-

UR

155 top A gold leaf helmet from the tomb of Meskalamdug, PG 755, in the Royal Cemetery, with an accurate reproduction of wavy locks held together by a ribbon and gathered into a braid on the nape of the neck.

155 bottom The Standard of Ur, from Tomb PG 779 of the Royal Cemetery, now in the British Museum. This is a sort of wooden panel with an inlay of shells and lapis lazuli against a bitumen ground. On one of the long sides are three registers depicting scenes of peace, while the opposite side has battle scenes.

eastern ones). These were underground mausoleums with a monumental stairway lined with false vaults, at the end of which were chambers with false domes that housed several tombs.

After the destruction wrought by the Elamites (ca. 2000 B.C.), the city of Ur was ruled by the kings of Isin and Larsa who set about rebuilding some structures in the sanctuary such as the Gipar and who probably also promoted the foundation of residential quarters. One of these, called the Isin-Larsa quarter, had narrow, irregular streets that converged in a small central area and often contained a type of house in which most of the rooms ran around a central courtyard, some of the rooms probably being family chapels and kitchens. These houses seemed to have a second floor that repeated the layout of the lower one, with the deceased family members buried under the floors.

Because of the ever-increasing importance of Babylon and the gradual degradation of the southern territory of Sumer, Ur began to decline, suffering a serious blow in 1740 B.C. when Babylon punished the southern cities for an unsuccessful rebellion. During the Kassite period, king Kurigalzu restored the ziggurat and rebuilt the Gipar by enlarging it to the south and moving the Temple of Ningal inside its grounds. He also completely rebuilt the E-dub-lal-makh with bricks, enhancing its function as a law court, and added new buildings that merged the E-nun-makh structurally with the ziggurat complex. During the Neo-Babylonian period, Nebuchadnezzar and Nabonidus committed themselves to building and restoration in Ur. The former built the wall that enclosed the entire sacred area, while the latter renovated the ziggurat, rebuilt the Temple of Ningal (adding other buildings in the tower precinct), rebuilt the E-non-makh, turning it into a temple, and rebuilt the E-bub-lal-makh, in front of which he placed the Gipar. Despite all this activity, the glory of Ur was clearly in decline, and in 400 B.C. the city was finally abandoned.

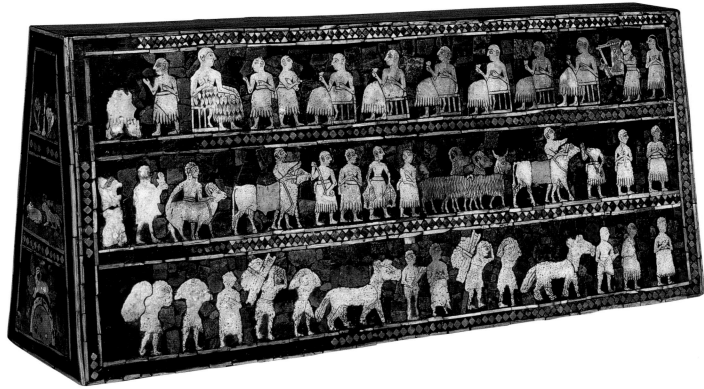

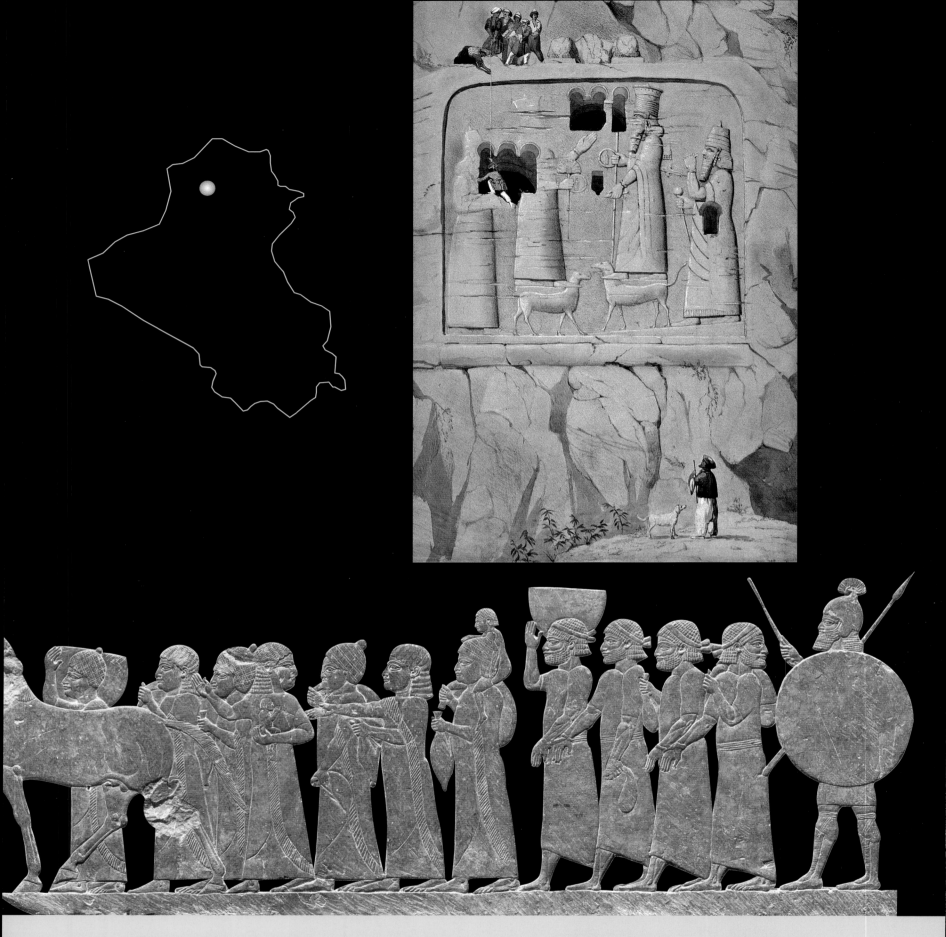

156 TOP A WATERCOLOR BY F.C. COOPER (1850) DOCUMENTS THE ARCHAEOLOGICAL EXPLORATION EFFECTED BY A.H. LAYARD AT BAWIAN, NEAR NINEVEH.

156 BOTTOM THIS RELIEF ON A FRAGMENT OF ALABASTER FROM HALL VVT' OF THE NORTH PALACE OF KUYUNJIK (MID-SEVENTH CENTURY B.C.) DEPICTS ELAMITE PRISONERS, CAPTURED DURING THE MILITARY CAMPAIGN OF 653 B.C., ON A CART ESCORTED BY ASSYRIAN SOLDIERS.

157 TOP WORKMEN AT A DEEP OPEN-AIR DIG ON KUYUNJIK HILL DURING THE 1931-32 CAMPAIGN. M.E.L. MALLOWAN, ASSISTANT TO THE LEADER OF THE EXCAVATION R. CAMPBELL THOMSON, FOUND TRACES OF THE MOST ANCIENT SETTLEMENT DURING THIS DIG.

157 BOTTOM AN ENGLISH PRINT EXECUTED IN 1849 RECREATES THE DISCOVERY OF A COLOSSAL HEAD, WHICH MAY BE THAT OF A BULL OR WINGED HUMAN-HEADED LION.

NINEVEH

NINEVEH

Text by ANTONELLA MEZZOLANI

"The city beloved by Ishtar," which Sennacherib made the capital of his kingdom, lay on the east bank of the Tigris River, opposite the city of Mosul and actually touching its outskirts. The first indications of the ruins came from the Spanish rabbi Benjamin of Tudela, who visited the site at some point between 1160 and 1173, from Pietro della Valle in the early seventeenth century, and from J. Otter, who in 1748 came upon two different oral traditions according to which the ancient site was situated either opposite Mosul or further north, on the right bank of the Tigris in the locality known as ancient Mosul. In the second half of the eighteenth centu-

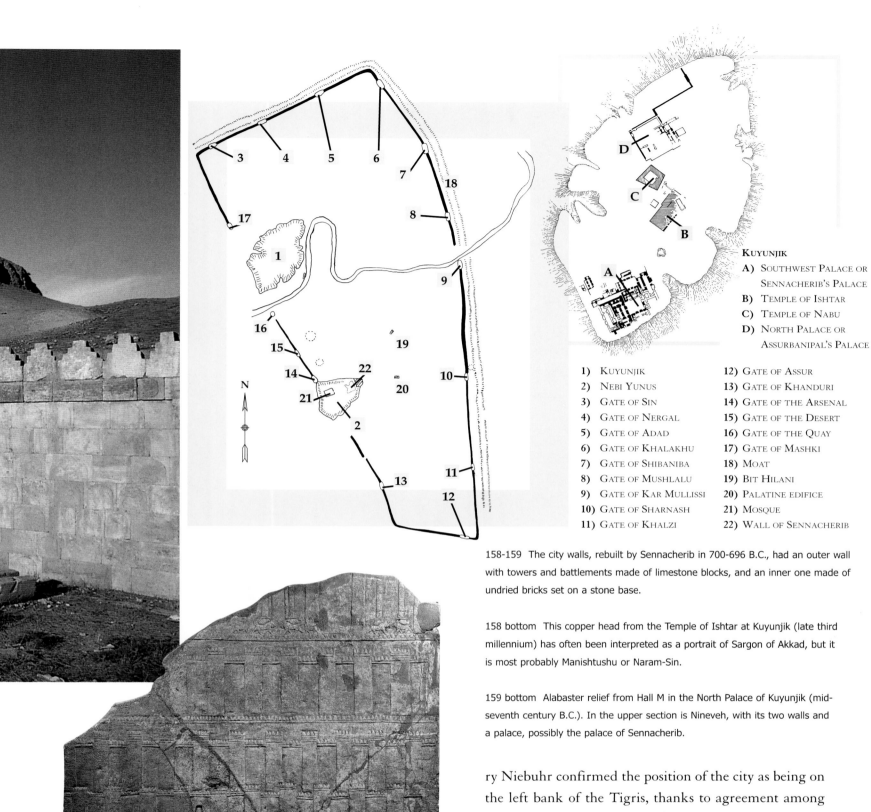

KUYUNJIK

A) SOUTHWEST PALACE OR SENNACHERIB'S PALACE
B) TEMPLE OF ISHTAR
C) TEMPLE OF NABU
D) NORTH PALACE OR ASSURBANIPAL'S PALACE

1) KUYUNJIK	12) GATE OF ASSUR
2) NEBI YUNUS	13) GATE OF KHANDURI
3) GATE OF SIN	14) GATE OF THE ARSENAL
4) GATE OF NERGAL	15) GATE OF THE DESERT
5) GATE OF ADAD	16) GATE OF THE QUAY
6) GATE OF KHALAKHU	17) GATE OF MASHKI
7) GATE OF SHIBANIBA	18) MOAT
8) GATE OF MUSHLALU	19) BIT HILANI
9) GATE OF KAR MULLISSI	20) PALATINE EDIFICE
10) GATE OF SHARNASH	21) MOSQUE
11) GATE OF KHALZI	22) WALL OF SENNACHERIB

158-159 The city walls, rebuilt by Sennacherib in 700-696 B.C., had an outer wall with towers and battlements made of limestone blocks, and an inner one made of undried bricks set on a stone base.

158 bottom This copper head from the Temple of Ishtar at Kuyunjik (late third millennium) has often been interpreted as a portrait of Sargon of Akkad, but it is most probably Manishtushu or Naram-Sin.

159 bottom Alabaster relief from Hall M in the North Palace of Kuyunjik (mid-seventh century B.C.). In the upper section is Nineveh, with its two walls and a palace, possibly the palace of Sennacherib.

ry Niebuhr confirmed the position of the city as being on the left bank of the Tigris, thanks to agreement among the ancient sources concerning the figure of the prophet Jonah, but it was only in 1820 that C.J. Rich identified with certainty the ruins of the ancient city on the hillocks of Kuyunjik and Nebi Yunus.

This period of debate and theories on the position of Nineveh was followed by the first digs. They were initiated by P.E. Botta, the French consul at Mosul, who in 1842 had some trenches dug, but the lack of results caused him to suspend the excavation. Work was continued with more perseverance in 1846 by A.H. Layard, who already the following year was rewarded with the discovery of the foundation terrace of Sennacherib's palace. Thanks to these promising finds, the British Museum told Layard to carry out a second campaign, which he did in 1849-51. The success of these digs, which for example brought to light Assurbanipal's library, encouraged the British Museum to continue the research, first with a brief mission headed by J.F. Jones in the spring of 1852, and then with a longer campaign from late 1852 to the spring of 1854 headed by H. Rassam. Among the other excavation campaigns at Nineveh, mention should be made of the fortunate exploration made by G. Smith, who in 1873 succeeded in finding the missing parts of the cuneiform tablet with the account of the Flood (the XI tablet of the Gilgamesh epic), which he found among the inscriptions now in the British Museum. From 1927 to 1932 R. Campbell Thomson resumed the digs on the Kuyunjik hill, aided by R.W. Hutchinson, R.W. Hamilton and M.E.L. Mallowan. In the following years, particularly from 1960 to the 1970s, the digs were suspended and restoration work was carried out on the site by the Iraqi Department of Antiquities, which concentrated on some stretches of the

160 top A relief on an alabaster fragment from the North Palace (perhaps Hall S') of Kuyunjik (mid-seventh century B.C.) representing a parade of archers, which some scholars have interpreted as Elamites and others as Persians.

160 bottom Another alabaster relief from Hall L of the North Palace of Kuyunjik (mid-seventh century B.C.). The various registers depict episodes from a campaign against the Arabs (650 or 644 B.C.), who are on camels and are being pursued by the Assyrian cavalry and infantry.

160-161 Alabaster relief from Throne Room M in the North Palace of Kuyunjik (mid-seventh century B.C.) depicting an episode in the Assyrian army's attack on an Egyptian city (perhaps Memphis) during the 645 B.C. campaign.

fortifications and on the area of the first throne room in the southwestern palace of Sennacherib. Lastly, in 1987-1990 the University of California at Berkeley promoted an archaeological campaign headed by D. Stronach that concentrated on the northeast sector, that is, the heart of the more ancient lower city.

The most ancient periods of the urbanization of Nineveh cover the entire period from the high Neolithic to the protodynastic age, as is demonstrated both by the se-

quence of pottery cultures identified by M.E.L. Mallowan in a wide-ranging excavation at Kuyunjik and by the finds in other areas. However, it was during the Akkad period (2350-2193 B.C.) that Nineveh seems to have acquired the fortified wall at the foot of the Kuyunjik citadel as well as the Temple of Ishtar, the patron of the city, which was built or rebuilt by Manishtushu of Akkad, according to an inscription of Shamshi-Adad. This was also the period to which belongs the splendid copper head of an Akkadian sovereign found in the central area of Kuyunjik and traditionally interpreted as an effigy of Sargon, although it is probably one of his successors.

As for the Old and Middle Assyrian periods, continuous building and restoration work was fostered by the Assyrian kings and from time to time consisted of renovation of the sacred precinct of Ishtar, the reconstruction of the walls and city gates, the erection of new palatial buildings, and water supply maintenance and sewage works. This fervent building activity in the city also con-

tinued in the Neo-Assyrian period and came to a turning point with Sennacherib, who, after ascending the throne in 704 B.C., decided to make Nineveh the capital of his empire. Many works were promoted by this Assyrian monarch (the excavation of canals, doubling the urban perimeter, the creation of fifteen city gates, work on the city walls, and enlargement of the squares and of the royal road) and reached their highest level with the construction of the palace complexes. The remains of an important edifice in the eastern sector of the lower city south of the Khusur can be attributed to Sennacherib. Other works by this king are the arsenal on the Nebi Yunus hill (which was enlarged and rebuilt by Asarhaddon), the "palace of succession" for the crown prince, mentioned by Assurbanipal in the passage in which he describes the work on the North Palace and perhaps located west of the temple of Ishtar, and, above all, the most monumental and striking work, the Southwest Palace, which Sennacherib himself called an "incomparable palace."

The beginning and the end of the construction work

on the Southwest Palace are known (703-691/690 B.C.) thanks to meticulous records made by the royal chancery which mention the subjugated populations that participated in the work, the vast foundation, the wealth of metal decoration, glazed bricks, and bronze images, and the intercession of the gods who showed the king the quarries for the building material and told him the secrets of fine casting. Nineteenth-century archaeological research brought to light a large amount of the inner sectors of this complex, but was not able to get as far as the sides (the first façade was found only in 1905 but was not accurately recorded).

Despite the incomplete layout, one can already note in Sennacherib's palace a marked spirit of innovation compared to the works of the earlier Assyrian monarchs. This is manifested in the original spatial layout, which tends to eliminate the distinction between interior and exterior. The main sectors of the complex, the ceremonial and residential, must have had a northeast-southeast orientation. The very decorative program of the palace, expressed in the vertical reliefs on the base, has innovative elements. Firstly, there is a choice of themes for the celebrative narration (already seen in Nineveh, for example in the painted, glazed clay slabs with military scenes, or in the White Obelisk with traditional religious, hunting, and military motifs that can probably be attributed to Assurnasirpal II) that favors battle scenes such as the famous conquest of Lachish in room 36, scenes of the construction of the palace, and the procession of court officials, guards, and servants. Then there is a connection between the architectural structure and the event depicted, which creates a unity of space and composition contained within a delimited structural element, with the sole exception of the throne room. Again, the visual perspective is wide enough to include events and backgrounds in a single figurative field, even though in some cases a division in levels makes the composition schematic. Lastly, the representation of the natural setting creates an element of actual space.

The architectural structure and decorative narration of the "incomparable palace" continued to be a standard for future monuments built by Sennacherib's successors. In particular, there are the works of Assurbanipal (668-627 B.C.), Sennacherib's grandson, who, besides renovating the "palace of succession" and completing the sculptural decoration of the "incomparable palace," also had a new palace complex built, again on the Kuyunjik citadel, which is traditionally known as the North Palace. De-

162 bottom A fragment of the head of a genii from Nineveh, dating from Sennacherib's reign, guards the city gates. It may be part of a statue of a bull or human-headed winged lion.

162-163 A relief on an alabaster fragment from Hall S' in the North Palace of Kuyunjik (mid-seventh century B.C.), showing Assurbanipal and his queen at a banquet in the royal park, surrounded by musicians and servants. This subject, which decorated the royal apartments, marked a drastic departure from traditional motifs.

163 bottom This alabaster relief from the archway of the Southwest Palace and the Temple of Ishtar at Kuyunjik (early seventh century B.C.) depicts two guards of Sennacherib, perhaps an Armenian and a Jew.

spite the rather summary account of the complex brought to light in the nineteenth century, it repeats the classic plan, and even the relief decoration seems to hark back to traditional motifs which are elaborated upon with a new vocabulary: there are hunting and military feats dominated by the presence of the sovereign, who is sometimes accompanied in the royal lion hunt by the

crown prince. And a previously unknown motif in royal figurative art can be noted in the depiction of the king and queen's everyday life. The composition is approached with different, original solutions, either in a single field or divided into levels. Then, the background is totally neutral or abstract and has no natural scenery in the case of the hunting scenes, or else it is harmoniously decorated with plants whose lines correspond to the human figures in the representations of the royal park. If the hunting and domestic motifs are to found only in the apartments, the military ones, such as those in Sennacherib's palace, are in the reception rooms, where a synthesis of events is provided in the throne room, while a detailed illustration of the individual campaigns decorates uniform complexes consisting of various rooms.

After this period of political importance and monumental and artistic splendor, Nineveh declined rapidly, so much so that in 612 B.C. it was besieged by the Medes, the Babylonians, and the Scythians, who brought about its dramatic destruction.

BABYLON

Text by ANTONELLA MEZZOLANI

The ancient city of Babylon, an extremely important religious and cultural center in antiquity, lay on both sides of the Euphrates, which divided it into two sectors connected by a bridge. Illustrious travelers such as Ibn Hawqal in the tenth century and Benjamin of Tudela in the twelfth century visited it and described its ruins. Others, such the abbot De Beauchamp and H.J. Bridge, tried to persuade the locals to sell them the large amount of material plundered from the ancient site. Only in 1811 did C.J. Rich, president of the East Indies Company, undertake the first systematic exploration of the area, which was followed by a description of the ruins of the individual hills and a series of maps. Various scholars who were engaged in archaeological research in other Mesopotamian cities began digs in Babylonia such as W.K. Loftus in 1849 and A.H. Layard in 1850. Then, in 1852 F. Fresnel and J. Oppert's mission brought to light the Euphrates bridge, which they succeeded in identifying thanks to the inscriptions of Nabonidus, and the following year Oppert published the first detailed map of the ruins. Later, more persevering research was

164 left The basalt "Lion of Babylon," executed by the North Syrian school, was found in the North Palace, which, because of the abundance of ancient sculpture pieces found there (most of which were military booty), was originally considered a museum.

164 right The head of a diorite statue (now in the Louvre) found at Susa, where it may have been brought from Babylonia. It portrays an Old Babylonian ruler, but no reliable documentation confirms the common identification with Hammurabi.

165 top Relief on enameled bricks of a passant bull which was part of the decoration of the Gate of Ishtar.

164-165 This lion, which was part of the wall decoration on the processional way, dates from the reign of Nebuchadnezzar.

carried out by the British Museum, which, thanks mostly to H. Rassam in 1876 and E.W. Budge in 1887, found cuneiform tablets, cylinder seals with inscriptions, and other objects of this kind. The most significant results were obtained during the expeditions of R. Koldewey (1899-1914), in which such leading scholars as W. Andrae, F. Wetzel, O. Reuter, and G. Buddensieg participated.

The inscriptions tell us that Sargon of Akkad destroyed Babylon in 2340 B.C. and that Shulgi of Ur (2094-2047 B.C.) sacked the E-sagila complex during his campaign, but we know very little of the city during the reign of Hammurabi (1792-1750 B.C.), who has remained in historic chronicles for his famous "code" of laws and because he made Babylon the capital of his empire. Little is also known, from an archaeological standpoint, of the Kassite period, while it is probable that the Assyrians built a fortification wall, perhaps during the reign of Sargon II,

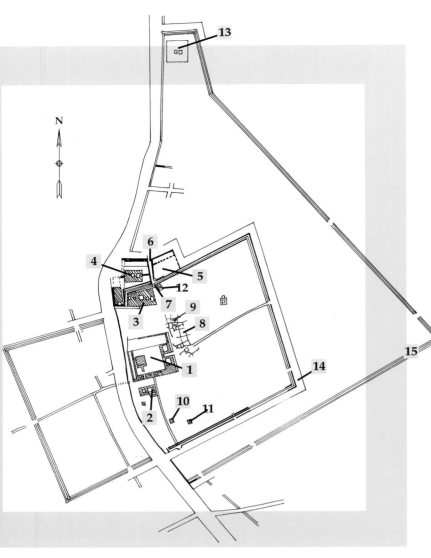

1) ZIGGURAT PRECINCT
2) E-SAGILA, TEMPLE OF MARDUK
3) SOUTH PALACE
4) NORTH PALACE
5) OUTPOST
6) PROCESSIONAL WAY
7) GATE OF ISHTAR
8) MERKÈS RESIDENTIAL QUARTER
9) TEMPLE OF ISHTAR OF AKKAD
10) TEMPLE Z
11) TEMPLE OF NINURTA
12) TEMPLE OF NINMAKH
13) SUMMER PALACE
14) OUTER DEFENSIVE WALL
15) INNER DEFENSIVE WALL

166 bottom This bronze and gold votive statuette from Larsa (first half of the nineteenth century B.C.) represents a man praying on his knees, possibly the dedicator Lu-Nanna and not King Hammurabi, as was commonly believed.

under the inner Neo-Babylonian wall, as well as the nucleus of the dried brick ziggurat which was part of the reconstruction work commissioned by Asarhaddon (680-669 B.C.) or by Assurbanipal (638-626 B.C.) after the cruel destruction of the city on the part of Sennacherib in 689 B.C.

The digs carried out by R. Koldewey, besides identifying the later periods of the site (Achaemenid, Seleucid, and Parthian) mostly through surface finds, also brought to light the Neo-Babylonian strata, which provided a rather clear picture of the city in which the first king to effect overall renovation work was Nabopolassar (625-605 B.C.), who concentrated on the fortifications, the reconstruction of various city temples, and the construction of palace complexes. In many cases Nabopolassar's building activity was integrated and completed by his successors, especially Nebuchadnezzar (604-562 B.C.) and Nabonidus (555-539 B.C.).

The Neo-Babylonian fortifications consisted of two walls: an outer one, seen only in the eastern part of the city, and an inner one, which was almost rectangular and protected both the eastern and western districts. The outer wall consisted of three juxtaposed walls, with alternating small and large watchtowers. The inner wall had two juxtaposed walls, also with alternating watchtowers, but there must have been a third wall a short distance from the other two with a wide moat that was begun by Nabopolassar and completed by Nabonidus,

as well as a wall to the west on the bank of the river that Nabopolassar rebuilt several times above a fortification line dating from Sargon II's time and rebuilt in dried bricks by Nebuchaddnezzar and Nabonidus. There were many gates along the inner wall, the most famous being the Ishtar Gate, a large arch between the bastions splendidly decorated with colorful bricks bearing figures of dragons and bulls. Three distinct decorative phases have been identified for their varying techniques, all dating from the Neo-Bablyonian period: in the first one the animal figures are in relief on unglazed bricks, in the second the animals are painted on enameled bricks, and in the third there are dragons and bulls in relief on enameled bricks.

From the north, a processional way lined with tall walls and decorated along the lower level with lions and rosettes in relief on enameled bricks passed through the Ishtar Gate and continued into the city, where, after arriving at the southern side of the E-temen-an-ki ziggurat, headed westward toward the river to the bridge that con-

166-167 Reconstruction of the Gate of Ishtar, with the glazed brick decoration with relief representations of bulls and *mushkhush*, the dragons of Marduk.

167 bottom The diorite lunette of the Code of Hammurabi (first half of the eighteenth century B.C.) portrays King Hammurabi paying homage to the enthroned god Shamash, while the middle registers contain the prologue, the 282 articles, and the epilogue of the famous code.

nected the two sides of the city. In the northern section of the city, on the west side of the processional way, placed against the outside of the inner wall, was the North Palace of Nebuchadnezzar, which stood around two courtyards, repeating the layout (like the northernmost Summer Palace in the northeastern corner of the outer fortifications) of the western sector of the South Palace. This latter, immediately inside the northern line of the inner wall and west of the processional way, had been built by Nabopolassar but had been radically changed by his son Nebuchadnezzar to include a monumental inner layout with five central courts around which were arranged chambers and halls of different sizes and small blocks of rooms. The westernmost block, with the throne room, was used for public and administrative purposes, while the easternmost one presumedly had living quarters.

In the middle of the city was the large precinct of the E-temen-an-ki, the ziggurat that inspired the image of the Tower of Babel. In reality, very few ruins of the tower have survived (there is only the nucleus in dried bricks, while the outer casing has been completely removed) and most of the information we have comes from historic sources, in particular Herodotus, and from the "E-sagila tablet," a cuneiform text dating from the Seleucid period. The ziggurat, built by Nabopolassar and Nebuchadnezzar, must have had seven stories of decreasing size, the last of which contained the Temple of Marduk, the patron god of the city. The ziggurat quarter had a monumental entrance on the processional way and smaller ones on the south side.

Immediately south of the ziggurat was the E-sagila, the Temple of Marduk, a complex laid out around a central court with monumental entrances and façades richly decorated with pilaster strips and towers in profile; an open annex preceded the east side of the temple.

Other minor temples found in the city, like the Temple of Ishtar of Akkad, repeated the typical layout scheme of

the E-sagila: a courtyard with walls and buttresses; an *antecella* and a *cella* with a shallow niche for the statue of the divinity, both latitudinal; small chambers around the courtyard; corridors around the *cella* block; and lastly, a secondary entrance on a long side. The residential quarter of Merkès was discovered in the eastern sector of the city. This proved to be highly interesting because it revealed the types of houses built at the time, which were centered around an inner courtyard often affording access to a reception room. After the Neo-Babylonian period, during which the city was quite prosperous, Babylon was conquered by Cyrus in 539 B.C., and under Artaxerxes II (409-359 B.C.) a columned building similar to the Persian Apadana type was added to the palatial structures. In 331 B.C. Alexander the Great entered Babylon and made it the capital of his empire. He had the ancient edifices (including the ziggurat) restored and built a Greek theater. During the reign of Mithradates I (171-138 B.C.) this latter was remodeled, the Summer Palace was transformed into a fortified complex, and private houses were built in the area of the ancient palaces. The decline of Babylon began with the foundation of Seleucia, and the Roman emperors Trajan and Septimius Severus found it deserted when they visited it in A.D. 115 and 199 respectively.

168 left The inside of the Gate of Ishtar, decorated with unglazed bricks with reliefs of bulls and *mushkhush* dragons that were executed in the first construction phase.

168 right The stela of Marduk-zakir-shumi dates from the tenth century B.C. and is now in the Louvre. In the upper lunette is a scene of a conversation between the king and an official, with the symbols of the Babylonian deities on altars in the background.

169 The modern reconstruction of the entrance to the South Palace of Nebuchadnezzar. It is an arched gateway flanked by two towers aligned with the processional way; later on, the fortified wall that enclosed the entire complex was built on either side of this entrance.

170 TOP LEFT AERIAL VIEW OF PERSEPOLIS IN 1933, WITH MOUNT KUH-I-RAHMAT IN THE BACKGROUND.

170 TOP RIGHT A PHOTOGRAPH TAKEN ON FEBRUARY 13, 1933 OF E. HERZFELD, DIRECTOR OF THE UNIVERSITY OF CHICAGO'S ORIENTAL INSTITUTE ARCHAEOLOGICAL MISSION FROM 1931 TO 1934.

170-171 BOTTOM THE SAKA TIGRAXAUDA DELEGATION, WHICH BROUGHT HORSES, JEWELS, AND CLOTHING AS A TRIBUTE TO THE KING.

171 THE TEAM OF THE UNIVERSITY OF CHICAGO ORIENTAL INSTITUTE RESTORING THE EAST STAIRWAY OF THE APADANA.

PERSEPOLIS

PERSEPOLIS

Text by ANTONELLA MEZZOLANI

In the present-day locality of Takht-i Jamshid (Fars province, Iran) is the city of Persepolis, founded in 500 B.C. by Darius I as the residence and ceremonial center of his dynasty and then destroyed by fire in 331 B.C. after Alexander the Great conquered it.

Only the monumental citadel of the city, already described in ancient chronicles, has been brought to light. Since the seventeenth century many travelers were convinced that the ruins were those of Darius I's capital, but the scientific confirmation arrived only when the Old Persian cuneiform texts from the site were deciphered by G.F. Grotefend, who identified the name of Darius and some of his successors.

In 1878 large-scale excavations were begun at the behest of the governor of the province of Fars, Farhad Mirza, but no documentation of this has survived. Only in 1924 did the Iranian government invite E. Herzfeld to prepare a map of the site and draw up an excavation plan. The work was financed by the Oriental Institute of the University of Chicago, under the supervision of Herzfeld from 1931 to 1934 and of E.F. Schmidt from 1935 to 1939. Later digs, headed by A. Godard, M.T. Mostafavi, and A. Sami for the Iranian Archaeological Service, brought new structures to light. In the last few decades activity has concentrated on the preservation and restoration of the monuments.

The citadel of Persepolis was part of a larger complex that also included edifices at

173 bottom This close-up shot shows the masterly execution of the bas-relief decoration in the Persepolis monuments. The hair of this guard or noble of Median origin with a bulb-shaped headdress was rendered with exquisite detail.

172-173 Stone relief of a lion killing a bull, a representation of the triumph of good over evil. This motif decorates the east stairway of the Apadana, the access stairways of the Tripylon, and the Palace of Darius I.

172 bottom The east stairway of the Apadana is decorated with elegant stone reliefs with a procession of guards. Here is a section of the row of Susian guards armed with spears who accompanied the Persian and Median courtesans.

174 top The north staircase of the Apadana: stone relief of a procession of Persian archers with long apparel and a cylindrical, flute headdress that resembles a feathered crown.

the foot of the terrace, probably a lower city that was never located and the royal tombs of the Achaemenid dynasties hewn out of the rock at Nasq-i Rustam, as well as the tombs of Artaxerxes II, Artaxerxes III, and Darius III, situated on the rise behind the citadel.

The ceremonial nature of the Persepolis terrace, connected to the New Year's Day Feast, exploits the complex layout of the buildings, all of which seem to have a theatrical civic role, even though they are palace structures that must have also been used as living quarters.

The most impressive building in the citadel, the Apadana or Audience Hall, erected by Darius I in 515-490 B.C. and completed by his son Xerxes I, who added sharply angled annexes and monumental entranceways, sits on a rather tall podium (8.5 feet) whose focal point is a vast central hall with 36 columns, with a perimeter in

1) ACCESS STAIRWAY
2) GATE OF XERXES
3) UNFINISHED GATE
4) APADANA
5) THRONE ROOM, OR HALL OF THE HUNDRED COLUMNS
6) PALACE OF DARIUS
7) TRIPYLON, OR COUNCIL HALL
8) HAREM OF XERXES
9) PALACE H
10) PALACE OF XERXES
11) TREASURY
12) RUINS OF THE EAST FORTIFICATION
13) RUINS OF THE NORTH FORTIFICATION
14) TOMB OF ARTAXERXES II

174-175 Overall view of Persepolis from the east: in the foreground, the military quarter; in the middle ground, the Throne Room or Hall of the Hundred Columns; in the background, the ruins of the Apadana, its tall columns crowned by bulls' heads.

175 top This capital in the shape of a griffon's head was executed with remarkable skill and much was attention paid to a create a truly lifelike appearance. The capitals, normally consisting of a pair of animals' heads, were set horizontally on the columns.

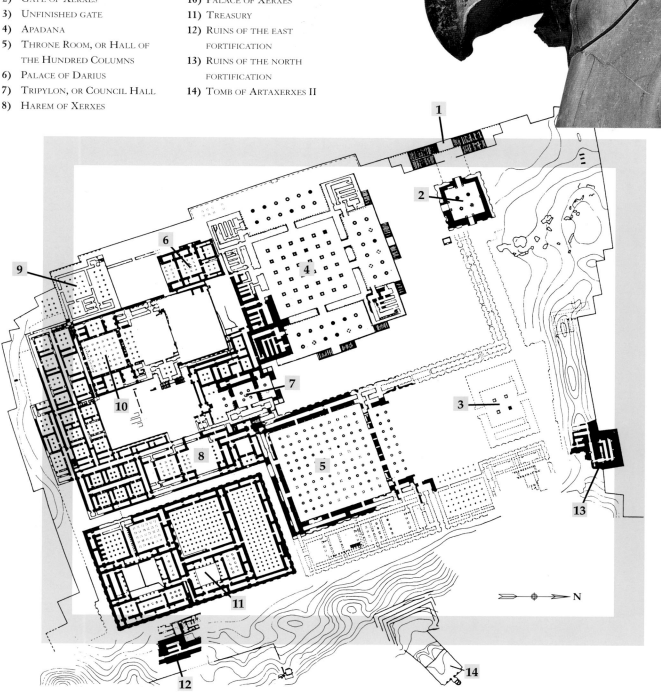

PERSEPOLIS

176 top The Gate of Xerses: the east portal, with human-headed winged bulls guarding the jambs and crowned by molding. Behind this are fluted columns on ribbed campaniform plinths that end in bell-shaped corollas and volutes.

176 bottom A bull's head capital. The sculptor paid special attention to the dimension and the graphic rendering of the details. The capitals with a double animal's head were often connected to the columns by a bell-shaped corolla and four large volutes.

176-177 Entrance to the Palace of Darius. The stairway, consisting of two independent flights, was decorated with reliefs with motifs such as the combat between a lion and a bull or the procession of guards, and it afforded access to the portico leading to the central hall with twelve columns.

which the four corner structures delimit three exterior colonnaded vestibules. The harmoniously painted reliefs that decorated the supporting walls of the podium and the stairways to the east and north seem to represent the phases of the ceremony: in the central façade there are eight guards presenting an inscription concerning the King of Kings, and at the end of this there is a battle between a bull and a lion, in the inner part of the ramp there are Persian guards lined up to form a double wing, and in the casing of the podium is a composite procession of the delegations of the 28 nations subjugated by the Assyrian empire along with the Persian and Median courtesans, accompanied by horses, royal carriages, and the Susian guards. The conceptual originality that developed in the Achaemenid sphere, especially in Darius I's time, is expressed not only in the layout, but also in the structural and compositional definition of the columns, whose square or bell-shaped bases support strongly upwardly thrusting fluted shafts that were masterfully crafted, with horizontal capitals in the shape of animal heads. The articulation between the round vertical element and the horizontal capital is sometimes achieved by connecting them by means of a bell-shaped corolla, on which was placed a quadrangular element with four pairs of volutes.

Between the Apadana and the Throne Room, or "Hall of the Hundred Columns," is a central building commonly known as the Tripylon or Council Hall, which is made up of a double staircase, a two-column portico, and a central hall with four columns, completed in the end by a back portico. It may be that this structure, which has often been interpreted as a connecting element between the Apadana, Darius' Palace, and the Throne Room, had other functions such as a banquet hall or council meeting hall. Among the relief scenes decorating the edifice, mention must be made of the one on the east door, in which Darius I is seated on the throne, accompanied by his son, and above the baldachin is the chief divinity of the Achaemenid Pantheon, Ahura Mazda.

PERSEPOLIS

178 top East stairway of the Apadana: stone relief of some of the tributaries of the Gandhara delegation, who are wearing a short garment and a longer mantle.

178 bottom East stairway of the Apadana: stone relief with a representation of a tributary of the Lydian delegation, wearing a tall turban and draped mantle, who is bearing a gift of two metal vases with ribbed curvature and handles with animals' heads.

178-179 Tripylon: detail of a stone relief depicting two Persian officials holding flowers.

179 bottom East stairway of the Palace of Darius: detail of a stone relief showing a servant with a lamb, which is probably an evocation of the banquet that must have taken place in the palace.

The Hall of the Hundred Columns or Throne Room, planned by Xerxes I but completed by Artaxerxes I, offers a seemingly infinite space that differs from the more symmetrical, balanced taste shown in Darius I's Apadana. The vast square hall, preceded by a large porticoed vestibule, has many more columns, which, though they also have the type of capital in the shape of animal heads, are much thinner, and all other chambers have been eliminated. The reliefs on the north and south portals feature, albeit with some variations, the image of the king on his throne with a baldachin held up by his bearers, while on the side entrances the image of the sovereign or the royal hero appears killing an animal.

The Palace of Darius, immediately south of the Apadana, was to be a constant model for the later palace

complexes in Persepolis. The rectangular structure is divided into a front sector, with a porticoed vestibule and a square central hall with twelve columns and symmetrical wings with small chambers, and a back one composed of two square, colonnaded halls with three wings with secondary chambers. The two-fold function of this complex, both ceremonial and residential, seems to be suggested by the relief motifs including the scene of the hero slaying the lion in the chambers adjacent to the central hall, and the rows of servants following the king featured in the jambs of the doors leading to the back halls.

The so-called Harem seems to have a similar layout.

This edifice should probably be attributed to Xerxes I and lies between the Treasury and the Tripylon. Xerxes' Palace also seems to have been modeled after his father's but with variations, as the central hall is larger, perfectly square, and has 36 columns, and the minor colonnaded chambers are now on the sides and no longer in the back. Even more striking variations in the plan of the·palace complexes (albeit modeled after the Palace of Darius) can be seen in later constructions such as Palace H, the residence of Artaxerxes I. In the last century of Achaemenid dominion, Persepolis was beautified with lesser buildings, restoration work, and sculptural renovation.

180 center Part of the east stairway of the Apadana: detail of a stone relief of a procession of tributaries offering sheep and fabrics to the King of Kings.

180 bottom and 181 East stairway of the Apadana: stone relief depicting the delegation of Lydian tributaries, with their long robes, draped mantle, and tall turbans, brings gifs of horses with chariots, jewels, and vases made of precious metals.

180 top East stairway of the Apadana: stone relief of the Bactrian delegation, whose members can be recognized by their baggy trousers. Preceded by a Median guard, they are bringing camels and vases made of precious metals as a tribute to the King of Kings.

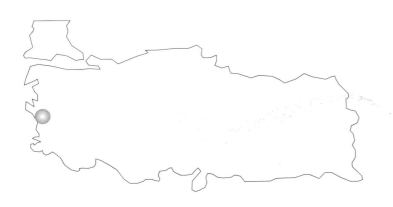

EPHESUS

Text by RICCARDO VILLICICH

The city of Ephesus, which according to tradition was founded by the Amazons or by the mythical Ephesus and Koressus, rose up and developed on the Gulf of Koressus on the western coast of Anatolia, an area heavily colonized by the Greeks, who founded the first settlement in the ninth or eighth century B.C. near an ancient sanctuary dedicated to an indigenous goddess of fertility who was later identified with Artemis. The city, enclosed within walls more than five miles long, occupied a vast coastal plain between the Marnas and Cayster rivers and the Bulbul and Panayr hills. This large metropolis, one of the wealthiest and most highly populated in the ancient world, was systematically brought to light thanks to archaeological digs that began in the mid-nineteenth century, following a long period in which all traces of Ephesus had been lost and it had fallen into oblivion after its gradual abandonment during Ottoman rule. The English archaeologist J.T. Wood's exploration and further research on the part of D.G. Hogarth led to the location and excavation of the Artemision, the great temple dedicated to Artemis that according to Strabo was destroyed and rebuilt seven

182 top According to a common interpretation, this marble bust is a portrait of the goddess Artemis. The sculpture, a Roman copy of the original Greek work of 460 B.C., dates from the second half of the first century A.D. and was found in the large city *palaestra*.

182 bottom Marble Corinthian columns like this one lie on top of the Doric columns of the basilica, which was built during the Augustan age along the north side of the civic Agora.

182-183 The entrance archway to the *pronaos* of the Temple of Hadrian on the Curetes Way is elegantly decorated. In the middle is a bust of Tyche (the city's tutelary goddess), the only remaining element of the triangular tympanum that once crowned the façade.

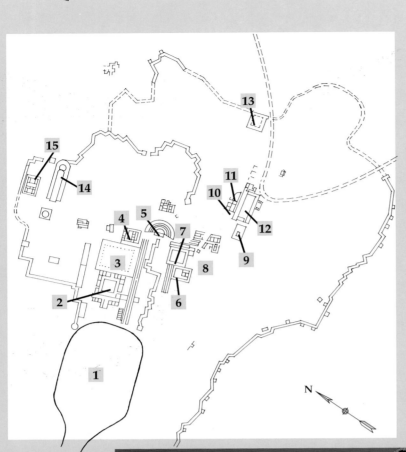

1) HARBOR
2) HARBOR BATHS AND
   PALAESTRA
3) VERULANUS SQUARE
4) *PALAESTRA*
5) THEATER
6) TEMPLE OF SERAPIS
   (SERAPEION)
7) SQUARE AGORA
8) LIBRARY OF CELSUS
9) "TEMPLE OF
   DOMITIAN"
10) PRYTANEUM AND
    DOUBLE TEMPLE
11) BOULEUTERION
12) CIVIC AGORA
13) EAST *PALAESTRA*
14) STADIUM
15) PALAESTRA OF VEDIUS
16) SACRED PRECINCT OF
    ARTEMIS

EPHESUS

184 The Fountain of Trajan, on the Curetes Way, was built in A.D. 102-104, as an inscription tells us, and was dedicated to the emperor. It was rebuilt on a smaller scale, as originally it must have been over 39 feet high.

184-185 The theater, seen here from the Arcadian Way, is one of the best preserved monuments in the archaeological site. The first building phase took place during the Hellenistic period. In Roman times many alterations were effected on different occasions in the *cavea* and the stage area.

185 top This river deity with a crown and a horn of plenty, sculpted in marble and found in the *natatorium* in the Palaestra of Vedius, dates from the Antonine period.

times. Later excavation campaigns carried out at intervals by the Austrian Archaeological Institute were equally illuminating, as they shed new light on the city's urban structure and its main monuments.

There were basically two centers of development in the original city: a small urban community near the port area and the sanctuary of the indigenous goddess identified with Artemis. The first two phases of the archaic Temple of Artemis are commonly dated to the eighth and seventh centuries B.C., a period when an altar and the remains of an *in antis* temple were also found. The Temple of Artemis took on its monumental form in the sixth century B.C., when the city had become one of the leading cities in the Greek world and was subject to the political and cultural influence of the kingdom of Lydia. In the mid-sixth century a new, very large Ionic temple was built and dedicated to Artemis. It was made entirely of marble and surrounded by 126 columns arranged in two rows. After the temple had burned down in 356 B.C., slow reconstruction began on what was to become the seventh wonder of the ancient world: a grandiose temple made entirely of marble that stirred the admiration of Alexander the Great. Praxiteles and Scopas were presumedly among the artists and architects who worked on the edifice. The cult statue of Artemis Ephesias, kept in the temple, was worshipped well into late Roman period.

EPHESUS

186-187 The construction of the Library of Celsus was undertaken in A.D. 114 by Gaius Julius Aquila, who dedicated it to his father, Celsus Polemeanus. The monument was finished about twenty years later, in A.D. 135.

186 bottom A side view of the Library of Celsus in Ephesus. Here can be seen one of the four niches used to house the allegorical statues representing the virtues of Celsus (valor, knowledge, wisdom, and destiny). In the background is the Gate of Mazeus and Mithridates (Augustan age), which gave access to the Agora square.

187 top This marble relief from the square of the so-called Temple of Domitian depicts a winged victory with a laurel crown in her left hand.

187 bottom Panoramic view of the Square Agora. In the background is the upper section of the Library of Celsus, while in the foreground are the ruins of the colonnade, built by the emperor Nero, that linked the Agora and the theater.

In 290 B.C. the city was redesigned in keeping with the Hippodamian scheme by Lusimachus, one of Alexander the Great's *Diadochi*. The new town plan basically, but not strictly, consisted of streets intersecting at right angles and remained unchanged even during the Roman age. The city was ruled by the Seleucids and then by the Attalids from Pergamum, and in 133 B.C. was bequeathed to Rome by the last king of the latter dynasty, Attalus III, together with the entire western part of the Anatolian peninsula. After the Mithridatic wars Ephesus became one of the power centers of Marc Antony, and then under Augustus became the capital of the Asian province in 29 B.C.

The Augustan age brought about profound changes in the hierarchy of the public areas, while at the same time leaving the spatial organization and the polycentric nature of the city unaltered. It was obvious that the aim was to transform the former organs of municipal autonomy into complexes that would be entirely under the aegis of the emperor and therefore marked by the symbols of his cult. After a series of works to improve the water supply network through the construction of new aqueducts, Augustus turned his attention to the central area of the city. The heart of city life were the square porticoed *agora*, the theater connected to the port by a large avenue called the Arcadian Way (later named after the emperor Arcadius, who rebuilt it), and another *agora* to the southwest used

for civic purposes, to which was added the Curetes Way, the ancient route that, proceeding westward, led to the Temple of Artemis.

The changes made in the *agora* during the Augustan age were quite emblematic, as this public area was completely reorganized in conformity with the emperor's ideological program. A long, narrow basilica was built on the north side and was dedicated to the princeps by a local benefactor, Sestilius Pollione. Two small twin dynastic temples dedicated to Rome and to the Divine Caesar were added to it and inserted between the Prytaneum and the Bouleuterion (council chamber), and a temple was erected in the middle of the large square that was dedicated to the deified Augustus. Another construction from the Augustan age is the monumental southeastern entrance to the square *agora*, which was commissioned by two citizens, Mazeus and Mithridates, in honor of Augustus, Livia, Agrippa, and Julia. East of the civic *agora* Domit-

ian later build a peripteral temple placed in a large peribolus and dedicated to his deified father Vespasian.

Between the first and second centuries A.D., Ephesus became one of the leading cities in the Empire for its prosperity and important monumental complexes. The city's Greek-Hellenistic town plan was combined with typical Roman grandiosity. New residential quarters, baths, and a gymnasia were laid out, and from the mid-first century to the second century the theater was enlarged with new tiers and an impressive *scaenae frons*. All these monuments manifest typically Eastern "giantism" and are characterized by striking and elegant architecture and decoration.

In the second century A.D. some of the city's most prestigious monuments were erected. These include the Library of Celsus at the square *agora*, the Temple of Hadrian along Curetes Way (a small *in antis* temple with rich and elegant architectural decoration), the large Veru-

lanus Square, and the Baths of Vedius. The library, the façade of which is much like a theater *scaenae frons*, was commissioned by the consul Gaius Julius Aquila with a two-fold purpose: as a center of learning and a mausoleum for his father, Gaius Julius Celsus Polemaenus. During the reign of Antoninus Pius a noteworthy monumental altar was built. Known as the Altar of Ephesus, it had a sculpture cycle commemorating the victories of Marcus Aurelius and Lucius Verus against the Parthians that reveals the high quality achieved by the Ephesian sculptors, which had already been revealed in many bust portraits and sculpture pieces. These altar reliefs combine classical sculpture and the analytical realism typical of Roman historic relief work.

Ephesus was also a major city during the rise of Christianity, as can be seen in the construction of St. Mary's Church in the fourth century and the large St. John's Basilica on the Ayasoluk hill commissioned by Justinian, which continued to be a popular pilgrimage site until the Turkish conquest in the tenth century.

188-189 The two columns distinguished by anthropomorphic sculptures were part of the decoration so characteristic of the Curetes Way. This old avenue crossed the heart of the ancient city.

189 top The monument erected in the first century A.D. in honor of Caius Memmius, Sulla's grandson, was articulated in a series of triumphal arches supported by caryatids to commemorate the city's capitulation to the Romans after the Third Mithridatic War.

189 bottom The decoration of many monuments in Ephesus (here we see an arch on the Curetes Way) is distinguished by its high quality. The fame of the Ephesian artisans and masons rivaled that of their colleagues in Aphrodisias.

GERASA

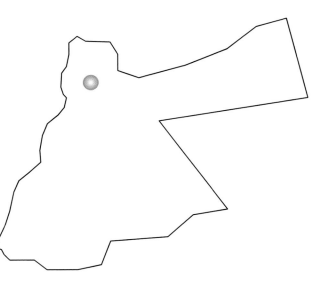

Text of RICCARDO VILLICICH

The city of Gerasa, also known during the Hellenistic age as Antiocha on the Chrysorrhoas, was founded by Antiochus IV Epiphanes (175-164 B.C.) on the banks of that river, 30 miles north of Amman in present-day Jordan. In the first century B.C. this Seleucid city was incorporated into Judea by Alexander Janneus and was shortly afterwards made part of the new Roman province of Syria when Pompey reorganized Rome's eastern territories in 63 B.C. Gerasa enjoyed great prosperity in the second half of the first century A.D. when it became an important caravan trade center in a territory that had abundant agricultural and mineral resources. During the second century the city experienced its most prolific period during which its most grandiose edifices were built, when Trajan made it part of the new province of Aragia in A.D. 106. In the following century, Gerasa was given the honorific title of colony. However, this period also marked the beginning of gradual economic decline that was interrupted briefly only during Justinian's age. Though it was no longer the florid economic center of preceding centuries, the city became a major hub for the diffusion of Christian culture and religion: in a little more than two centuries, from 400

190-191 The oval Agora, seen here from the south, was the starting point of the large colonnaded avenue that was the city's *cardo maximus*.

191 top Among the ruins of the colonnaded avenue are the monumental columns crowned by splendid Corinthian capitals.

191 bottom The monumental arch with three openings was built to celebrate the emperor Hadrian's visit to Gerasa in A.D. 129-130. Four half-columns placed on tall plinths frame the two side openings and the central one; this latter has a large arch that makes the entranceway quite spacious.

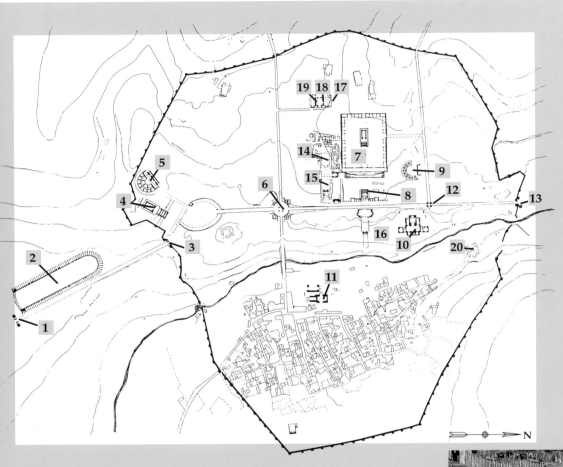

1) ARCH
2) HIPPODROME
3) SOUTH GATE
4) TEMPLE OF ZEUS
5) SOUTH THEATER
6) SOUTH TETRAPYLON
7) TEMPLE OF ARTEMIS
8) PROPYLAEA
9) NORTH THEATER
10) WEST BATHS
11) EAST BATHS
12) NORTH TETRAPYLON
13) NORTH GATE
14) CATHEDRAL
15) ST. THEODORE'S CHURCH
16) NYMPHAEUM
17) SS. COSMAS AND
    DAMIAN CHURCH
18) ST. JOHN'S CHURCH
19) ST. GEORGE'S CHURCH
20) CHURCH OF THE
    PROPHETS AND MARTYRS

192 bottom The definitive form of the Temple of Zeus dates from A.D. 163. Scattered here and there are the drums of columns and other architectural elements from the temple.

192 center In keeping with Roman tradition, the *scenae frons* of the theater was "animated" by particularly elaborate architectural elements.

192-193 The south theater of the city, dating from the second century A.D., had a seating capacity of more than 3,000 and is still in a good state of preservation. Here the *cavea* and orchestra are pictured with the stage in the background.

to 600, more than thirteen churches were built in the city. After the Arab conquest, the city was gradually abandoned, partly because of a terrible earthquake in 746. When the Crusaders occupied Gerasa in the first half of the twelfth century, some of its monuments, including the great Temple of Artemis, were turned into fortresses. The virtually total abandonment of the city, which was repopulated only in 1878 by a group of Circassians, was responsible for the excellent state of preservation of the

archaeological ruins, which were gradually brought to light during the excavation campaigns (most of which were carried out by British missions) that began in the 1920s.

Gerasa is divided into two sections separated by the Chrysorrhoas River, which crosses through the entire city. The eastern part, the ancient ruins of which have been covered by the modern town, corresponds more or less to the residential quarter and seems to have been distinguished by a town plan that is only partly regular because of the geo-morphological features of the site. The western section, which we could call the true heart of the city, is dominated by the gigantic Temple of Artemis and contained the monumental area with its su-

perb public buildings. Like Apamea, Palmyra, Bosra, and many other Near Eastern cities, Gerasa also has a *plateia*, a spectacular colonnaded avenue that traverses the city from one end to the other and that functioned as the main hub of city life, where the city's main monuments stood. In the case of Gerasa, the great colonnaded way, which begins in the south at a vast and singular oval square, has two very large tetrapyla (the southern one is particularly impressive) at the intersection with the two main *decumani*. These monuments, which consist of four portals with four columns each, are often seen in the crossroads (*quadrivia*) of Near Eastern cities and are an original architectural means of regularizing the street network, at times serving to conceal the axes of

the streets, which are not always perfectly perpendicular. As demonstrated previously, the construction, and rebuilding, of most of the prestigious monuments we see today are to be dated to the second century and were often due to the generosity of wealthy citizens. For example, the triumphal arch south of the city was erected during Hadrian's time outside the walls in an area adjacent to the grandiose hippodrome (801 x 167 feet, with a seating capacity of more than 15,000), to celebrate the visit the emperor made in A.D. 129-130. Inside the city walls, in the southern sector, is a large public area consisting of the round Forum from which the colonnaded *plateia* begins, one of the two theaters (in the Roman style, with 14 tiers, four entranceways, and a seating capacity of 3,000), and the Temple of Zeus, which was rebuilt in its present

194-195 The *nymphaeum* in the large colonnaded avenue, which dates from the second century A.D., has a façade similar to the *scenae frons* of a Roman theater, with two rows of niches that were originally framed by jutting columns.

194 bottom The large north tetrapylon, in the shape of a four-façade arch with a central opening and two side ones, indicated the junction of the north *decamanus* and the *cardo* and the course of the street from the North Gate.

195 left The monumental entrance to the Cathedral, the first church built in Gerasa (fourth century A.D.). This is a common three-aisle basilica with Corinthian columns which, like the other churches, stood in the middle of town, around a fountain considered miraculous.

195 right The grandiose Temple of Artemis–the main sanctuary in Gerasa–is a hexastyle peripteros with Corinthian columns on a podium that rose up in the middle of a large colonnaded sacred precinct (*temenos*) and dates from the Antonine age.

form in A.D. 163 as an octostyle peripteros with columns 46 feet high.

As impressive as this temple is, the Temple of Artemis (the tutelary deity of the city) is absolutely spectacular. It lies at the halfway point of the grand colonnaded avenue, dates from the second century, and is one of the largest religious complexes in the Eastern Roman Empire: the colonnaded *temenos* is 787 x 394 feet. Huge *propylaea* directly facing the *cardo maximus* led to a grandiose stairway 62 feet wide that in turn led to the *temenos*. In the middle of this sacred precinct was the Temple of Artemis, a hexa-

style peripteros with 11 columns on the long sides and six on the façade and back side. The buildings in this complex were completed by a *nymphaeum*, also facing the *cardo*.

A second theater was built north of the Temple of Artemis during the Antonine period, and opposite it, on the other side of colonnaded way, was one of the largest bath complexes in the city, the so-called West Thermae. Among the many churches built during the Christian period (most of them common three-aisle basilicas), mention should be made of the Basilica of Saints Cosmas and Damian with its magnificent well-preserved mosaics.

PALMYRA

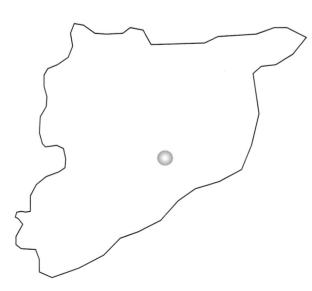

Text by RICCARDO VILLICICH

Palmrya, the ancient caravan city of Syria, rose up in an oasis situated halfway between Homs and Abu Kermal on the Euphrates River, along a trade route that went from the Mesopotamian region, through the desert, and on to the Mediterranean. The name of the city dates from the Greco-Roman period: the ancient community, which was first settled at the dawn of the second millennium B.C., was called Tadmor and was inhabited by a

196-197 The monumental, three-opening arch built in A.D. 220 had a console with statues of important persons over the entranceways. In the background is the fortress built by the Ayyubid emir Al-Malik Shirkuh in 1230.

197 top View of the ruins of Palmyra showing the grand colonnaded avenue that ran the entire length of the city, linking the various quarters–and the impressive sanctuary of Bel.

197 bottom left The Temple of Nebo has been dated to the mid-second century A.D. The northeast corner of the temple façade was cut in order to align the central segment of the colonnaded avenue with the *scenae frons* of the theater.

197 bottom right This funerary stela portrays Queen Zenobia bedecked with jewels, including a *lunula*, a typical crescent-shaped pendant. To her right is Tyche, or Fortune, with a turreted crown and palm branch.

population that can be traced back to the Amorites and then the Aramaeans. However, it was in the Roman period that Palmyra enjoyed the extraordinary prosperity that made it one of the wealthiest cities in the eastern Roman Empire.

The first contact this desert metropolis had with the Romans occurred in 41 B.C. when Antony, as Appian tells us, tried to sack this city of rich merchants. From

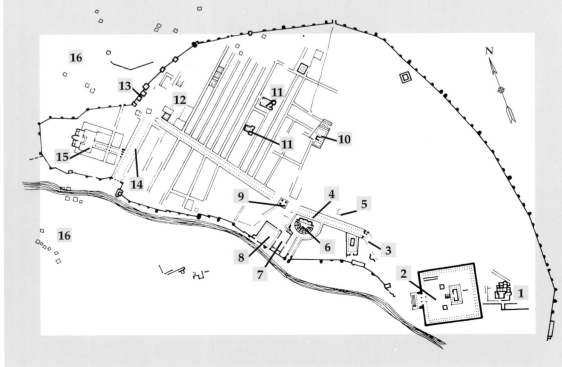

1) ANCIENT HOUSES
2) TEMPLE OF BEL
3) ARCH OF THE SEVERAN
    EMPERORS
4) COLONNADED AVENUE
5) BATHS OF DIOCLETIAN
6) THEATER
7) "HAREM"
8) AGORA
9) TETRAPYLON
10) TEMPLE OF BAAL-
    SHAMIN
11) CHRISTIAN BASILICAS
12) RESIDENTIAL AREA
13) TOMBS INCORPORATED
    INTO THE RAMPARTS
14) TRANSVERSE PORTICO
    AND SQUARE
15) CAMP OF DIOCLETIAN
    AND TEMPLE OF
    ATHENA-ALLAT
16) NECROPOLIS

198-199 The theater, the stage area of which faces the colonnaded avenue, was originally enclosed in an semicircular porticoed square whose shape was modeled after the theater cavea.

199 top The *scenae frons* of the theater, in keeping with Roman architectural canons, has a very elaborate façade made up of niches and jutting elements framed by columns. An architrave crowned by a pediment distinguishes the main entrance to the *pulpitum* from the minor entrances.

199 bottom At this point the colonnaded avenue is connected to the monumental tetrapylon. In the foreground is the west sector of the square outside the theater; at right is one of the accesses to the avenue.

myrrh, incense, and gems from Arabia, and polychrome glass and purple-dyed wool from Phoenicia. In A.D. 129 the Emperor Hadrian visited the city and granted it full fiscal independence; in his honor the city took on the name of Hadriana Tadmor. After a period of great prosperity under the Severan emperors (Caracalla granted Palmyra the status of a Roman colony), during the decades of anarchy in Rome after the death of Alexander Severus, prince Odenathus, governor of the province and the leader of a decisive victory over the Persians that earned him the title of "king of kings," made Palmyra the capital of a true Oriental despotate that was politically independent. After Odenathus, his widow, Queen Zenobia, and their son Vaballatus, taking advantage of the crisis in the Roman Empire, tried to extend the boundaries of their

the fist century A.D. on, Palmyra, at first an autonomous city and a tributary of the Roman province of Syria, played a major role in the Roman Empire's eastern *limes*, both as a barrier against Parthian raids and as a dominant caravan and trade center. The long caravans, which passed in a continuous flow from east to west and vice versa, followed the route that started off from the Persian Gulf, went up along the Euphrates, and from Dura Europos passed through Palmyra to reach Emesa and the Mediterranean. The merchants of Palmyra traded all kinds of refined and exotic products: precious stones, cotton, and aromas from India, silk from China,

new kingdom to the detriment of the Romans by invading Egypt, Syria, and part of Anatolia. The defeat of Zenobia at the hands of the emperor Aurelian in A.D. 273 and the conquest of the city marked the beginning of the decline of what had been one of the richest cities in the East. Despite some initiatives by Diocletian, who reinforced the city walls, reduced the perimeter of the city, and set up a military camp there, Palmyra never regained its commercial pre-eminence. The vitality of the new Christian culture also died out in 634, when the Arabs conquered the city.

Archaeological digs and research were carried out at

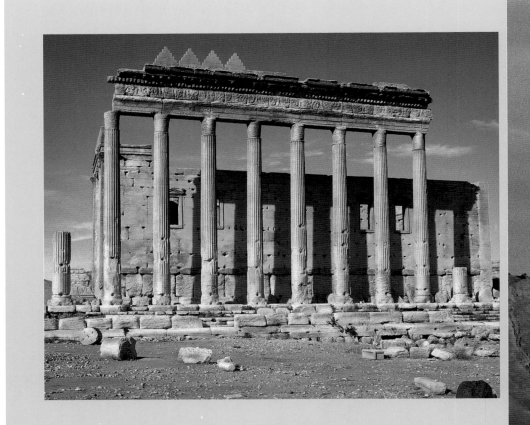

200 top The columns of the Temple of Bel supported an architrave crowned by unique triangular pinnacles.

200 bottom This relief from the Temple of Bel depicts the three main gods of the Palmyra pantheon: in the middle is Bel, to his right Aglibal, the moon, and to his left is Yarhibal, the sun. The three gods are wearing Roman military dress.

200-201 The small Temple of Baal-shamin was built during Hadrian's reign in the northeast sector of the city. This edifice has a façade with four columns, which like those in the colonnaded avenue, have consoles used to support statues.

Palmyra from the early 1900s on (mention should be made of the German mission from 1902 to 1917, and then the French, Syrian, and Swiss missions, followed in 1959 by excavations by the Polish team headed by K. Michalowski). The city has an irregular urban layout characterized by nuclei and quarters that developed in chronological sequence and therefore varied to quite a degree. A large colonnaded street marks the attempt to lend regularity to a complex that is very disjointed, while at the same time providing continuity to the varied range of monuments that line it. This broad avenue (3,600 feet long, with a carriageway 36 feet wide), characterized by two rows of columns with consoles used to support statues of illustrious persons, is not rectilinear

but is divided into at least three rather clear-cut junctions that are concealed by two monuments: a tetrapyle and an arch with a triangular plan used as a connecting link. While the former, a four-front monument consisting of sixteen granite columns on sixteen square supports, had a basically decorative function, the monumental, three-opening arch, built in the third century, was, thanks to its triangular plan, an ingenious expedient that allowed the monument to have a perpendicular façade on both the diverging sections of the colonnaded avenue. In the middle stretch of the avenue, between the tetrapyle and the arch, were the most representative public edifices in the city: the square agora, the theater, the Temple of Nebo (a god in the Babylonian pantheon

202 top This temple tomb, a Corinthian hexastyle, had an architrave and pediment, just like a true sanctuary.

202 bottom left One of the impressive tower tombs in the west necropolis has consoles on the façade that were probably used to support statues.

identified with Apollo), and the Baths of Diocletian. From the arch, proceeding along the southeastern section of the avenue (which was rebuilt from A.D. 200 on and perhaps never finished), one reached the grand sanctuary of Bel, which consisted of a large, almost square porticoed *temenos* (673 x 394 feet), in the middle of which was a peripteral temple with eight columns on the façade.

The temple, built in A.D. 32 and dedicated to the supreme god Bel (later identified with Zeus), is an interesting mixture of classical architectural elements, such as the Corinthian columns and the two pediments, and reworkings of more ancient Mesopotamian traditions. The

202 bottom right The funerary bust of Aqmat, the daughter of Hairan, comes from the Shalamatt hypogeum in the west necropolis and was built in the second half of the second century A.D.

202-203 View of one of the necropolises of Palmyra. In the distance are the typical tower tombs, one of the most common architectural types in the city together with the so-called temple tombs and hypogeum tombs.

pediments, which in the classical orders are structural elements, the terminal part of a sloping roof, in this case have a purely decorative function, since the temple was covered with a terrace. This latter, on which special cult rituals were performed, was accessed via a series of spiral stairs inside the *cella*. Other Oriental architectural motifs were used at the entrance to the *cella*, which was not on a short side of the temple, as is customary, but on one of the long sides, on the original trabeation surmounted by a row of dentate merlons, and in the two facing chapels (*thalamoi*) in the *cella*.

An important monument built in Hadrian's time was the Temple of Baal-shamin, set in an earlier Oriental-type sanctuary in the place where Diocletian's mili-

tary camp was later situated. This temple is yet another example of the assimilation of an Oriental god into the Greco-Roman pantheon. Other characteristic monuments in Palmyra are linked to the cult of the dead and figurative art such as the tombs in the form of either mausoleum-temples, funerary towers, or hypogea, inside which there were many loculi that were sealed off mostly by sculpted stone slabs, and the so-called Palmyra stelae, which often depicted funerary banquet scenes with the deceased among his relatives. These stelae also frequently bore portraits of the deceased in Roman dress, but more often, especially in the case of female figures, Oriental hair styles and apparel were preferred.

This city in Syria, in the valley between Lebanon and Anti-Lebanon, at 3,840 feet above sea level, owes its present name Baalbek (documented from A.D. 400 on) to the cult of the god Baal, the supreme deity in the Eastern pantheon who was often identified with Jupiter. In the Hellenistic and Roman periods the city was known as Heliopolis, a name that is also connected with the religious traditions of the city, where it seems that the cult of Hadad–in Hellenistic times identified with the Sun–was deeply rooted. Thus religious syncretism was responsible for the cult of Jupiter Heliopolitanus, which documents have dated to the Roman period and which is evidently a transposition of the ancient indigenous cult of the Sun. The name of the city has also been documented in some brief passages of ancient literary sources. In fact, Heliopolis is mentioned by Flavius Josephus in his description of Pompey's expedition in 64 B.C. and by Strabo, who placed it near Apamea, an ancient Seleucid city in Syria. In the Julio-Claudian period Heliopolis became a Roman colony with the title of Colonia Iulia Augusta Felix Heliopolitana (a title often seen in coins and milestones).

Because of its position, the city was never a trade center, and we do not know whether it was particularly im-

BAALBEK

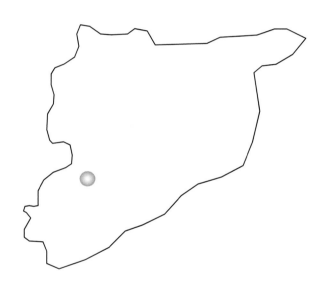

204 A lion's head in the entablature of the Temple of Jupiter Heliopolitanis was not purely decorative; its mouth was used as a sort of spout for rainwater.

205 top A panoramic view of the archaeological area. In the background is the large Temple of Jupiter Heliopolitanis.

205 bottom An variety of architectural material is scattered over much of the archaeological area. In the background, still in their original position, are the remains of a colonnade. The central entrance has a wide archway.

206-207 The large central courtyard gives access to the Temple of Jupiter. In the middle of the colonnaded square are the ruins of the altar and the tower monument.

206 bottom In the foreground is one of the two longitudinal basins at the edge of the central court of the sanctuary. In the background, at left, is the grand stairway that led to the Temple of Jupiter.

207 The round Temple of Venus is not large and has a horseshoe-shaped colonnade with a tetrastyle *pronaos* on its façade and four columns in the back section of the round *cella*. Statues were placed in the niches.

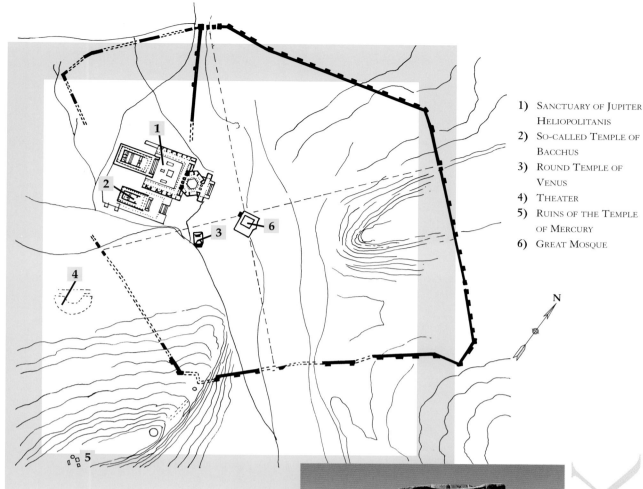

1) SANCTUARY OF JUPITER
   HELIOPOLITANIS
2) SO-CALLED TEMPLE OF
   BACCHUS
3) ROUND TEMPLE OF
   VENUS
4) THEATER
5) RUINS OF THE TEMPLE
   OF MERCURY
6) GREAT MOSQUE

portant politically or economically. However, it seems that Baalbek played a major role as a religious center. The fame of the Heliopolitan sanctuary, the construction of which lasted for centuries, can be seen in the spread of this cult throughout various provinces of the Roman Empire. Even at Rome, a temple was built on the Janiculum hill and dedicated to the Heliopolitan triad. Under Septimius Severus the colony obtained *ius italicum* status. During the reign of Caracalla, memorable games were established in honor of Jupiter Heliopolitanis, who was totally identified with Jupiter Capitolinus. The first Christian community presumably grew up under Constantine, who built a church in the city that was destroyed thirty years later by the pagan emperor Julian the Apostate. Compared to other Near Eastern cities, the citizens of Baalbek were more reluctant to accept the new Christian religion. Despite the fact that the city was an Episcopal See, paganism continued to dominate until the bloody repression of 579 ordered by the Byzantine emperor Tiberius II to eliminate pagan rites once and for all. In 637 the city was conquered by the Arabs and in 1175 was taken by Saladin at the expense of the Crusaders. In 1260 what remained of the old city was razed to the ground by the Mongol military chief Hulagu Khan. Present-day Baalbek, which has been Lebanese since 1920,

occupies only the eastern part of the ancient city.

A complete detailed picture of the town plan does not exist and what is available was brought to light only partially through a series of excavation campaigns on the site, which began in the early 1900s. However, it would seem that it was not perfectly regular because of various pre-Roman elements that inevitably conditioned the Roman layout. In itself the town plan of Baalbek does not appear to be particularly significant, however there is a series of monuments erected mostly between the first and third centuries A.D., including a Bouleuterion, a round temple built in the early third century, a hippodrome, and a theater, as well as private houses with noteworthy mosaic floors. While the town plan and the above-mentioned

BAALBEK

208 left The *pronaos* of the so-called Temple of Bacchus. In the foreground is one of the Corinthian capitals that stood on top of the colonnade columns.

208 right The short back side of the so-called Temple of Bacchus, which is thought to have actually been dedicated to Venus-Atargatis.

208-209 In the interior of the *cella* in the Temple of Bacchus are the lovely walls, their half-columns framing niches crowned by pediments in the upper register and small arches in the lower one.

209 bottom Elegant decoration with plant motifs enhances the jambs of portal of the *cella* in the Temple of Bacchus.

monuments are not especially distinguished, the western sector of the city is on the other hand literally dominated – for its dimensions and the quality of the architecture – by the sanctuary of Jupiter Heliopolitanus, which towers over the entire city because of its enormous plan (886 x 394 feet) and height (the temple alone is 151 feet high). From the beginning of the first century until at least the third century, many architectural structures were placed around this gigantic temple dedicated to Jupiter-Baal (the combined manifestation of the supreme Roman deity and the main Eastern god), thus forming a spectacular, dazzling mixed complex laid out on different levels and animated by the many minor monuments and the exuberant decoration.

The Great Temple (295 x 117 feet) is a decastyle peripteros standing on a colossal podium. It was built in the second half of the first century A.D. and faces a large colonnaded court probably dating to the Antonine period, along the perimeter of which are open spaces and *cellae*; a tall tower, enormous basins, and an altar lie in the open space in the middle of the courtyard. Access to the temple court and the temple is afforded by a monumental propylon (early third century) that has twelve columns on the façade at the top of a tall stairway. This structure is con-

nected to the colonnaded temple courtyard by a singular octagonal court built in the mid-third century. A little further south of the Great Temple, in a long, narrow colonnaded courtyard, was the so-called Temple of Bacchus (really dedicated to Venus-Atargatis, a Syrian goddess), which has been dated on the basis of its style to the mid-second century. This is an octastyle perpiteral Corinthian temple which, although smaller than the colossal Great Temple, has impressive proportions: 214 feet long, 110 feet wide, and placed on a 15-1/2-foot high podium preceded by a 34-step stairway. The *cella* consisted of a chamber with barrel vaulting and a three-aisle adytum, access to which was afforded by a nine-step staircase.

FAR EAST

HAMPI

PAGAN

AYUTTHAYA

ANGKOR

THE DIVINE AND THE HUMAN IN SOUTHEAST ASIAN CITY PLANNING

TEXT BY

MARCO CERESA

Since very ancient times the idea of the Orient in European cultural circles was fraught with conceptions that went well beyond the empirical knowledge Westerners had of this land. In ancient Greece, Aeschylus and Euripides described the Orient as the land of sworn enemies and obscure religions that were potentially subversive to the stability of the West. Painting the Orient as weak, decadent, and corrupt was a reassuring lie used to assuage the anxiety of the West, even though actual experience of this "other" reality was really quite limited. The Orient remained remote, difficult to explore and interpret, and the fantasies and fears of Westerners were projected in chaotic fashion onto this distant land. Fabulous stories were told of immense riches and magnificent and fascinating cities governed by cruel sovereigns. People had direct knowledge only of the bordering territories of the Orient, which they tried to keep at bay and control; the rest was left to the imagination. The Bible, Herodotus' *Histories,* and the scarce information garnered from travelers and merchants were used to solve the riddle of the mysterious Orient, but in vain as they merely added fuel to the legends. With time the Orient was divided into the Near, Middle, and Far East. Everything

Far East

that early visitors had seen and related was taken for granted, and every successive traveler tried to corroborate and recreate this myth, thus adding to this inventory of mirages and fables. The closest and best-known Oriental countries, the Holy Land and Egypt, had already become part and parcel of Western imagination. One of the most overwhelmingly intriguing characteristics of the Orient was Islam.

However the Far East, the most distant Orient, was another world entirely. Up to the age of colonialism, the Far East was considered the last frontier, the end of the Earth, the vague repository of memory and fantasy.

Besides its distance and antithetical relation with the West, the Far East is also delimited and separated from the rest of the world by a geographic gap that has produced a long-lasting historic separation. The Himalayan mountain chain, the Central Asian deserts to the north, and river basins to the south covered with forests have always been a barrier obstructing penetration via land routes, while navigation in the Indian Ocean was made difficult by seasonal monsoons. These particular circumstances made contact between the Far East and the Western world both difficult and sporadic, at least until the arrival of Vasco da Gama at Calicut in 1498, which marked the beginning of Western colonialism in the East.

Historic-geographic conditions have produced two vast cultural regions in the Far East, the Chinese and Indian, that are separated by the Indochinese peninsula and the Indonesian archipelago, and which have been influenced by them respectively. Further east, the Japanese islands were the most distant objective of Western economic and cultural currents, beyond which lies another immense natural barrier, the Pacific Ocean.

This very remote and composite universe is divided into the inhospitable mountains of the north inhabited by nomadic tribes and the fluvial plains of the south, more suitable for large communities. Given this geographic configuration, the birth and rise of large nations corresponded to the capacity to control the menace of the northern populations and to channel and exploit the water resources needed for agriculture, the primary means of subsistence for the people of the plains.

In this context, the rise and organization of cities was not linked with local autonomy but was rather the tangible manifestation of a centralized power and the mark this power makes on its domain. And just as centralized power is the human representation of a cosmic or religious order (the emperor who rules in virtue of a heavenly mandate, for ex-

213 top A *vyala*, a fantastic composite animal, graces a column of the Temple of Vittalasvami at Hampi.

ample the *devaraja* who is a "celestial king"), cities are the architectural representation of this order. The layout of the city and the arrangement of its buildings reflect the cosmological principles of the civilization that produced it; walls, gates, streets, and axes are often oriented with the cardinal points, the five elements, or the constellations. Inside the city the hierarchy of the buildings and diversification of their functions reveal the details and specific nature of the civic and religious rituals that guaranteed orderly social life.

This Orient that Westerners dreamed of, feared, disparaged, but on the whole knew very little about, was for centuries the cradle of civilizations that were much more sophisticated from a scientific and technological standpoint than the civilization of their detractors. The scientific superiority of Oriental civilization was lost only after the scientific revolution that took place in Europe in the seventeenth and eighteenth centuries. Furthermore, the Far East was also the home of a great religion, Buddhism, which was the connective tissue and vehicle of civilization for all the Oriental cultures, from India to Japan, and which also gave rise to an ethical-political system, Confucianism, which sustained one of the largest empires in the world for over two thousand years.

But as Italo Calvino relates in his *Invisible Cities*, every empire is destined to fall and its very foundation holds the seeds of its demise. The same feeling of helplessness, transience, and melancholy felt by Kublai Khan in Calvino's novel in "an evening with the smell of elephants after rainfall and of sandalwood ashes turning cold in the braziers," must have also been felt by Jayavarman VII, Narai, and Anawrahta. Their capitals—Angkor, Ayutthaya, Lopburi, and Pagan—were certainly as rich, splendid, and sumptuous as any city described by Marco Polo, and yet they began to decline soon after their foundation. Ayutthaya was burned, Lopburi was abandoned, Pagan became a lair of thieves and ghosts, and Angkor was strangled by the jungle.

Cities created out of the void by the determination and ambition of a single ruler were inevitably returned to oblivion by other kings, other men, other armies.

Cities were abandoned, forgotten, and even lost only to be rediscovered centuries later, as in the case of Angkor, with no Marco Polo to describe them.

It is this book's aim to discover "the thread of a subtle design" (in the words of Calvino) in the harmony of proportions, the profound silence of vast courtyards, the faded grace of sculpture, and the proud towers and domes that time and enemies have not managed to wholly subdue of these grand cities.

The scenery in this region is spectacular, and there is surely one of the most moving landscapes in southern India. Rocky hills consisting of masses that seem piled up by chance, extend in fantastic shapes all around. Here and there are large patches of luxuriant vegetation, and the brilliant band of the Tungabhadra River flows in wide bends. Hampi, which is the ancient local name still used today, or Vijayanagar, the "city of victory" as it was christened in its heyday, is now an enormous and extremely fascinating stretch of ruins.

It was founded around 1336 by the brothers Harihara and Bukka, probably the sons of a sovereign deposed by the Muslim conquerors. The siblings were former Hindus who converted to Islam and thus secured themselves important posts, but then rebelled and returned to Hinduism and set up an independent reign in the territories assigned to them by the Muslim rulers. In the two centuries that followed, the city was the brilliant capital of the last Hindu empire in India, the final bulwark against the Muslim conquest of southern India.

In its golden age Hampi occupied a surface area of at least eleven square miles, and many Western travelers such as the Italian Niccolò de Conti and the Portuguese Domingo Paes and Fernão Nuniz wrote enthusiastic descriptions of its magnificence and luxury. In the fifteenth century, the Persian Abdu'r Razzaq wrote, "All the inhabitants, be they nobles or commoners, including the artisans in the bazaar, wear jewels and gilded ornaments on their ears and around their necks, arms, wrists, and fingers." Paes, at the beginning of the following century, compared Hampi to Rome and was spellbound by a chamber in the palace completely faced with ivory. When in 1565 Talikota was de-

HAMPI

214 The plinth of this column in the Temple of Vitthalasvami is decorated with figures of lions, the ancient symbol of regality. Every column in the temples at Hampi is an elegant, elaborate sculpture in itself.

215 bottom left This small building, a replica of a processional cart (*ratha*), is one of the most famous monuments at Hampi. It was built with such perfection that some say its wheels can actually move.

215 right The columns of the temple at Hampi, like this one in the Temple of Vitthalasvami, often bear a sculpted *vyala* (or *yali*), a fantastic, composite animal that is depicted rearing up and reined in by a human.

216-217 The Temple of Acyutaraya was certainly one of the most important sacred sites in the city. Its setting is still quite fascinating.

216 center The colonnaded hall (*mandapa*) of the Temple of Acyutaraya manifests all the refined skill of the Hampi sculptors, who executed extremely elegant works.

216 bottom The Temple of Hazara Rama comprises two *sacraria* that end in the topmost structure so characteristic of southern Indian temples, a sort of stepped pyramid whose steps consist of miniature replicas of edifices.

feated and his empire doomed, Hampi was subjected to six months of pillage and the city was abandoned forever. But some buildings, both religious and secular, have survived, which makes Hampi the only traditional Indian city whose structure can still be admired. The city had a sacred quarter, an area reserved for the king and his court, and residential quarters. It was surrounded by seven walls, according to contemporary historic sources; the three outermost ones protected cultivated fields, while the other four sur-

rounded the inhabited areas. Some stretches of the walls still stand, some as much as thirtythree feet high. There is also a broad processional way that starts off from the great temple of Virupaksa, from where the carriages of the divinities proceeded during solemn feast days.

The urban area seems to have been well provided with canals and basins used as reservoirs. The large-scale use of perishable building materials such as wood, rocks, and plaster, as well as thatched roofs, accounts for the lack of examples of ancient private houses. As was common in India the most important constructions were made of stone, which in this particular case consisted of granite with a rather coarse grain. The many religious buildings constructed by the kings of Vijayanagar, both in the capital and in the rest of the empire, are testimony to one of the most important chapters in the history of Indian art.

The temple architecture of the period, which followed the already established tendencies in southern India, marked a definite step toward ever more complex and impressive structures. The temple was no longer a single edifice but a vast complex of structures. The sacred area was generally a rectangular walled enclosure with entrances at the cardinal points, these latter being surmounted by sculpt-

HAMPI

1) TEMPLE OF VIRUPAKSA, OR PAMPAPATI
2) ANCIENT PROCESSIONAL WAY AND BAZAAR
3) TUNGABHADRA RIVER
4) TEMPLE OF ACYUTARAYA
5) TEMPLE OF KRISHNA
6) TEMPLE OF VITTHALASVAMI
7) TEMPLE OF HAZARA RAMA
8) ELEPHANT STABLES
9) UNDERGROUND TEMPLE
10) WOMEN'S QUARTERS (ZENANA) AND LOTUS MAHAL
11) "QUEEN'S BATH"
12) TEMPLE OF PATTABHIRAMA
13) GATE OF TALARIGATTU
14) SULE BAZAAR

Vithoba, who was an extremely popular deity in southern India. This temple dates from the reign of Krsnadevaraya (1509-30), the greatest monarch of Vijayanagar, who presumedly promoted the construction of many other sacred buildings in his empire. Inside the sacred quarter one notes above all a small edifice in the shape of a cart, a charming stone replica of the wooden processional carts that are still popular in many regions of India. The temple itself is in the middle and consists of two *mandapa,* or colonnaded halls, and the *cella*. One of the halls has "musical"

ed *gopura*, or towers, with a strange shape. There were a great number of colonnaded halls, and the columns themselves each became an elaborate sculpture that often portrayed characteristic figures such as fantastic animals or rampant horses mounted by horsemen. The most famous and acclaimed temple in Hampi is the Vitthalasvami, dedicated to a form of the great god Vishnu called Vitthala or

columns, which emit different notes when struck. The major temples in southern India are completed by other edifices including the sanctuary of the goddess-consort (the Amman, or "Mother") and the so-called *kalyana mandapa,* or "wedding pavilion," which is exquisite for its form and sculptures. In this latter the bronze statues of the god and his consort were exhibited on particular religious holidays.

218-219 Some platforms probably served as bases for buildings, which, having been built with perishable materials, are lost to us today.

218 bottom The gem of Hampi's domestic architecture is this small building called Lotus Mahal, or Lotus Palace, because its shape is similar to a lotus with open petals.

219 top Even though nobody is sure what its use was, this large edifice near the royal citadel is known as the Elephant Stables because of its huge rooms.

219 bottom In the reliefs of the largest platform elephants and dancers figure, magnificently sculpted despite the poor quality of the local stone, a type of coarse-grained granite.

Other important temples in ancient Hampi are the Virupaksa, or Pampapati, dedicated to the god Shiva, which has paintings on the ceilings, the Acyutaraya, and the Hazara Rama in the royal citadel, which was probably used for the king's private worship.

Some monuments in this area of the city are still obscure, such as certain large platforms that once supported structures that have since disappeared. The most majestic of these is decorated on its sides by long friezes depicting battles, horse rides, and women dancers in a rather vernacular style. Other buildings reveal a considerable Islamic influence. At least in the field of architecture, Vijayanagar could not completely ignore the Muslim kingdoms as sources of inspiration, ironically the very kingdoms that would bring about its downfall. Thus, large domes crown the structure known as the "Elephant Stables" and an elegant building called Lotus Mahal (Lotus Palace) is completely inlaid with elegant cusped arches. Scattered throughout the city are impressive sculptures representing Hindu deities (Vishnu, Narasimha, Ganesa, and the bull Nandin). The Temple of Virupaksa is still a popular place of worship and is visited regularly by many Indians, both pilgrims and tourists alike.

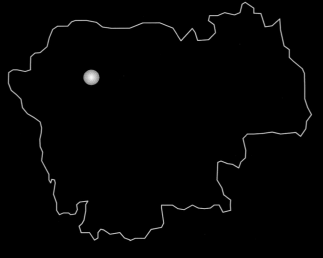

ANGKOR

220 THE BAYON TOWERS, WITH A SQUARE BASE, CONSIST OF FOUR LEVELS CROWNED BY A LOTUS FLOWER. ON EACH SIDE IS A SCULPTED HUMAN FACE BETWEEN SIX AND EIGHT FEET HIGH.

220-221 THE ENGRAVINGS BY THE FRENCH ARTIST LOUIS DELAPORTE PUBLISHED IN *VOYAGE AU CAMBOGE: L'ARCHITECTURE KHMER* (1880) SHOW THE STATE OF THE RUINS OF ANGKOR WHEN IT WAS DISCOVERED BY WESTERN TRAVELERS.

ANGKOR

Text by MARCO CERESA

The name Angkor, which in the Western world evokes images of grandiose temples, luxuriant and treacherous forests, and unsolved archaeological mysteries, designates an area in Cambodia that for more than 500 years was the political center of the Khmer Empire. Situated in a wide basin delimited to the south by the large Tonle Sap lake and to the north by the Kulen mountains, the Angkor zone lies about 204 miles north of Phnom Penh, the present capital.

The Angkor period (802-1432), the most glorious in Khmer history, began with the ritual ceremony that bestowed the title of *devaraja* (celestial king) on Jayavarman II (802-850) and ended when the capital was first moved to Basan, on the east bank of the Mekong River, and then to Phnom Penh, in southern Cambodia.

After a period spent as a hostage of the royal court in Indonesia, the future king Jayavarman returned to Cambodia in 790, where he consolidated his power with a series of military campaigns. At first he chose the city of In-

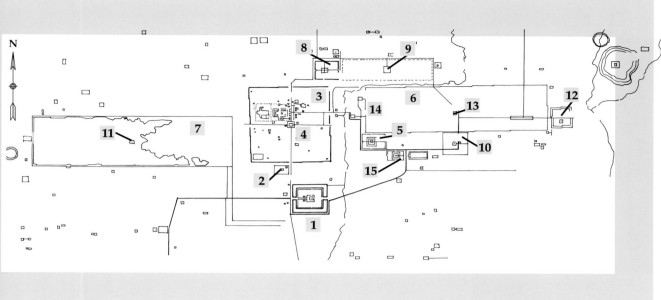

N

1) ANGKOR WAT
2) PHNOM BAKENG
3) ANGKOR THOM
4) BAYON
5) TA PHROM
6) EAST BARAY
7) WEST BARAY
8) PREAH KHAN
9) NEAK PEAN
10 PRE RUP
11) WEST MEBON
12) BANTEAY SAMRE
13) EAST MEBON
14) TAKEO
15) BANTEAY KDEI

222-223 The moat surrounding Angkor Wat is 3.4 miles long. It is crossed on the west side by a long paved sandstone bridge and on the east side by a simple earthen causeway.

223 center The Angkor Wat temple proper lies inside the first city wall, on a vast terrace surrounded by palm and mango trees.

223 bottom The outer façade of Angkor Wat consists of a tall laterite wall interrupted in the middle by a *gopura* (gateway) articulated in three sections. A colonnade connects the *gopura* to the towers at each end of the wall.

drapura as his capital, but around the beginning of the ninth century he moved it to area of Mount Kulen, 25 miles northeast of Angkor Thom. Here King Jayarvarman proclaimed himself *devaraja*, thus initiating a new religious rite based on the cult of the "celestial king."

The year 802 marked the beginning of the unification of the Khmer state, independence from Indonesia, and the beginning of the Angkor period, which saw 39 kings. Jayavarman II was succeeded by his son Indravarman I (877-889), who inaugurated the Angkor architectural tradition by building the "mountain temple" of Bakong, another temple in honor of his ancestors, and one of the two reservoirs (called *baray*) near Roulos. These three types of public works became, from this period on, symbols of royalty and useful tools for legitimizing royal power. Indravarman's successor Yasovarman I (889-900) made Yasodharapura—

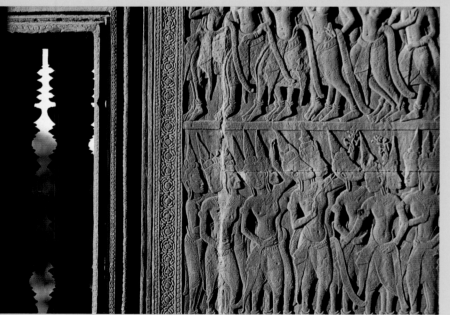

ANGKOR

later on called Angkor—the definitive capital of the kingdom.

Of the rulers from the golden age of Angkor, outstanding figures were Suryavarman II (1113-1150), the founder of the Angkor Wat temple, and Jayavarman VII (1181-1220), considered the greatest king of the Angkor period. An indefatigable builder, this king constructed more monuments, bridges, and roads than any other Angkor ruler and instilled the principles of Mahayana Buddhism, of which he was a fervent follower, throughout his kingdom. The death of Jayavarman VII marked the beginning of Angkor's gradual decline. During the reign of Indravarman III (1295-1307), Theravada Buddhism became the state religion. This religious sect, which came from Sri Lanka, opposed the doctrine of the *devaraja* (celestial king), which had played such a major role in the consolidation of the royal power at Angkor. The decline of royal authority, together with the economic difficulties caused by the architectural projects pursued during Jayavarman VII's reign and mounting pressure from bordering states, the Champa and the emerging Thai reign of Ayutthaya, accelerated the end of Angkor.

After a long siege, in 1431 Angkor was captured by the Thais from Ayutthaya, who occupied it briefly. As soon as the occupation ended the Khmer decided to transfer the capital further south, and the jungle slowly began to encroach upon Angkor.

Fourteenth-century Portuguese, Spanish, and Japanese travelers documented the existence of grandiose ruins in the middle of the jungle. However, it was the posthumous publication of the journals of Henri Mouhot, a French naturalist who had visited Cambodia in 1860, which truly aroused great interest in the ruins of Angkor. At first it was only the exoticism and romantic fascination of the ruins covered with vegetation that attracted visitors, but later, thanks above all to the efforts of the archaeologists and restorers sent by the Ecole Française d'Extrême-Orient, the temples of Angkor began to be appreciated as masterpieces of world architecture.

The monuments of Angkor are scattered over a radius of dozens of miles. Starting from the town of Siem Reap, the closest to the city, and heading north, the first temple one sees is Angkor Wat. North of Angkor Wat is the walled city of Angkor Thom, to the east and west of which are the two *baray*, the large cisterns that supplied the entire capital with water. East of Angkor Thom are many other temples, including the famous Ta Prohm, while to the north is Preah Khan and farther on to the northeast, Banteay Srei. East of Siem Reap are the temples of the Roulous group, which date from the early years of the Angkor period.

Angkor Wat is the largest and best preserved of the Angkor temples. It is rectangular, covers a surface area of almost 494 acres, and is surrounded by a moat 650 feet wide. A causeway 820 feet long leads to the main entrance. The temple faces the west, unlike all the other edifices at Angkor, which face the east, and this has given rise to many theories

concerning its function. Recent studies have demonstrated that Angkor Wat was a mortuary monument built to house the ashes of Suryavarman II; the direction of the ancient Brahmin funeral processions was in fact from east to west.

The temple, 213 feet high, has three concentric levels. On the third level there is a quincunx of five towers–four at the corners and one in the middle–that constitute the distinguishing feature of the silhouette of Angkor Wat.

According to scholars, the temple is a stone replica of the universe. The central tower represents mythical Mount Meru, situated in the middle of the universe, while the other four towers are its peaks. The enclosure wall symbolizes the mountain chain at the edge of the Earth and the surrounding moat the oceans.

Along the innermost enclosure wall of the first level, in the part of the temple open to worshippers, is the famous gallery of bas-reliefs. Entering from the main entrance of the temple, the progression of the scenes is counterclockwise.

The west gallery features realistic scenes of the mythical battle of Kuruksetra, celebrated in the Indian epic poem *Mahabharata*. The south gallery, the so-called historic gallery, contains no mythical scenes but depicts the parade of the army of Suryavarman II. The bas-reliefs in the east gallery illustrate one of the most famous and most repre-

226-227 The bas-reliefs in the south wing of the west gallery depict the battle of Kurukshetra between the Kauravas and the Pandavas, which is described in the Indian epic poem *Mahabharata*.

227 The bas-reliefs in the north wing of the west gallery depict the battle of Lanka, during which Rama, with the help of his monkey allies, rescued his wife Sita, who had been kidnapped.

ANGKOR

sentative motifs in Khmer art, *Churning the Sea of Milk*, in which gods and demons are engaged in churning the Sea of Milk to make the elixir of immortality emerge from the depths. The north gallery features Khrishna's victory over Bana, the king of demons. Lastly, in the stretch of the west gallery left of the main entrance is another battle from the poem *Ramayana*: the struggle between Rama and the demon king Ravana, at Lanka.

The city of Angkor Thom, built by Jayavarman VII and situated one mile north of the main entrance of Angkor Wat, has a surface area of about four square miles. Walls 26 feet high surround it, forming a square about two miles long per side. Along the outer perimeter is a wide moat. Bridges flanked by enormous statues of demons and gods lead to the five monumental city gates, each of which is decorated with two enormous stone faces.

In the middle of the city is the most important monu-

228 bottom The outer perimeter of the Bayon temple is characterized by four gateways and four corner pavilions. Left of the east gateway is the beginning of the bas-reliefs gallery, which surrounds the entire edifice, albeit damaged in many spots.

229 The stone face of the deified king of Bayon, with his lowered eyelids and slightly curled lips, epitomizes the famous "Angkor smile."

228 top The faces sculpted in stone on the 54 towers of Bayon, each facing a different cardinal point, symbolize the omnipresence of the Bodhisattva Avalokitesvara, the alter ego of King Jayavarman VII.

228 center The complexity of the Bayon temple and the intricate arrangement of its edifices are a consequence of the many alterations made as early as the reign of Jayavarman VII.

230 top In the middle of the main basin in the Neak Pean temple (second half of the twelfth century) is a small round island with the sanctuary of Avalokitesvara.

230 bottom The bas-reliefs of the south wing of the east gallery of Bayon, divided into three registers, depict a military parade with a forest in the background.

203-231 The south platform of the Elephants' Terrace is bordered on both sides by three stone elephant heads. The animals' trunks, resting on a lotus flower, serve as pillars.

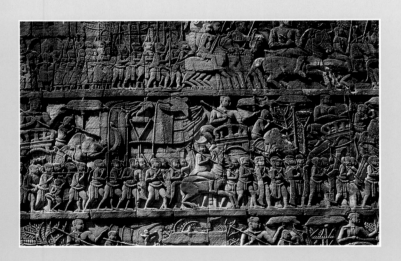

structure becomes well defined and its most famous characteristic clearly emerges: from the top of the towers, 200 huge stone faces look down at the visitors with a faint, enigmatic smile. This is the "smile of Angkor," characterized by a slight curling of the lips that is the main feature of Bayon sculpture.

According to different interpretations, the stone faces portray the Bodhisattva Avalokitesvara or his earthly manifestation, King Jayavarman VII himself. Conceived by a great king and a fervent holy man, Bayon is at once symbol of Jayavarman VII's regality and the achievement of his mystical vision.

North of the Bayon is the Royal Square, delimited by two parallel roads. West of the square are such famous monuments as the Baphuon Temple, the Terrace of the Elephants, the Royal Palace, the Phimeanakas Temple, and the Terrace of the Leper King. The Royal Square was used for royal parades and processions that could be watched from the two terraces. The former was named after the almost life-size bas-relief elephants on the façade. The second terrace owes its name to the statue of a seated man, probably the god of the dead, Yama, covered with a crust of lichens that make him look like a leper.

ment in Angkor Thom after Angkor Wat, the Bayon, where the four roads that divide the city into four quarters converge. This temple is considered the most important monument in Angkor after Angkor Wat, situated in a rectangle of 460 x 525 feet and with 54 towers moving upwards like jets of lava that have solidified in the air. Seen from a distance, because of the effect of the light the Bayon looks like an indistinct heap of stone blocks in perpetual movement upward. But the closer one gets to this monument, its

231 bottom The anterior façade of the Elephants' Terrace is decorated with a procession of elephants, which are represented in profile with extraordinary realism and are of almost natural size.

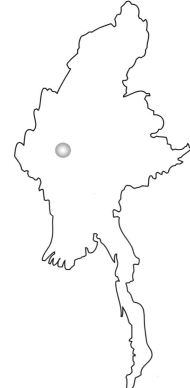

PAGAN

Text by MARCO CERESA

There are two religious capitals in Southeast Asia, Pagan (or Bagan) in Burma and Angkor in Cambodia. Internationally famous for the number and magnificence of their temples, these two cities experienced an entirely different pattern of urban development. While Angkor is hidden in the midst of the jungle, where Nature inexorably tries to regain the space conquered by Man, the ruins of Pagan lie in an arid, barren plain with nothing to hide it from view. The latter city has thousands of temples that are perfectly distinguishable from one another and that extend as far as the eye can see over a surface area of 9,800 achers.

Situated 298 miles north of Yangon (formerly Rangoon) and 120 miles south of Mandalay, Pagan lies on the east bank of the Irrawaddy River and dominates the central plain of Burma. Although the traditionally established date of the foundation of Pagan is A.D. 849, archaeological sources have demonstrated that at that time Pagan was already a very large settlement founded by the Pyu, an ethnic group that had migrated either from the Tibetan-Burmese plateau or from India. The Pyu were then driven away or assimilated by the invaders from Yunnan in the tenth century, and without them central Burma had no leadership. On the other hand, southern Burma, in particular the area of the Irrawaddy Delta, had

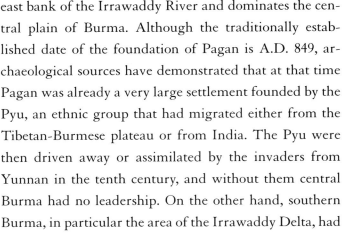

233 The Shwesandaw stupa, built by Anawrahta in 1057, was the first monument in Pagan with external stairs giving access to the round base of the stupa. The upper terrace has a fine view of the entire archaeological zone of Pagan.

232 top Minnhathu is one of the main towns in the area of present-day Paga. Around it are important thirteenth-century temples.

232 center The façade of the Tayok Pye Paya temple abounds in stuccowork depicting famous persons in a rather detailed fashion.

232 bottom In the Minnhathua area are the Leimyethna Patho (1222), Thambula Pahto (1255), Nandamannya Pahto (mid-thirteenth century), and Tayok Pye Paya (thirteenth century) temples, as well as the Payathonzu complex (late twelfth century).

PAGAN

since the sixth century been under the dominion of the Mon, a population from East India, or, according to another theory, from Southeast Asia.

In the eighth and ninth centuries the Bamar, or Burmese, from the east Himalayas filled the power vacuum left by the Pyu in central Burma and occupied the site of present-day Pagan, which they chose as their capital.

Pagan began to take on importance when King Anawrahta ascended the throne. At that time the Bamar, who initially practiced a religion that combined Tantrism and Mahayana Buddhism, gradually converted to the Theravada school of Buddhism. Manhua, the Mon king

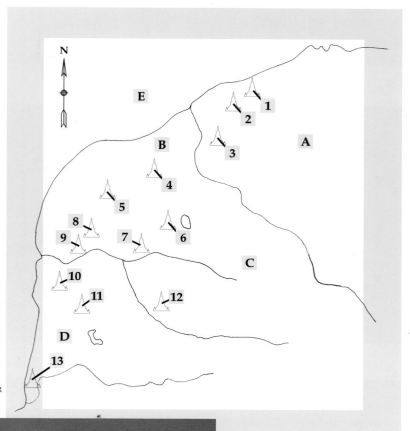

TEMPLES:

1) SHWEZIGON
2) KYANZITTHA
3) GUBYAUKGYI
4) HTILOMINLO
5) ANANDA
6) SULAMANI
7) DHAMMAYANGYI
8) SHWESANDAW
9) GUBYAUKGYI
10) MANHUA
11) APEYADANA
12) DHAMMAYAZIKA
13) LOKONANDA

ARCHAEOLOGICAL ZONES:

A) NYAUNG-U
B) WETKKI-IN
C) MINNATHU
D) NEW PAGAN
E) IRRAWADDY RIVER

234-235 The Ananda Pahto temple, built in 1090, marks the transition from the early to the middle architectural style in Pagan.

234 bottom The Shwezigon Paya was built by Kin Kyansittha around 1086-90 to house one of the copies of Buddha's tooth kept in Kandy, Sri Lanka.

235 The spires and stupas of the Ananda temple were gilded in 1990 to commemorate the 900th anniversary of its foundation. The outer walls are periodically whitewashed.

of Thaton, managed to convert King Anawrahta to Theravada, but when the latter demanded that the Buddhist writings and relics kept in Thaton be delivered to him, Manhua, mistrustful of the convert's zeal, flatly refused. Anawrahta therefore conquered Thaton in 1057 and took the Mon king prisoner. Anawrahta's triumphant return to the capital—with the defeated Manhua in his train—marked the beginning of the first Burmese empire and the glory of Pagan.

The Pagan empire enjoyed three centuries of peace and prosperity, during which the culture and religion of Burmese civilization flourished to an unprecedented degree. The extraordinary quantity of temples and the exceptional quality of the sculptures and paintings that have survived, make this the most important period of Burmese art.

The decline of Pagan coincided with the rise of Kublai Khan in North China. In 1287 the Mongols passed through Yunnan and invaded Burma. Marco Polo visited Pagan in 1298 and gave the following description of the kingdom:

You must know that at the end of this fifteen days' journey lies a city called Mien, which is the capital of the kingdom. The inhabitants are idolaters and speak a language of their own. They are subject to the Great Khan. And, in this city is a very remarkable object of which I will now tell you:

There once lived in this city a rich and powerful king. When this king came to die, he commanded that above his tomb or monument there should be erected two towers, one of gold and one of silver, such as I will describe. One tower was built of fine stones and then covered with gold, a full finger's breadth in thickness, so completely that it appeared as if made of gold only [...] In form it was circular, and round the whole circuit were set little gilded bells which tinkled every time the wind blew through them. The other tower was of silver and was built on the same plan as the golden one and of the same size and structure. This structure was designed as a token of the king's greatness and for the sake of his soul. And I assure you that the towers were the fairest to be seen in all the world and were of incalculable value.

(The Travels of Marco Polo, translation by Ronald Latham, Penguin, 1958; p.188-189)

The reasons for the decline of Pagan are still being debated. According to official Burmese historiography, the devastation wrought by the Mongols weakened the empire, while other sources seem to indicate that the seeds of decadence had already taken root in the last years of the empire. The fact is that, at the end of the thirteenth century, the growth of the city suddenly ended and a great many temples were demolished to make room for fortifications, while other temples were sacked. With its population drastically reduced, Pagan virtually became a ghost city for three centuries, where thieves and temple profaners ran amok. Toward the end of the nineteenth century, during the British occupation of Burma, the area was garrisoned to protect the temples, and the city slowly began to come to life.

According to an official count made in 1978, 2,127 temples are still identifiable and in good condition in the Pagan area. If we add the unidentifiable ruins, the number of archaeological sites increases to 4,000. The edifices belong to two main architectural types: the *chedi* (or stupa) and the *patho* (or temple).

The *chedi* is a solid brick structure in the shape of a bell usually placed on a stepped platform and crowned by a dome. The temple is the prevailing architectural structure, having from one to four entrances. The one-entrance temple has a main corridor, or vestibule, that leads to a central sanctuary in which is an image of Buddha. The four-entrance temple, on the other hand, has four identical corridors leading to a central *cella* on the sides of which are chapels housing statues of Buddha.

The Shwezigon is the most famous stupa in Pagan. It was built by King Anawrahta to house the relics of Buddha and was completed by King Kyansittha (1084-1113) around 1086-90. Despite repeated restoration, the Shwezigon has maintained its original form and served as a model for later *zedi*.

The Ananda is a typical temple with four entrances built by Kyansittha in 1090; it is the largest and best-preserved temple in the city. The Dhammayangyi Pahto, usu-

236-237 The Dhammayangi Pahto temple, the construction of which is attributed to King Narathu (1167-70), is considered the best example of dry masonry in Pagan.

237 top The Thatbyinnyu temple, built by Alaungsithu in 1144, is a typical example of Pagan middle period architecture, with its monumentality and upward thrust. The absence of scenes from the life of Buddha presumedly means that the temple was never consecrated.

237 bottom The stucco friezes in the Sulemani temple, which was built by Nadaungmya (1211-34), are among the masterpieces of Pagan decorative art and are still in a good state of preservation.

ally attributed to King Narathu (1167-1170), is similar in plan to the Ananda but much more massive. This temple harbors an architectural secret that has not yet been solved. One of the two corridors in the central section of the temple is entirely occupied by rubble that hides from view most of the stuccowork and fresco decoration. According to legend, the slaves who were building the temple filled this corridor with pieces of brick to get revenge for the terrible treatment they received at the hands of the king.

The Pahtothamya, Apeyadana, and Gubyaukgyi temples are a fine example of the style of the small temples in fashion in the period before the great architectural innovations effected in the twelfth century.

In fact, the Shwegugy and Thatbyinnyu temples, both built by King Alaungsithu (1113-1163), marked the transition from the massive, closed, and dark structure of their predecessors to a more spacious and illuminated one and represent a classical example of Middle Pagan architecture.

The Sulamani temple, constructed by King Narapatisithu in 1181, together with the Htilominlo, built by King Nadaungmya (1211-1234), are the best examples of the late Pagan style. They combine the horizontal plan of the first period temples and the tendency to verticality of the middle period, thus creating a sort of stepped pyramid that is surmounted by a miter-shaped tower. The apogee of late Pagan architecture is the Gawdawpalin temple, which was finished by Nadaungmya. King Mon Manhua, during the many years he spent at Pagan as a hostage of the victorious King Anawrahta, was allowed to build the Manhua Paya temple in 1059. The temple is relatively small and contains three large images of the seated Buddha and another enormous recumbent Buddha. The obvious lack of proportion between the size of the statues and the space they are located in, lends a sense of constriction and suffocation to the interior which—at least according to legend—reflects the mood of this king in a state of captivity. The only note of serenity is afforded by the smile of the recumbent Buddha, who is about to enter Nirvana: only by abandoning earthly things would the king free himself from his prison in Pagan.

238 The Htilominlo Pahto temple was built by King Nadaungmya in 1218 on the spot where, years before, he had been chosen, from among his father's five sons, to be crown prince.

239 top The Gawdawpalin Pahto is one of the most impressive temples in Pagan. Construction began during the reign of Narapatisithu and was completed under King Nadaungyma. The temple was badly damaged by the 1975 earthquake.

239 bottom A pilgrim praying in front of the a gigantic statue of the recumbent Buddha.

AYUTTHAYA

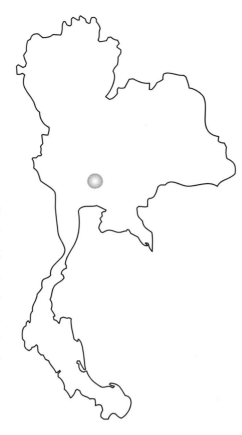

Text by MARCO CERESA

The city of Ayutthaya, situated about fifty three miles from Bangkok, was the capital of the Ayutthaya kingdom from 1350 to 1767, when this kingdom was the leading power in the Chao Phraya river basin. During its heyday, Ayutthaya had more than one million inhabitants and was considered one of the wealthiest and most luxurious cities in Asia, compared to which–according to the 17th-century foreign ambassadors–London and Paris were mere villages. The area, which is now an archaeological park, was included in the UNESCO World Heritage list on 13 December 1991.

The name "Ayutthaya," an abbreviation of Phra Nakhon Si Ayutthaya ("Sacred City of Ayodhya"), derives from the Sanskrit "Ayodhya" ("the invincible"), the birthplace of the god Rama, the protagonist of the Indian poem *Ramayana*.

Although a settlement was in this area before 1350, the importance of Ayutthaya in Thai history began when a cholera epidemic forced Phya U Thong, the prince of U Thong (today Suphan Buri) to move the population to a healthier locality. The choice of a new site fell on Ayutthaya, which offered many advantages. In fact, the city was founded on an island at the confluence of Lopburi, Pa Sak and Chao Phraya

240-241 Only these impressive piers remain from the destruction of the Vihara of the Wat Phra Mahathat temple.

241 bottom left This granite statue of Buddha at the Wat Phra Si Sanphet shows the influence the Sukhothai style had on the Ayutthaya artists, who initially drew inspiration from the Mon and Khmer cultures.

241 bottom right The Wat Phra Si Sanphet was the largest temple in the city and was used as a royal chapel and residence by many kings of Ayutthaya. It has three large stupas, built in the fifteenth century to house the ashes of the kings.

rivers, an ideal position for river transport and trade. Furthermore, the rice paddies in the vicinity supplied food to the population and, during the rainy season, was also a barrier that made the city impregnable. In 1350 Phya U Thong officially settled in Ayutthaya and ascended the throne as Ramathidibodi I (1350-1369). Thus began the kingdom of Ayutthaya, which lasted 417 years and was ruled by 33 sovereigns before being destroyed by the Burmese.

River and maritime trade made Ayutthaya one of the richest emporia in all of Southeast Asia and soon attracted foreign settlers to Ayutthaya. The first to arrive were the Asians: Chinese, Japanese, and Persians, followed by the Portuguese, who arrived in 1511. They were joined by the Spanish toward the end of the 16th century, and then by the Dutch and the British of the East Indies Company in the 17th century.

The reign of King Narai (1656-1688), the most cosmopolitan of all the rulers in Ayutthaya, witnessed the arrival of the French, at first merchants and mis-

242 top In the Wat Phra Mahathat precinct, a head of Buddha seems to be imprisoned in the roots of an enormous pipal tree (*Ficus religiosa*), the tree under which Siddhartha attained enlightenment.

sionaries and then diplomats from Louis XIV's court. The French tried in vain to convert the king to Christianity and to set up a military outpost in Thailand by sending troops to Mergui and Bangkok under the pretext of protecting Siam from the expansionist aims of England and Holland. They were aided in this by Constantine Phaulkon, a Greek adventurer who had become the right-hand man of King Narai. His influence on the king and his partiality for the French cause made him unpopular with the court nobles. One of them, Phra Phetracha, the Commander of the Regiment of Royal Elephants, took advantage of the wave of anti-French

242 center right The Wat Phra Mahathat precinct contains 185 stupas of different shapes and sizes.

243 The Wat Phra Mahathat temple, built in 1384, and the Wat Ratchabaurana (mid-fourteenth century) with its tall *prang*, are considered the two most important architectural complexes in Ayutthaya.

242 center left The impressive *prang* (tower) of Wat Phra Mahathat is all that remains of one of the most important and ancient temples in Ayutthaya.

1) ROYAL PALACE OF AYUTTHAYA
2) WAT PHRA SI SANPHET
3) WAT MONGKHON BOPHIT
4) WAT PHRA RAM
5) WAST PHRA MAHATHAT
6) WAT RATCHABURANA
7) WAT NA PHRA MEN (OR WAT PHRA MERU)
8) WAT CHAI WATTANARAM

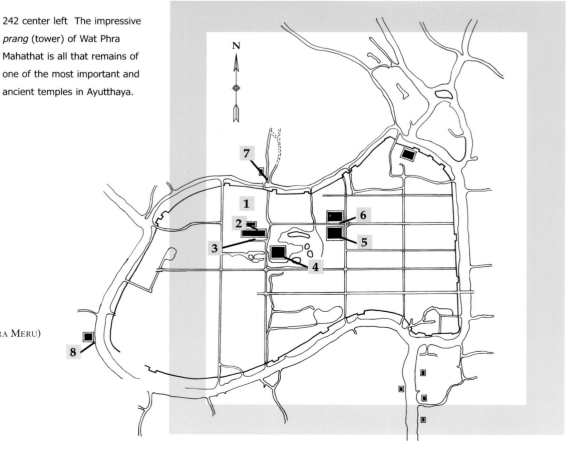

244-245 The tall tower of the Wat Ratchaburana temple dominates the two *chedis* (stupas) commemorating the death of the brothers of King Borom Rachathirat II (1424-48), who died in fratricidal combat.

244 bottom This Buddha making the typical *abbaya mudra* gesture was sculpted in the Uthong style. It is now in the Ayutthaya National Museum.

and anti-Christian sentiment among the nobles and of the king's illness to have Phaulkon killed and usurp the throne in 1688. With the advent of Phetracha and the expulsion of the French, contacts between Ayutthaya and the Western nations decreased. In 1569, the Burmese king Bayinnaung captured Ayutthaya, thus beginning a decade of Burmese dominion. Ayutthaya regained its independence after the battle of Nong Sarai (1592), but after about a century of relative peace, the Burmese resumed hostilities. In April 1767, after a long siege, the Burmese troops sacked and burned the city, putting an end to one of the richest cultural periods in the history of Thailand.

At present, little remains of the capital described by foreign visitors in the 17th century. The destruction wrought by the Burmese left only some masonry buildings, stupas (*chedi*), tow-

ers (*prang*) and the mutilated statues of Buddhas. All the wooden buildings were destroyed, as were the manuscripts and documents kept in the libraries in the monasteries. This is the reason why dating the edifices in Ayutthaya on the basis of documentation is extremely difficult, while the accounts of foreign travelers have proved to be valuable in this regard.

The Old Royal Palace was almost completetely destroyed by the fire started by the Burmese. The only remaining edifices in its complex is the Wat Phra Si Sanphet, with three large *chedi* (stupas) built in the 15th century to house the ashes of the kings. The Wat Phra Mahathat, built during the reign of King Ramesuan in 1384, is one of the most ancient and celebrated temples in Ayutthaya, although the devastation wrought by the Burmese left only a *prang* (a Khmer style tower) of breathtaking proportions. Opposite the Wat Phra Mahathat are the two *chedi* of the Wat Ratchaburana temple, built at the behest of King Borom Rachathirat II (1424-1448) to commemorate the death of his two brothers, who died in combat on elephants at the site of the temple itself.

Only one major temple escaped the fury of the Burmese: the Wat Na Phra Men (or Wat Phra Meru), the date of which is uncertain. The temple was not destroyed because of its position: it stands opposite the Old Palace, separated from it only by a canal, and the Burmese king Chao Along Phaya therefore stationed his artillery there to fire on the palace. However, one cannon exploded unexpectedly, accidentally killing the king and interrupting the destruction of the city.

AYUTTHAYA

245 bottom left From the gate of the Wat Ratchaburana *bot* one has a glimpse of the steep stairs leading to the main entrance of the tower, which houses images of Buddha.

245 bottom right The Wat Yai Chai Mongkon complex, built in 1357, was named after the large stupa (literally, *yai* means "large") in its interior.

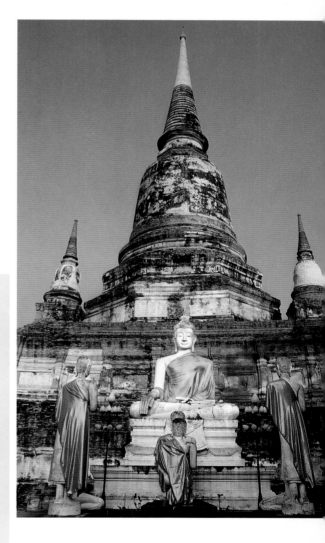

THE AMERICAS

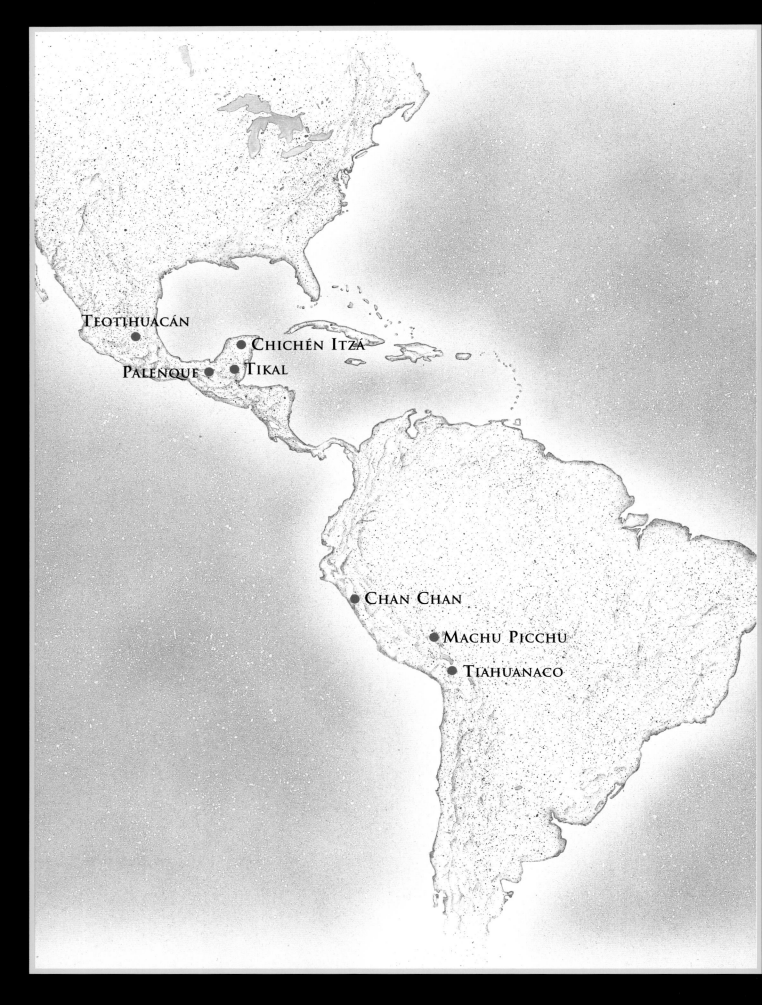

TEOTIHUACÁN

CHICHÉN ITZA

PALENQUE   TIKAL

CHAN CHAN

MACHU PICCHU

TIAHUANACO

247 top Palenque: stucco head of the wife of Pacal.

247 bottom Detail of Stela H at Copán.

NATIVE AMERICAN URBANISM

TEXT BY
DAVIDE DOMENICI

The cities of the Americas have features that clearly distinguish them from those in the Old World. In many cases, the fact that there is very little difference between them and that they had small populations have sometimes led scholars to say that some of the leading settlements in America were not true cities. It is obvious that the difficulty in fitting the American cities into a universal definition of a city is due to the great singularity of the Amerindian world whose cultures followed different courses from those of other regions of the earth. The cities in the Americas thus become mirrors in which, all ethnocentric prejudice aside, it is possible to observe the radical differences of the American world. At the same time, the very definition of a city, in order to be universal, must be reevaluated and "broaden its horizons" to encompass the cities that rose up in the two main centers of urbanization in the Americas: Meso-America and the Andes. If it is true that cities are manifestations of larger and more complex institutions such as nations, kingdoms, or empires, the true nature of the Amerindian city is to be sought in the social, political, and economic functions they had rather than in their exterior configuration. According to Richard Blanton, a city is "a manifestation of the growth of institutions capable of organizing vast regions into integrated systems." The distinction between a city and a village therefore lies in the function of the community: the city is a concentration of non-productive services that the village cannot provide, especially in the political-social and religious fields. Above and beyond this, the criteria

THE AMERICAS

usually used to define a city (size, population density, inner differentiation that indicates the division into classes, specialization of handmade goods, political organization not based on families or dynasties, writing, etc.) can be considered as common, but not necessary, tendencies of urban development. The basic function of the American cities was doubtless of a political and religious nature. Many cities in the Americas therefore fit into the category of what Richard Fox called ritual-royal cities. They were the seats of a political-religious elite and of family groups connected to it, and generally consisted of a monumental district with temples and buildings around which were smaller residential structures that gradually "evaporated" into the surrounding farmland, often without any clear-cut separation. The monumental precinct was a sort of "model of the cosmos" whose very shape legitimized the city's political system, which was the terrestrial equivalent of an analogous supernatural order. Although administrators and manufacturers of luxury goods also usually lived in this type of city, their activities were clearly secondary compared to the political-religious function, which is reflected in the negligible difference in the city structures. It is evident that while the definition of a ritual-royal city has the virtue of comprising many of the American urban communities that are often denied the status of a true city, it does not permit a clear distinction between the first, small monumental grounds that rose up right from the first agricultural periods and the large cities that grew up in governmental contexts. Though the difference between these two extremes of the urbanization process is purely quantitative and not qualitative, it may be that we are dealing with a continuum that is difficult to divide into stages that are not merely conventional. A second category established by Fox is that of the administrative cities. Here the primary function is of a political-administrative type, since these cities were often capitals or administrative centers in a political system that comprised several cities. This does not mean that the ideological-religious function is not present, but merely that the growing importance of administration, along with an increasing number of officials, administrators, and soldiers who lived in the city, led to a great differentiation, stratification, and heterogeneity of the city structures. Side by side with temples, major edifices, and residential complexes, there are now administrative buildings, military headquarters, and warehouses. In general these cities, which are clearly separated from the rural world around them, are also potential seats of commerce or trade of handmade products (especially luxury goods), but economic activity is still secondary with respect to the city's political function. All the major American cities probably fit into this category including Tenochtitlan, Teotihuacán, Monte Albán, Tula, Cholula, Chan Chan, Cuzco, and Machu Picchu. It is important to stress that the development of administrative functions did not at all replace the ideological-religious function of the city which, given the close connection between political power and religion in the Americas, was still of fundamental importance. The great capitals of the American empires were like "cities in the center of the world" and always maintained the symbolic features typical of ritual-royal cities such as extraordinary monuments, areas reserved for collective rituals, and a specific astronomical orientation that "anchored" the city structures to the heavenly and supernatural order.

However, the other three categories established by Fox appear to be absent in the native American world. While this is all too obvious with regard to colonial cities and industrial cities,

THE AMERICAS

the case of the so-called mercantile cities is remarkable in this context. A basic feature of these last-mentioned cities is that the volume of goods produced by commercial transactions, stockpiling, and other analogous activities is greater than that of the goods deriving from the control of agricultural activities. Large sea or river ports and distribution centers located at the junction of trade routes are scarce in the Americas, and the few known cases consist of small towns that never achieved the importance of, for example, certain medieval and modern cities in Europe. This was probably due to the technological limits of the Americas (for example, the lack of draft animals and hence of transport by means of wheels) as well as the state's constant and severe control of commercial activities, a factor that obstructed that "administrative freedom" that seems to be one of the necessary conditions for the prosperity of a mercantile city.

Thus, the true propelling force behind urbanization in the Americas was the close connection between political power and religious power that characterized this world. The aims of town planning projects were of a political rather than commercial nature and therefore the cities of Meso-America and the Andes are to be interpreted for the most part as a story of power, its administrative organization, and its strategies of communication and propaganda.

MESO-AMERICA

In Meso-America, the large cultural area that extended from northern Mexico to Costa Rica, the first monumental cities date from the Middle Pre-classical Period (ca. 1200-300 B.C.), when, in the sphere of the Olmec civilization and other related cultures, the birth of monumental regions such as San Lorenzo (Veracruz) or La Venta (Tabasco) reveals the emergence of new forms of political aggregation. These monumental areas were organized in keeping with cosmological models in which monuments such as thrones and portraits of rulers were distributed throughout a territory that was artificially modified by means of the construction of pyramids and earthen structures. It is quite probable that the population was small and that these cities were communities for a small elite in which the concentration of many persons occurred only on occasion of ceremonies or pilgrimages. The development and differentiation of regions that characterized the Late Pre-classical Period (ca. 300 B.C.-A.D. 300) throughout Meso-America led to the birth of larger and more complex monumental cities – true ritual-royal cities – and administrative cities. Furthermore, this period witnessed a deviation from the traditional form of urbanization that would continue for many centuries. In Central Mexico and Oaxaca urbanism clearly rose with the foundation of cities such as Teotihuacán and Monte Albán, large and vastly differentiated urban communities with a dense population and, at least in the first case, with an organizational system that seems to have been based on territorial criteria that were added to, and perhaps replaced, those based on the family unit. In southeastern Meso-America, on the other hand, especially in Maya territory, the ancient tradition of the monumental quarter as the seat of a dynastic-hereditary type of political power developed continuously until it reached

THE AMERICAS

its peak in such large Maya cities as Tikal and Copán. These splendid monumental cities lie in the middle of vast rural areas with a low population density and an organizational structure that seems to reflect the organization of society based on family and blood ties. These features have led some scholars to speak of Mayan culture as a "civilization without cities." It is probable that the difference between the town-planning traditions of the two areas is due as much to purely cultural reasons as to the less productive potential of the tropical forest compared to the semi-arid valleys of Central Mexico. Maya urbanization has often been considered "incomplete," mirroring a society "not yet" wholly state-organized, but this appears to be an opinion that imposes criteria of evolution (and implicit value judgments) on a reality that is actually only different, and not "backward" with respect to a process of development. However, there is no doubt that urbanization in Central Mexico had a strong influence on the rest of Meso-America. Probably from the Classical Period (ca. A.D. 300-900) Teotihuacán enjoyed the status of a "holy city" superior to that of any other Meso-American city. In the Post-classical Period (A.D. 900-1521) the urban tradition in Central Mexico gave rise to the idea of a sort of city par excellence, usually called Tollan ("the Place of the Reeds"), which became the ideal model of many Meso-American cities such as Tula, Cholula, and Chichén Itzá, the great city that dominated the Maya world for about three centuries.

The splendor of the Meso-American cities is mirrored in what the first Spanish explorers saw when they went over the mountain pass that offered a view of the Basin of Mexico and its large lake system. On an islet in the lake stood Tenochtitlan, the capital of the Aztec empire with about 300,000 inhabitants, divided into quarters where family groups with specific working activities, known as *calpulli,* lived. This city, linked to the land by large elevated roads, was soon called the "Venice of the West" and to this day, even though it has been virtually annihilated by the growth that led to the rise of Mexico City, it still reminds Old World observers that other peoples also knew how to build cities as extraordinary as theirs.

THE ANDEAN WORLD

From the first period of agricultural development, the construction of imposing monumental cities on the Peruvian coast such as Aspero (ca. 2500 B.C.) and Sechín Alto (ca. 1400 B.C.) shows that various agricultural village communities merged into a city whose primary function was to "mediate" between human beings and the supernatural world. These were probably places that became major pilgrimage sites and the venue of collective rituals during special festivities, which strengthened the social relations of mutual dependence that were the basis of Andean social organization. The monuments that were the heart of these "prototypes" of ritual-royal cities were *wakas*, earthly manifestations of the sacred around which communities were grouped and where the burgeoning political-religious elites of the Andes installed themselves. These elites saw to the gathering of goods as offerings and their ritual redistribution, in keeping with a pattern in which political-religious factors seem to have been greatly superior to the purely economic one. This tradition was the context in which some of the main ritual-royal Andean cities such as Chavin de Huantar, Pachacamac, and Cahuachi rose up, becoming splendid

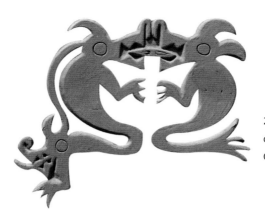

monumental centers that dominated the political-religious scene until the end of the First Intermediate Period (100 B.C.-A.D. 600).

The foundation of Tiahuanaco, over 12,467 feet above sea level on the Titicaca plateau, and its development from A.D. 100 on as the capital of a great agricultural-pastoral empire marked one of the most important stages in the history of Andean urbanization. Tiahuanaco was perhaps the first great administrative city in the Andes and its period of splendor had repercussions that went far beyond its sphere of influence. It was the link with Tiahuanaco and the encounter with the Mochica and Sicán kingdoms on the northern coast of Peru – where such important cities as Moche, Galindo, and Pampa Grande rose up – that so influenced the administrative nature of Wari, the capital of the empire of the same name that from A.D. 600 to 800 dominated most of the Peruvian archaeological area. Impressive buildings, walled residential areas, warehouses, and streets made up the heart of Wari, which probably had a population of over 50,000. But the real urban innovation at Wari was that it became the hub of a road network that linked a great number of planned administrative centers such as Viracochapampa, Azángaro, Jincamocco, and Pikillakta and had numerous storehouses that accumulated goods collected as levies from various provinces that were then transported to the imperial capital. This sort of urban network comprising the capital and its satellite cities would become one of the basic features of Inca urbanism. The fact that some of the main administrative centers in the Americas grew up in the Andes region, where writing was unknown and calculation was effected by means of strings with knots called *quipu*, is further proof of the singular nature of American urban development. With the decline and collapse of the Wari Empire the urban innovations already developed on the northern coast of Peru were adopted for the construction of the most splendid administrative city in the Andean world, Chan Chan, the capital of the Chimú Empire (ca. 900-1470) which, with its complex stratification of public buildings and residential complexes is perhaps the best example of the framework of Andean cities.

The expansion of the Inca Empire from the fourteenth to the sixteenth century led to the rise of a new form of that typically Andean urban network that originated in the Wari period. More than 25,000 miles of roads linked a series of planned administrative centers such as Huánuco Viejo, Vilcaswaman, and Hatun Jauja, as well as Cuzco, the capital of an empire with a surface area of 1,544 square miles, from present-day Ecuador to Argentina. Despite the size of this empire, Cuzco was a relatively small city (the population was from 40,000 to 100,000) whose main function was certainly ritual-royal. The central square, which divided the city into the traditional upper and lower halves (*hanan* and *hurin*, respectively), was the starting point for the four roads that divided the entire empire into four areas, and for the *ceques*, the 42 ideal lines that connected 328 *wakas* with Qorikancha, the Temple of the Sun at Cuzco. This city was the home of the Sapa Inka, the emperor, the city nobles, and part of the provincial nobility, who were like "privileged hostages," as were the main idols of the conquered regions. Cuzco was thus the physical and symbolic center of the entire Inca Empire. Despite being the strictest and best organized of the Andean empires, the city, whose administrative network astonished the Spanish who came to conquer it, continued to carry out a basically ritual and royal function, in keeping with the indigenous tradition that went back to the most remote periods in the history of the Americas.

TEOTIHUACÁN

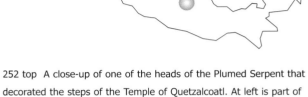

252 top A close-up of one of the heads of the Plumed Serpent that decorated the steps of the Temple of Quetzalcoatl. At left is part of the plumed body, while at right is the rattle of the serpent.

252-253 The Avenue of the Dead, the major street in Teotihuacán, is seen here from the top of the Pyramid of the Moon. In the foreground, the Plaza of the Moon, and at left, the Pyramid of the Sun.

Text by DAVIDE DOMENICI

Teotihuacan was undoubtedly the most extraordinary urban phenomenon in Pre-Columbian America. Its impressive ruins are testimony to a grandiose past and an epoch, from the beginning of the Christian era to the seventh century B.C., during which Teotihuacán was the principal political, economic, and religious center of all of classical Meso-America. In A.D. 500 this metropolis in Central Mexico covered a surface area of over 5,000 acres, and with over 125,000 inhabitants it was the sixth largest city in the world. Over 80 percent of the entire population of the Valley of Mexico lived in Teotihuacán or its environs in the wake of a process of urbanization of the rural population that was to remain unique in the history of Meso-America.

Teotihuacán was undoubtedly the main city of ancient Mexico, the place where some of the basic elements of Meso-American urbanization and its mythical and cosmological connotations were elaborated on over the course of more than 600 years of history. The position of Teotihuacán in the political scene of classical Meso-America, which had many cities, was clearly unique and unparalleled. Teotihuacán gave birth to a concept of the city and of its political organization that permeated most of contemporary and later Meso-American culture. Yet despite all this, many aspects in the ancient life of Teotihuacán are still obscure. For example, its original name, the language that was spoken there, and the ethnic identity of its inhabitants are still unknown. This is one of the reasons why we use the name that the Aztecs gave it many centuries later and the conventional name of Teoti-

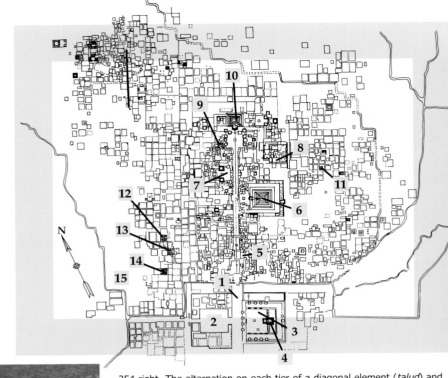

1) AVENUE OF THE DEAD
2) GREAT COMPLEX
3) CITADEL
4) TEMPLE OF QUETZALCOATL
5) AVENUE OF THE DEAD COMPLEX
6) PYRAMID OF THE SUN
7) PLAZA OF THE COLUMNS
8) XALA COMPLEX
9) PALACE OF QUETZALPAPÁLOTI
   PALACE OF THE PLUMED SHELLS
   PALACE OF THE JAGUARS
10) PYRAMID OF THE MOON
11) TEPANTITLA
12) YAYAHUALA
13) ZACUALA
14) TETITLA
15) ATETELCO

254 left The Pyramid of the Moon, perhaps the most ancient structure in Teotihuacán, is thought to have been dedicated to a female aquatic deity that predates the Aztec Chalchiuhtlicue.

254 right The alternation on each tier of a diagonal element (*talud*) and a vertical panel with a quadrangular frame (*tablero*) is a sort of "trademark" of Teotihuacánian architecture.

254-255 The presence of a cave sanctuary and the discovery of children's bodies suggest that the Pyramid of the Sun may have been dedicated to a water deity analogous to the Aztec Tláloc.

huacáns when referring to its citizens, since we cannot use ethnic and linguistic definitions as we do in the case of the Maya, the Zapotecs, and the Nahua.

In the early first century B.C. Teotihuacán was a simple farmers' village in the northeastern part of the Valley of Mexico. Within 200 years that village became the most important settlement in the Valley, probably thanks to the extraordinary development of irrigated agriculture. At the end of the first century A.D. the city already had a population of 50,000 and its monumental quarter began to take shape with the construction of the Pyramid of the Sun and the Pyramid of the Moon, the city's two major religious structures. From the second to the fourth century the main street (now known as the Avenue of the Dead) was laid out and Teotihuacán was divided into four quadrants thanks to the deviation of the course of the San Juan River. Building activity increased greatly: the

Great Complex and the Temple of Quetzalcoatl were constructed south of the river, large public and administrative complexes were laid out along the Avenue of the Dead, and outside the monumental quarter proper the city began to expand with the construction of the typical walled residential complexes that were one of the most unique features of the city's architecture. Teotihuacán achieved its maximum splendor between the fourth and sixth centuries, when the monumental precinct we see today was surrounded by over 2,000 residential complexes and when the city was at least ten times larger than other cities in the Valley of Mexico.

Besides intensive farming in the entire valley, the economy of Teotihuacán was based on the mineral resources and fauna in the marshy zones, rivers, freshwater and saltwater lakes, and vast woods. Control of the mineral deposits was of crucial importance, particularly ob-

TEOTIHUACÁN

sidian, which became one of the main commodities in the vast pan-Meso-American trade network. In fact, the location of the city was extremely favorable, being close to the trade and communication routes linking the Valley of Mexico with the Puebla-Tlaxacala region, and beyond this, the Oaxaca valley, the Gulf of Mexico, and the Maya region.

However, it is estimated that about two-thirds of the city population did farm work, while the other third was involved in religious, political-administrative, and above all, handicrafts activities, among which pottery and obsidian manufacture stood out. It is easy to imagine that urbanization, specialized work, and an active part in the economic network of Teotihuacán was quite advantageous for the inhabitants of the Valley of Mexico when compared to simple farm life. This is to be seen in the proliferation of the typical Teotihuacánian residential

255 center This dead Sun was found in the Plaza of the Sun in Teotihuacán.

255 bottom View of the northern sector of Teotihuacán, with the two large pyramids dominating the Avenue of the Dead.

256-257 The pillars of the central patio of the Palace of Quetzalpapálotl are decorated with bas-reliefs of raptors surrounded by aquatic symbols.

256 bottom The central plaza of the Palace of Quetzalpapálotl was almost completely restored, so that we can appreciate many of its architectural details. Note the painting decoration on the pediment surmounted by the *almenas*, sculpted "merlons" depicting the Meso-American symbol for the year.

257 bottom left The Temple of Quetzalcoatl, a pyramid in the middle of the Citadel, was built around A.D. 150 with decoration referring to the role played by the Plumed Serpent in the creation of time. The images of reptiles alternate with headdresses depicting the alligator god that was called Cipactli during the Aztec period, a name corresponding to the first day of the ritual calendar.

complexes, most likely the headquarters of family groups that shared a common economic activity as well as a specific tutelary divinity.

There is no doubt that the impressive development of Teotihuacán was also due to the strong religious character of the city. Along the main city axis, the Avenue of the Dead, the monuments are arranged in an order that obviously alludes to a corresponding cosmic order. The northern sector of the city is dominated by the two main pyramids and the grandiose temple plus administrative and residential complexes. At the end of the Avenue of the Dead, in the focal point of the spectacular monumental quarter, the Pyramid of the Moon is framed by the profile of the Cerro Gordo, the mountain that supplied the city with its water and that was traditionally known as Tenan, "the Mother of Waters." It is probable that the temple on the top of the pyramid was dedicated to a goddess of terrestrial water, the "prototype" of the Aztec Chalchiuhtlicue.

East of the Avenue, the majestic Pyramid of the Sun rises over a grotto which is probably artificial and must have been one of the most sacred sites in Central Mexico. In Meso-America, in fact, grottoes were considered access ways to the underworld located in the bowels of the sacred mountain which is the home of the aquatic divinities and the "germs" of life. They are therefore sites symbolizing origin and birth. The grotto-sanctuary of Teotihuacán must have been perceived as the access into the heart of the sacred mountain represented by the Pyramid of the Sun, probably associated with the kingdom of a high aquatic divinity similar to the Aztec Tláloc.

Around these marvelous monuments were countless temples and administrative and residential complexes that meticulously followed the layout of the town plan, "anchored," as it were, to the cosmic order by a particular astronomical orientation. Teotihuacán was evidently a "City in the Center of the World" that drew energy and justification from its cosmological status.

In the lower quadrants of the city, south of the San Juan River, there are monuments that seem to be connected to the city government and politics. In the middle of the Citadel, the Temple of Quetzalcoatl is decorated with multicolored sculptures of plumed serpents and headdresses that probably represent the face of a terrestrial god in the guise of an alligator, known in the Aztec periods as Cipactli. The symbolism of the temple decoration, as in the over 200 sacrificial tombs under its base, seems to allude to a myth of the calculation of time and holy war. According to some experts, the temple is a manifestation of the ideological demands of a particular power group united under the "protection" of the

257 bottom right The access way to the Palace of Quetzalpapálotl, at the southwest corner of the Plaza of the Moon. This palace, built over the more ancient Palace of the Plumed Shells, was probably the residence of one of the most influential power groups in Teotihuacán.

plumed serpent. If this theory were true, the second dressing of the temple – a little more than a century after its construction – would indicate an important substitution of the priestly caste at the top of the city's power hierarchy that occurred around the third century A.D.

The difficulty in interpreting the political organization of Teotihuacán is closely related to the special character of the local power as a "public language." Unlike other large Meso-American cities, here individual portraits of rulers or their ancestors, as well as inscriptions narrating their feats, are totally lacking. The painting cycles at Teotihuacán, in fact, consist of very impersonal images and elements that seem to be place names or emblems that refer to the origin or the function of particular groups in the city. It may very well be that a political structure originally based on family relationships was gradually replaced by a classical type of structure, with an increasing difference in status among the citizens and the rise of a highly bureaucratic ruling class. Political power at Teotihuacán is manifested in the representation of rows of identical priests dressed with elements that refer to "patron divinities." This suggests that the city was governed by groups of priests who probably wielded territorial rather than dynastic power that was substantiated by their association with particular patron divinities.

It is thought that because of this power the priestly caste received the surplus products from the Valley of Mexico agricultural communities as offerings for the temples, which they used to support a large portion of the artisans. These products, such as obsidian implements and special types of ritual ceramics, were then exported to distant lands in exchange for such luxury goods as minerals, feathers, cocoa, cotton, etc. The sacerdotal class would therefore have run a sort of redistribution network that was probably manifested publicly by means of the wide-ranging collective distribution of food and goods. According to supporters of this theory, the so-called Great Complex that rises in front of the Citadel is not the seat of a market, as many maintain, but the place where this massive ceremonial redistribution was effected.

The great political, economic, and religious power of Teotihuacán had major repercussions throughout Meso-America. While the Valley of Mexico and perhaps the Toluca Valley were the territories directly controlled by the metropolis, it also wielded a strong influence in areas much farther away, such as the Gulf of Mexico, Oaxaca, the Isthmus, the Pacific coast of Chiapas and Guatemala, and the Mayan region. In some areas Teotihuacán seems to have had real colonies whose purpose was to control trade routes or certain resources, as was the case with Matacapan (Veracruz), Chingú (Oaxaca), Escuintla (the Guatemala coast), and Kaminaljuyú (Guatemala). In such important places as the Zapotec capital, Monte Albán, or

258 and 259 bottom Details of the wall painting known as "Tlálocan" in the Tepantitla residential complex, which portrays men playing and butterflies. For a long time it was thought that this mural represented the "Paradise of Tláloc," an otherworldly site for those whose deaths were in some way related to water. Now this interpretation is disputed, above all because the deity dominating the scene is not the god of water but the so-called Great Goddess, perhaps his female counterpart.

259 top "Reticulate" jaguars and coyotes alternate on the talud of the White Patio in the Atetelco complex. These animals, with headdresses and feathered bodies, are depicted in the act of devouring a bleeding heart out of which emerges a "comma of the word." The "reticulate jaguar" was a very widespread motif in the latter periods in Teotihuacán and may have been the symbol of one of the power groups that dominated the city during its heyday.

in large Maya cities such as Tikal or Copán, Teotihuacán's presence seemed to be on a more ceremonial level, connected with prestige. Representations of "ambassadors" from Teotihuacán have been found in these locations, and in some cases the local rulers seemed to boast of these connections, be they real or not, with the great metropolis. These intense relations with all of Meso-America must have been reflected in the ethnic composition of the city population, which during its long age of splendor attracted people from various regions. It has been confirmed, for example, that in Teotihuacán there was a Zapotec, Veracruzan, and probably, a Michoacan quarter.

After centuries of glory, the first perceivable signs of crisis between the late sixth and early seventh century led to a sudden collapse. Around 650 most of the monumental quarter was burned and destroyed and the city was abandoned by most of the population, which left for the Valley of Mexico. Despite the fact that Teotihuacán was occupied again almost immediately afterward, perhaps partly by northern populations, and remained the most populated city in the Valley of Mexico for three more centuries, the city never regained its former splendor. Its fall triggered a crisis in the entire political and economic system of Meso-America which over three centuries led to the abandonment of almost all the great classical capitals.

Among the many reasons offered to explain the collapse of Teotihuacán, mention should be made of the excessive bureaucracy and inflexible political system, defor-

TEOTIHUACÁN

estation and the erosion of the soil that resulted, the invasions of northern "barbarians," and the closure of trade routes on the part of cities that were former allies of Teotihuacán. In many of these cases is it not easy to distinguish between the causes and effects of a crisis that most certainly was not brought about by a single factor and which may never be fully explainable.

In any case, we know for sure that although Teotihuacán had an inglorious end, its heritage was never forgotten. Certain aspects of its social and political system, such as its multi-ethnic character and the collective government of a territorial nature, would become characteristic features of the Post-classical Period in most of Meso-America. But above all, the memory of the great holy city that was the seat of the Plumed Serpent would be perpetuated in the myth of Tollan and in many post-classical cities that aspired to the role of the terrestrial Tollan. Almost 900 years after the fall of Teotihuacán, the Aztecs, the new rulers of the Valley of Mexico, went on pilgrimage to the ancient city and excavated the ruins, which they called Teotihuacán, the "Place Where One Becomes Divine," and narrated that the gods had met there to create the Sun, which gave rise to the fifth cosmic era. Teotihuacán was therefore still the City where Time Began.

261 top A typical "death mask" from Teotihuacán made of greenstone, a very precious material in Meso-America. The value of this stone (a generic name given to different rocks) was due to its symbolic association with water.

261 bottom This clay mask was the main element in one of the so-called "theater censers" in Teotihuacán, complex burners for copal made of various terracotta elements. The large earrings and nose ornament, perhaps referring to the Butterfly God, are symbols of high rank.

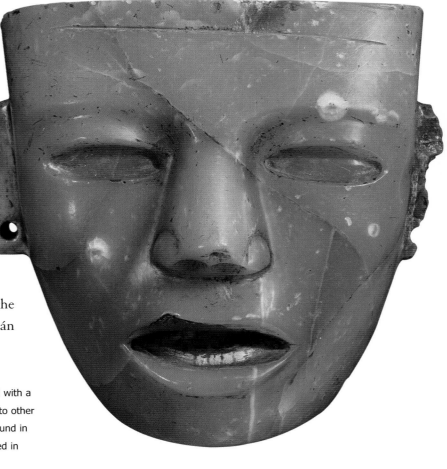

260 This "death mask" from Teotihuacán made of greenstone is covered with a turquoise, shell, and obsidian mosaic. Despite its name and its similarity to other Meso-American death masks, none of the many masks in this city was found in a mortuary context, therefore the function of these objects is still wrapped in mystery.

262-263 AND 262 BOTTOM THE JOURNEYS JOHN LLOYD STEPHENS AND FREDERICK CATHERWOOD MADE BETWEEN 1839 AND 1842 MARKED A REVOLUTIONARY TURNING POINT IN OUR KNOWLEDGE OF THE MAYA WORLD. THIS ACCOMPLISHMENT WAS PARTLY DUE TO CATHERWOOD'S ILLUSTRATIONS. IN THESE VIEWS OF PALENQUE ARE THE TEMPLE OF INSCRIPTIONS AND THE PALACE (ABOVE) AND THE PATIO OF HOUSE C IN THE PALACE (BELOW).

263 TOP THIS PLATE EXECUTED IN 1786 SHOWS PLANS AND SECTIONS OF THE TEMPLE OF THE CROSS AND THE TEMPLE OF THE SUN.

263 BOTTOM NOTE HOW THE REPRESENTATION OF A PALENQUE BAS-RELIEF, THE "BEAU RELIEF" DRAWN BY WALDECK, CONTAINS INCONGRUENT ELEMENTS SUCH AS A PHYRGIAN BONNET, A PANPIPE, AND CUNEIFORM SIGNS. THIS NEO-CLASSIC STYLE EXEMPLIFIES THE MENTALITY OF THE FIRST EXPLORERS IN THE MAYA REGIONS, WHO ASSOCIATED THE MAYA CITIES WITH ANCIENT GREECE.

PALENQUE

265 TOP LEFT THE TEMPLE OF THE SUN AT PALENQUE IN ONE OF THE PHOTOGRAPHS MAUDSLAY TOOK DURING HIS TRIPS THERE, DEVELOPING THE FILM INSIDE THE CHAMBERS OF THE MAYA MONUMENTS.

265 TOP CENTER THE PHOTOS TAKEN BY MAUDSLAY, SUCH AS THIS ONE OF THE PALACE TOWER, SHOW US THE STATE OF MANY MAYA MONUMENTS BEFORE THE RESTORATION WORK (OFTEN CONTROVERSIAL) WAS CARRIED OUT.

265 TOP RIGHT THE RESEARCH EFFECTED BY MAUDSLAY, SEEN HERE ON THE PALACE PATIO, WERE PUBLISHED IN CENTRAL-AMERICAN BIOLOGY (1889-1902).

Text by DAVIDE DOMENICI

Of the classical cities in the Maya lowlands, Palenque is perhaps the one whose monumental quarter affords the most accessible key to the interpretation of the history, ideological, and propagandistic aims of a royal Maya dynasty. Although archaeologists concentrated for a long time on the edifices in the monumental sector, in particular those built during the reigns of the two most famous rulers of Palenque, today new research is bringing to light different aspects, many of which provide a clearer picture of the urban nature of the site.

The exploration carried out in the environs of the monumental precinct have in fact demonstrated that the ancient city covers a surface area of about 865 acres, almost all invisible to modern visitors and thickly occupied by residential complexes, public buildings, and temples.

The most ancient periods of Palenque show a remark-

264 The great explorer Alfred Percival Maudslay traveled throughout the Maya regions from 1881 to 1894, as his curiosity was aroused by the works of Stephens and Catherwood. In this photograph, Maudslay is standing inside the Palenque Palace tower.

265 bottom The funerary mask that covered Pacal's face was made of green stone mosaics, shells, and obsidian. Masks of this type are rather common in the royal tombs of the classical Maya world.

266-267 This view of the monumental center of Palenque shows the Palace, the Temple of the Inscriptions, and the Temple of the Cross. This area, like the entire area now open to visitors, is only a tiny part of the ancient city.

267 top The Palace and the Temple of the Inscriptions are the heart of Palenque's monumental center. Their construction was mostly due to the political and propagandistic needs of Pacal, the most famous monarch of this city.

267 center This stucco bust, which perhaps portrays Pacal, was found under the sarcophagus of the great sovereign, together with another bust that may be of his wife.

267 bottom The collapse of the façade of the Temple of the Foliated Cross, in the Group of the Crosses at Palenque, exposed the rooms inside. The name of the temple derives from the corn plant in the shape of a cross with leaves that represents the center of the world in the central bas-relief.

able tendency toward population density, something rather unusual in the Maya world. The city was founded around A.D. 150 at the edge of a fertile plain traversed by waterways north of the present-day Mexican state of Chiapas. This was a strategic position between the basin of the Usumacinta River and the Gulf of Mexico coastline. The city soon began to attract people and became an important regional center. The foundation of a local dynasty by K'uk Bahlum (Quetzal Jaguar) in 431 triggered the rise of Palenque in the classical Maya political scene.

When in 615 a 12-year-old boy, whose original name was Lakamha though he was soon called K'inich Janahb' Pacal (Great Sun Shield), ascended the throne, Palenque, or "Broad Waters," was already the leading political center of the lower Usumacinta region. During the reigns of Pacal (615-683) and his son Chan Bahlum (684-702), Palenque became one of the most important cities in the Maya world, and its influence rivaled that of cities like Tikal, Calakmul, and Copán. The political strategies of these two ingenious sovereigns materialized in a town planning project that changed the configuration of the city for ever, generating an inextricable tangle of myth, history, and political propaganda that can be perceived in the inscriptions and the splendid bas-reliefs that exemplify the most characteristic feature of

PALENQUE

Palenque's art. The extraordinary beauty of the city's monuments thus reveals the main function of Maya cities, true manifestations of political power and of its presumed supernatural character.

Pacal built the Temple of the Count and the Forgotten Temple and beautified the Palace, the large complex of rooms, corridors, and courts that were the heart of the city and served as residence to the royal family, whose members are portrayed in the stucco bas-reliefs that decorate the pilasters. The bas-reliefs in House C of the Palace narrate political-religious events (wars, sacrifices, and the observation of eclipses) in which the rulers of Palenque participated together with sovereigns and nobles from Tikal and Yaxchilán, the two principal allies of Palenque in the turbulent Maya political panorama. The scene of the coronation of Pacal, who receives the royal headdress from his mother Sak Kuk (White Quetzal), is

reproduced in the famous Oval Tablet that adorns one of the Palace corridors.

The high point of Pacal's construction program was the Temple of the Inscriptions, the pyramid that this king had built to house his tomb. Inside the temple that crowns the pyramid, Pacal commissioned the creation of large panels with a long inscription narrating the history/myth of the Palenque dynasty, whose origin, thanks to the ingenious Maya calendars, was related to a remote mythical past populated by divinities. Some scholars think that this complex propagandistic operation was set into motion by Pacal to justify his right to the throne, which was in question because he had inherited power from his mother and not from his father, as Maya royal tradition prescribed.

A stairway that descends through nine steps or terraces – an obvious allusion to the nine levels of the world

268-269 The Palace, in the central plaza, was for centuries the residence of the royal family.

269 top The palace's tower may have functioned as an observatory from which astronomical phenomena could be observed and then given a powerful political-religious connotation. For example, an inscription in the palace records that on August 7th in A.D. 659 Pakal observed a lunar eclipse with the king of Tikal and the prince of Yaxchilán.

269 center The labyrinth of chambers, corridors, and courtyards of the Palace is the result of the various alterations made in this residential complex. The two courtyards were perhaps the venue for civic-religious ceremonies, as several glyphic inscriptions indicate.

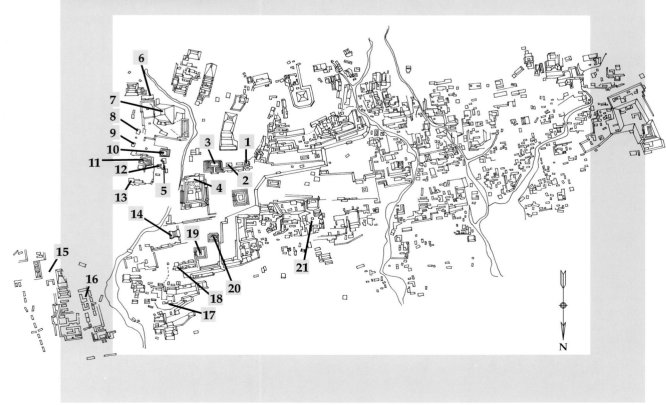

1) TEMPLE XII
2) TEMPLE XIII
3) TEMPLE OF THE INSCRIPTIONS
4) THE PALACE
5) TEMPLE XIV
6) TEMPLE XIX
7) TEMPLE XX
8) TEMPLE XVII
9) TEMPLE OF THE FOLIATED CROSS
10) TEMPLE OF THE SUN
11) TEMPLE OF THE CROSS
12) GROUP XV
13) GROUP XVI
14) BALL COURT
15) GROUP C
16) GROUP B
17) OLOTUM RIVER
18) GROUPS I AND II
19) NORTH GROUP
20) TEMPLE OF THE COUNT
21) TEMPLE X

270 top This stairway descends into the Temple of the Inscriptions and then into the crypt of Pacal. Note, to the left of the stairs, a hollow conduit (the so-called psycho-conduit) connecting the burial chamber and the exterior of the temple.

270 center In Pacal's burial chamber is the sarcophagus, with its monolithic lid partly opened.

270 bottom The Temple of the Inscriptions was built to house Pacal's tomb. In fact, his monolithic sarcophagus was placed in its present location even before the temple was constructed. The nine steps of the pyramid symbolize the nine levels of the world of the dead.

270-271 In the background of this view of the Group of the Crosses is the Temple of the Inscriptions. The Group was built by Chan Bahlum as the linchpin of his propagandistic strategy, which was linked to the one initiated by his father Pacal.

of the dead — leads to the true burial chamber of Pacal, where the king's skeleton was found inside a large monolithic sarcophagus. The body of the king was accompanied by rich funerary furnishings consisting of hundreds of jade objects. A complicated series of bas-reliefs on the walls of the crypt and on the sides of the sarcophagus represent Pacal's ancestors, while the huge monolithic lid bears the image of the sovereign, here associated with god of corn, descending into the bowels of the underworld.

After Pacal's death, Chan Bahlum initiated a new building program that called for the construction of the Group of Crosses, the architectural complex dominated by the Temple of the Cross, the Temple of the Foliated Cross, and the Temple of the Sun. The bas-reliefs in the

three temples have various portraits of Chan Bahlum receiving the royal insignia from his dead father, which can be interpreted as a veritable glorification of royal power and of its celestial, terrestrial, and warlike connotations.

In recent years archaeological excavations have brought to light new art treasures from Palenque such as the Tomb of the Red Queen (which lies next to the Temple of Inscriptions) and buildings XIX and XX in the Group of Crosses, all decorated with bas-relief panels whose motifs are always connected to political power.

Of particular interest is the recent dig of Group XVI, which has been identified as the temporary residence of the "provincial governors" of settlements that were in the sphere of influence of Palenque such as Tortuguero and Jonuta. The fact that these nobles, blood relations of the Palenque dynasty, had their own residence in the city is further proof of how Palenque was the seat, both real and symbolic, of political power in the region.

However, some experts say that the portrayal of even minor nobles in the city's art is a sign of the gradual weakening of the Palenque dynasty. After the death of Chan Bahlum, the new king, Kan Xul II, was captured in a battle and sacrificed on the altars of the enemy city of Tonina. The kings that succeeded him ruled a kingdom that became weaker and weaker until at the end of the eighth century the city was abandoned and the tropical forest took possession of what was probably the most elegant and sophisticated earthly manifestation of the sacred power of the Maya kings.

PALENQUE

272 top The composition of monumental texts by means of assembling stucco glyphs is one of the most typical features of Palenque.

272 center These two figures are the only elements in the date of the Long Count and mean "zero days." The figure at left stands for "zero," as the flowers on his arm indicate, while the one at right is a monkey indicating "day." This method of writing dates and numbers, known as the whole figure system, was the most formal and aulic of those used by the Maya scribes. Below right is part of the glyph of Pacal's name.

272 bottom In this detail of the Panel of the Palace (A.D. 721), Kan Xul, Pacal's second son, is receiving the regalia from his deceased parents. At right is his mother, Ahpo Hel. On either side of the central figure are columns of text.

273 Detail of the Panel of the Slaves (A.D. 730) depicting the face of the mother of Chak Zutz' (Red Bat), who is handing a shield-flintstone, the traditional sign of power, to her son.

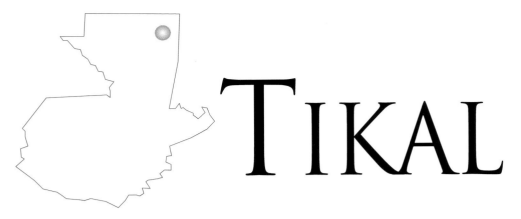

TIKAL

Text by DAVIDE DOMENICI

The urban nature of the Mayan cities has been the subject of a long and articulate discussion, and Tikal is certainly the site that has furnished the most debatable items. The population density of the city was in fact quite low, which was a typical characteristic of what can be called Maya urbanization; but the size, monumentality, and population of Tikal make it a model case in which it is possible to single out the dynamics of the

274 right A death mask made of greenstone, shells, and pyrite found in a royal tomb at Tikal. These precious materials were imported from distant regions for this kind of object, which were symbols of status and power.

275 The Pyramid of the Lost World in Tikal and, in the background, the top of Temple V. This part of the city has yielded some of the most ancient architectural ruins in the city.

formation and growth of the most important Maya city. The unmistakable central plaza of ancient Motul ("Hair Bun"), with tall pyramids towering over the jungle, was the main venue of most of the political and religious life of the Maya in the Classical Period. The kings who built it were the protagonists of centuries of alliances and wars that allowed Tikal to rule a kingdom so vast and important that it was unequalled in the Maya world.

274 left The central plaza of Tikal seen from the Northern Acropolis. The most impressive and powerful Maya city dominated the political scene of the Maya lowlands for most of the classical period.

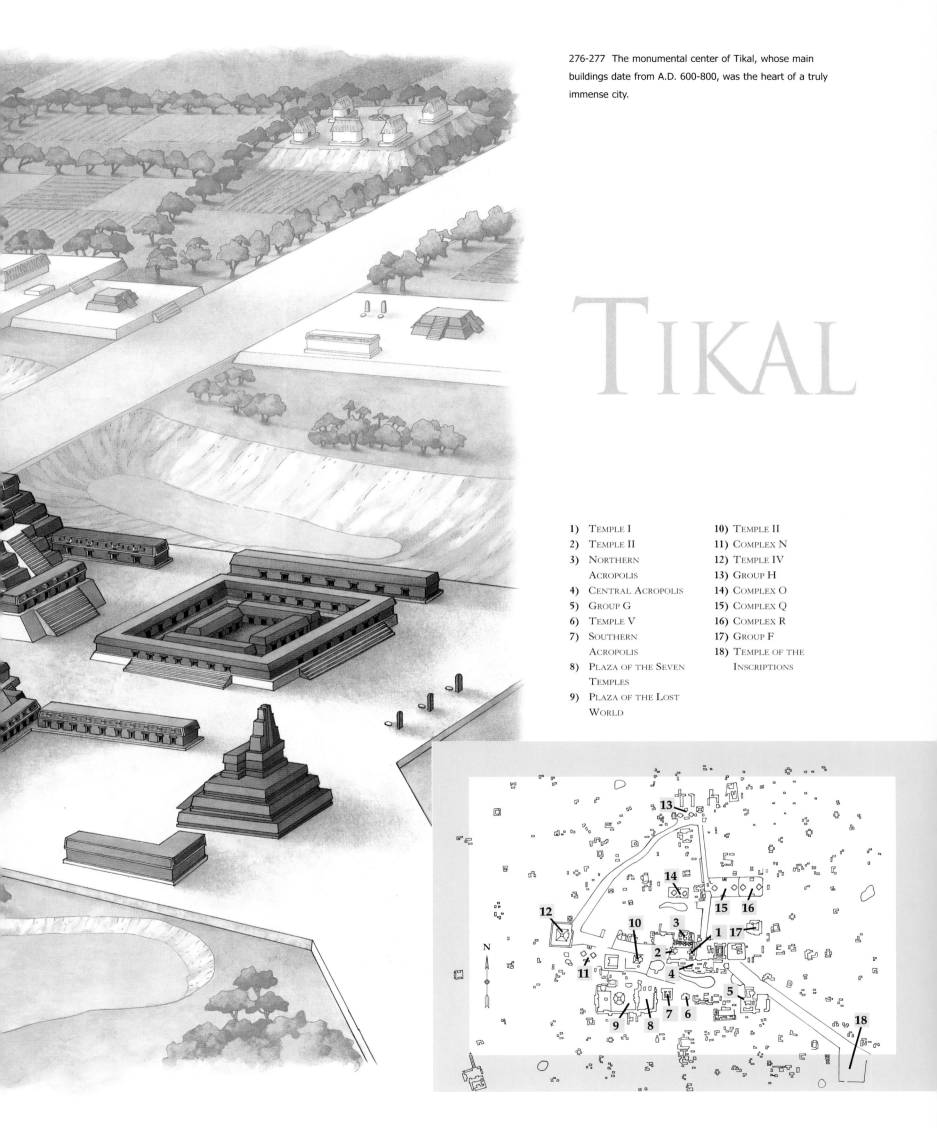

276-277 The monumental center of Tikal, whose main buildings date from A.D. 600-800, was the heart of a truly immense city.

TIKAL

1) TEMPLE I
2) TEMPLE II
3) NORTHERN ACROPOLIS
4) CENTRAL ACROPOLIS
5) GROUP G
6) TEMPLE V
7) SOUTHERN ACROPOLIS
8) PLAZA OF THE SEVEN TEMPLES
9) PLAZA OF THE LOST WORLD
10) TEMPLE II
11) COMPLEX N
12) TEMPLE IV
13) GROUP H
14) COMPLEX O
15) COMPLEX Q
16) COMPLEX R
17) GROUP F
18) TEMPLE OF THE INSCRIPTIONS

278-279 View of the central plaza, with Temple I and, at left, the Northern Acropolis. This latter complex, the result of eleven centuries of construction, was the monumental center of the city used to house the tombs of kings and nobles. This long tradition was interrupted by Hasaw Chan K'awil with the construction of Structure 5D-33-first, the first "streamlined" pyramid in Tikal, built above the tomb of his father Skull Shield and that of the great king Siyah Chan K'awil.

278 top View of one of the twin pyramids in Complex Q, inaugurated on January 20, 771 during the reign of Yax Ain II to commemorate the conclusion of a 20-year calendar cycle, in keeping with a tradition initiated by Hasaw Chan K'awil. In the foreground appear pairs of stelae-altars.

278 bottom left View of Temple I from the Northern Acropolis. Hasaw Chan K'awil built this temple to house his tomb, which was the first royal tomb outside the Northern Acropolis precinct. The nine steps of the temple refer to the nine levels in the underworld. A large portrait of the king on his throne stood on the crest of the temple.

278 bottom right Temple II, standing opposite Temple I in the Tikal plaza, also dates from the reign of Hasaw Chan K'awil, who may have had it built to house the tomb of his wife, Lady Twelve Parrot. The pyramid is less streamlined than the one on Temple I and its corners are "embedded" in keeping with the canons of Tikal architecture before the "revolution" effected by Hasaw Chan K'awil.

The political centrality of Tikal was partly due to its geographic position, as the city was founded on the watershed separating the basin of the Usumacinta River from the Caribbean side of the country, in the true heart of the Maya lowlands. In 800 B.C. several villages merged in this favorable position near two large humid areas known as *bajos*. 500 years later the construction of monumental edifices began in what was to become the Northern Acropolis, the great mortuary complex facing the Central Plaza where for over a thousand years the rulers of Tikal were buried.

Toward the end of the second century A.D., Yax Ch'aktel Xoc founded a local dynasty that was destined to have a great future. Its monarchs lived in the buildings in the so-called Central Acropolis, the large architectural complex opposite the Northern Acropolis, on the other side of the Central Plaza. During the reign of Chak Toh

Ich'ak ("Jaguar Claw"), Tikal managed to defeat and politically dominate nearby Uaxactún in A.D. 378, placing
on the throne of the defeated city the military chief who
had led the war. His name was K'ak' Sih ("Born in the
Fire"), but is better known as Smoking Frog. He was an
enigmatic person "from the West" who may have come
from Teotihuacán. In any case, he enjoyed prestige in
some way due to this highland metropolis.

In the centuries immediately following this event, the
rulers of Tikal manifested their bond with Teotihuacán
in the city monuments, albeit following the canons of
Mayan art and political propaganda. It is not clear what
role this city played in the dynastic vicissitudes of Tikal
(which decades later would be governed by kings related
to Jaguar Claw), but the continuous iconographic reference to the great city probably had something to do with
a legitimization of political power deriving from the status of "holy city" that Teotihuacán enjoyed and that in

turn conferred exceptional prestige and status to Tikal in
the context of Maya politics.

The main "Teotihuacanized" kings at Tikal were Yax
Ain I (First Crocodile), who ascended the throne a little
more than a year after the conquest of Uaxactún, and his
son Siyah Chan K'awil, also known as Stormy Sky. During the 45 years of the latter's reign (411-457), Tikal enjoyed its golden age, being constantly involved in complicated and aggressive political-military activity in the lowlands. Upon his death, in keeping with a centuries-old
tradition, the king was buried under a building in the
Northern Acropolis. It was precisely during the extenuat-
ing wars among the cities of Petén that, a century later,
Tikal was defeated by Caracol, which had entered into an
alliance with Calakmul, the powerful and historic rival of
Tikal. This military defeat, which occurred in 557, left an
indelible mark on the urban fabric of Tikal: apparently
for 125 years no monuments were built and no inscrip-

TIKAL

tions were carved in the city, while the few events identified during this period (including the war with Caracol) are narrated in the monuments of the victorious cities.

Although this decline involved only Tikal and not the other large cities, it still marked an important threshold in the political and cultural evolution of the lowlands, which in the Late Classical Period (ca. 600-900) was characterized by the absence of elements from Teotihuacán and by the full development of the Maya dynastic system.

It was no accident that Tikal re-emerged from its long architectural "silence" under Hasaw Chan K'azil, better known as Ah Cacaw, the greatest ruler in the history of the city. During his reign (682-734), when Tikal was undoubtedly the most powerful Mayan city in the lowlands, this king promoted an extraordinary revival of building activity in the city, and in 695 he took revenge for the defeat of his city by capturing the king of Calakmul. Monumental structures were built, as were the complexes of twin pyramids to celebrate the end of the 20-year calendar cycles. But Cacaw left his most definitive mark on the architectural heart of Tikal, where he built a large temple over the ancient tomb of Stormy Sky, thus establishing a link between his reign and that of his great predecessor. After having "sealed" the Northern Acropolis – which was never again used as a mortuary site – the king ordered the construction of the two large temples I and II that now tower over the

280 top left The Mundo Perdido (Lost World) Pyramid shows the influence Teotihuacán had on Tikal during the Classical Ancient period. For example, the steps consist of alternating *taluds* and *tableros*.

280 top right Unitl the seventh century, the Great Lost World Pyramid (105 feet high) was the tallest structure in Tikal. Its origins date back to 500 B.C., when a platform was built for astronomical observation and over the centuries was enlarged until it attained its present form.

280 bottom Under the late-classical buildings lining the east side of the Mundo Perdido, three platforms have been identified that, together with the first version of the Great Pyramid, constituted an astronomical observation complex.

280-281 The large Structure C5-54 dominates the center of the Mundo Perdido Pyramid, which from the Middle Preclassical period on was one of the most important complexes in Tikal, rivaling the Northern Acropolis.

Central Plaza. Temple II was probably meant to house the tomb of Cacaw's wife, while Temple I (or the Temple of the Great Jaguar), a magnificent example of the new "vertical" architectural style in Tikal, housed the tomb of the king himself. Found in 1962, the burial chamber still contained the body of the king accompanied by an extraordinary series of jade and ceramic objects.

During the reign of Hasaw Chan K'awil, the size of Tikal reached its maximum, becoming a true urban "colossus." Around one of the most articulated and stratified monumental complexes in the Maya world, the city of Tikal extended for six square miles, around which was a belt of patrician residences and other residential areas

that covered 25 square miles. It has been calculated that in the year 700 "Great Tikal" had a population of more than 20,000.

For over a century Hasaw Chan K'awil's successors continued the architectural program he had initiated, building complexes of twin pyramids and above all of large, slender temples (Temples III, IV, and V) that are still the distinguishing feature of the city's architecture. But the great crisis that struck the Mayan lowlands was looming over the city, and in 869 the last monument in Tikal was built. For reasons that are basically still unknown, the city was abandoned to the suffocating embrace of the green jungle of Petén.

CHICHÉN ITZÁ

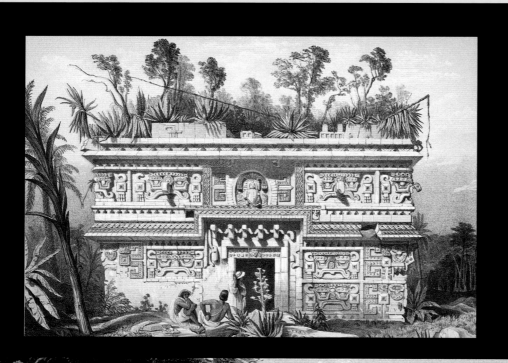

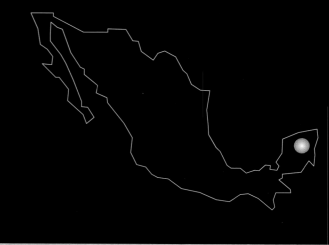

282 THESE ILLUSTRATIONS BY FREDERICK CATHERWOOD SHOW THE HOUSE OF THE NUNS (ABOVE) AND THE CASTILLO (BELOW).

283 TOP AND CENTER RIGHT CATHERWOOD ALSO REPRODUCED THE MURAL PAINTINGS, SUCH AS THOSE OF THE UPPER TEMPLE OF THE JAGUARS.

283 CENTER LEFT THE FAMOUS SELF-PORTRAIT OF ALFRED PERCIVAL MAUDSLAY IN HIS "STUDIO" INSIDE A BUILDING IN CHICHÉN ITZÁ IS PERHAPS THE BEST IMAGE AND SYMBOL OF THE PIONEERING WORK DONE BY THE FIRST EXPLORERS OF THE MAYA WORLD.

283 BOTTOM THE SO-CALLED CHURCH, ONE OF THE MOST ELEGANT PUUC EDIFICES IN CHICHÉN ITZÁ, IN A PHOTOGRAPH BY MAUDSLAY.

CHICHÉN ITZÁ

Text by DAVIDE DOMENICI

Chichén Itzá is the Maya city whose monumental quarter best exemplifies the important changes made in the Maya royal cities after the "collapse" of the Classical Period. It attests to both the regional flourishing of the Puuc style and to the rise of the new political-religious order of the Yucatán and of all of post-classical Meso-America at the same time as Chichén Itzá became one of the leading cities in the Americas.

One of the most evident features of the Maya cities in the Yucatán during this period is the remarkable scarcity of historic inscriptions, which makes it impossible for us to become familiar with the details of its political history. Fortunately, the documentation of the first colonial period makes up for this to some degree. We know that Chichén Itzá was the home of a group of Itzá Maya who from the late seventh century to the early tenth century shared power in the north of the Yucatán with the other Maya groups from settlements such as Sayil, Kabah, and powerful Uxmal of the Xiu Maya. Edifices in Chichén Itzá such as the Red House group, the Akab' Dzib, and the Casa de la Monjas (House of the Nuns), bear similarities with the typical Puuc style, characterized by build-

284 bottom right A turquoise mosaic disk with four plumed serpents' heads. This type of object, called *tezcacuitlapilli*, is often associated with the war iconography at both Chichén Itzá and Tula, the Toltec capital.

285 Detail of one of the large masks that decorate a corner of the House of the Nuns. These masks of gods with long noses are one of the characteristic features of Puuc architecture in the Yucatán peninsula.

284 left View of the monumental center of Chichén Itzá, with the Caracol, or astronomic observatory, in the foreground.

284 top right Detail of the face of a Chac-Mool. This type of statue, which was used to receive offerings, was created in the Classic period, in the context of the Chalchihuiteña culture of Zacatecas and Durango, in northern Mexico, and was then assimilated by the Toltec and Post-Classical Maya traditions.

1) CASTILLO
2) TEMPLE OF THE WARRIORS
3) GROUP OF THE THOUSAND COLUMNS
4) PLATFORM OF THE EAGLES AND JAGUARS
5) PLATFORM OF VENUS
6) TZOMPANTLI
7) BALL COURT
8) OSSUARY
9) RED HOUSE GROUP
10) CARACOL
11) HOUSE OF THE NUNS GROUP
12) INITIAL SERIES GROUP
13) MARKET

ings decorated with complex mosaic panels that often have impressive rows of masks of deities.

The monumental style during the heyday of Chichén Itzá in the ancient Post-classical Period (900-1250) is quite different, even though it partly coincides chronologically with the Puuc style. While the economic base of the city did not differ much from that of its Classical Period predecessors, since it was based on the gathering of products from a vast rural hinterland of over 12 square miles, there were profound changes in the political order, as can be seen in the monuments in the majestic central plaza. These are in fact quite similar to the models and styles from the central plateau in Mexico, in particular from the Toltec world of Tula. The individual portraits of sovereigns almost totally disappear, and the most recurrent motif in the monuments at Chichén Itzá is the Plumed Serpent, the great divinity who had already been the protector of the rulers of Teotihuacán and then of Xochicalco and Tula.

El Castillo, the main pyramid in Chichén Itzá, in the

286 In front of the entrance to the Temple of the Warriors, flanked by two large columns in the shape of plumed serpents with wide-open jaws, is a Chac-Mool. This name, which means Red Claw, is a modern invention that has nothing to do with the figure depicted in the statue.

287 left The top of the Temple of the Warriors stairway is decorated with heads of plumed serpents. Standards or flags were probably placed in the hands of the top anthropomorphic figure.

287 top right Sculpture of a telamon in the guise of a warrior. It may be that the jaguar on his chest is a symbol of a warrior caste much like those described in historic sources concerning the later Aztec world.

287 bottom right The Temple of the Warriors has quadrangular pillars decorated with figures of warriors.

middle of the plaza with monumental stairways flanked by impressive plumed serpents that on the equinox seemed to descend from the pyramid thanks to a play of shadows created by an ingenious architectural solution, was in fact dedicated to Kukulkan, or "Quetzal Serpent," the Yucatán translation of the Toltec Quetzalcoatl.

The same god is marvelously depicted in the columns flanking the entrance to the Temple of the Warriors, the sacred building that looks very much like the famous Temple B at Tula and that shows how the military iconography of northern origin spread to the Maya world. The temple, like its Toltec counterpart, was probably dedicated to Tlahuizcalpantecuhtli, or Venus the Morning Star, one of the manifestations of the Plumed Serpent.

This god is portrayed on the nearby Platform of Venus, while on the Platform of the Eagles there are eagles and jaguars devouring human hearts, a widespread motif in the central plateau area. Equally macabre is the *txompantli*, the podium of Toltec origin where the skulls of slain ene-

mies or sacrificial victims were put on display on wooden racks. The rows of bas-relief skulls that decorate its platform clearly refer to the function of this structure.

Sacrifice rituals are also represented in the complex bas-reliefs that decorate the face of the Ball Court, where one can see two teams at the sides of a scene in which a player is being decapitated.

But the main sacred site in Chichén Itzá is certainly the Sacred Cenote, or Well of Sacrifices, a large natural karstic well where the ancient inhabitants of Chichén Itzá (which in fact means "Near the Well of the Itzá") threw sacrificial victims and offerings from around the Americas to honor the aquatic divinity of the underworld.

The undeniable "Toltec" style of the monuments in Chichén Itzá led scholars to believe for a long time that the city had been conquered by armies from the north that imported the cult of the Plumed Serpent, a theory supported by the religious iconography, which is permeated with military motifs. Today, however, it is thought

that the Itzá Maya of Chichén shared a political-military ideology based on the figure of the Plumed Serpent with the Toltecs from Tula and with other peoples in post-classical Meso-America. This ideology served to legitimize multi-ethnic and expansionist governments that were replacing the more ancient dynastic-family order. One of the crucial elements in this ideology, which some call Zuyuana, was the image of a holy city par excellence, mythical Tollan, the seat of the supreme government under the aegis of the Plumed Serpent and the residence of powerful warriors and skillful artisans. Though many scholars have associated Tollan with Tula of the Toltecs, it is probable that many post-classical cities aspired to the role of a terrestrial "replica," as it were, of the mythical city, whose origin perhaps lies in the memory of the enormous prestige of ancient Teotihuacán. Tula, Chichén Itzá, and Cholula then became versions of Tollan, cities with an exceptional urban status that guaranteed specific prerogatives. For example, the rulers of many other regions went to these cities to have their noses pierced with

CHICHÉN ITZÁ

288-289 The Castillo, the main pyramid in Chichén Itzá, was dedicated to the plumed serpent Kukulkan, the Yucatán Maya equivalent of the Toltec and Aztec Quetzalcoatl.

289 left The sides of the Platform of Venus, in the main plaza of Chichén Itzá, are decorated with bas-reliefs bearing the figure of Tlahuizcalpantecuhtli, Venus as the Morning Star. We know that the appearance of the morning star was associated with the custom of holy war.

289 top right Below the Castillo archaeologists found a more ancient version of the same pyramid. Inside its temple on the top are a Chac-Mool and a throne/altar in the shape of a jaguar with deposits of green stone and shell crusts on which was placed a turquoise mosaic disk.

289 bottom right The modern name "Colonnade of the Chichén Itzá Market" really has no relation at all to the original function of this structure, which was probably used to host important collective rites connected to holy war.

290 top left View of the Temple of the Jaguars from the Platform of the Jaguars and the Eagles, decorated with heads of plumed serpents.

290 top right The Ball Court in Chichén Itzá is the largest in all Meso-America. The tall central edifice is the Temple of the Jaguars. The ball game was a ritual game that represented the descent into the underworld of the Sun and Venus, identified as mythical hero twins.

290 bottom Detail of the decoration on the Platform of the Jaguars and Eagles, in which the animals are feasting on human hearts. In a later period the two animals became the symbols of the two main Aztec warrior castes and they may have had a similar function at Chichén Itzá as well.

the turquoise ornament that confirmed their power, conferring more prestige and importance to them than their dynastic origin did.

The Itzá Maya of Chichén therefore lived in a holy city, near that sacred well of sacrifice that must have been the most important sanctuary in southeastern Meso-America, and this afforded them a great deal of prestige in their political and military relations with other Maya family groups that settled in cities like Izamal, Edzná, and Mayapán. According to tradition, it was precisely Hunac Ceel, the Maya Cocom sovereign of Mayapán, who conquered Chichén Itzá in 1221 with the aid of mercenaries from Central Mexico. Although we are unable to separate legend from reality in this late historic tradition, we do know that around 1200-1250 Chichén Itzá was abandoned and the political scene in the Yucatán was dominated by Mayapán, a newer copy of Chichén Itzá and, ultimately, of mythical Tollan.

290-291 A throne/altar in the shape of a jaguar at the entrance to the Lower Temple of the Jaguars. The walls and piers of the temple are decorated with intricate bas-reliefs, among which it is possible to make out the warrior who is reproduced in a drawing by Frederick Catherwood.

CHICHÉN ITZÁ

292-293 The House of the Nuns and part of the Church, two of the Puuc edifices in Chichén Itzá. Originally one of the many Puuc cities in northern Yucatán, Chichén Itzá soon became one of the most important terrestrial "Tollans" in all Meso-America.

293 top One of the typical Puuc masks. The god's long nose is an exaggerated representation of a serpent's head and is a generic attribute of a divinity. Once it was thought that all these masks depicted the rain god Chak, but it is now clear that they represent various gods.

293 center The Caracol seen from the stairway of the Temple of the Carved Panels.

293 bottom The Red House is less decorated that the other edifices in Chichén Itzá, but it is still a fine example of Puuc architecture, as can be seen by the frieze at the top.

294 TOP THIS PHOTOGRAPH, TAKEN IN THE EARLY 1900S, SHOWS OSGOOD HARDY, THE NATIVE INTERPRETER OF HIRAM BINGHAM'S EXPEDITION, UNDER ONE OF THE MONOLITHIC GATES OF THE PUMAPUNKU.

294 BOTTOM A GILDED COPPER OBJECT REPRESENTS A PERSON WEARING THE TYPICAL ANDEAN COSTUME, MADE OF LLAMA WOOL: A CAP WITH EAR-FLAPS AND A TUNIC WITH GEOMETRIC MOTIF DECORATION.

295 DETAIL OF THE GATEWAY OF THE SUN, THE MOST FAMOUS MONUMENT IN TIAHUANACO. NOTE THE WINGED "ATTENDANTS" CONVERGING TOWARD THE CENTRAL FIGURE OF THE GOD OF THE STAFFS.

TIAHUANACO

Text by DAVIDE DOMENICI

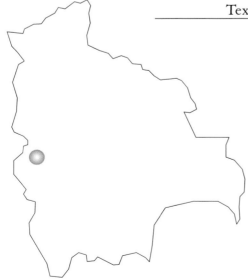

For almost a thousand years Tiahuanaco was the largest and most important native city in the Andean world. Situated 12,598 feet above sea level (a higher altitude than Lhasa and Katmandu), Tiahuanaco was a true symbolic center of the sacred geography of the highlands, between Lake Titicaca and the snow-capped peak of Illimani, and "connected" to the celestial order thanks to the astronomical orientation of its buildings. The magnificent monuments of ancient Taypikala ("The Stone of the Center," the original Aymara name of Tiahuanaco) were the heart of the city that was the seat of one of the

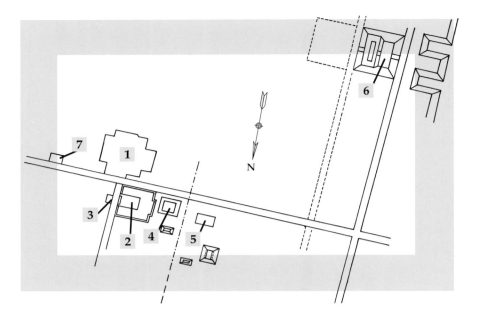

1) AKAPANA
2) KALASASAYA
3) HALF-SUNKEN TEMPLE
4) PUTUNI
5) KERIKALA
6) PUMAPUNKU
7) KANTA TAYITU

largest and most long-lasting Andean states.

Originally a farm village that cultivated mostly potatoes and quinoa in 400 B.C., Tiahuanaco soon acquired the heritage of cities such as Chiripa and Pukara, and in A.D. 100 it began to grow prodigiously, becoming, in a few hundred years, a splendid city whose monumental district of around 1000 acres was surrounded by residential structures that extended for a radius of almost six miles. This was probably a "patrician city" populated by about 45,000 persons (most probably native speakers of Aymara), many of whom were aristocrats, bureaucrats, and servants. From 550 on, Tiahuanaco went through another phase of expansion, becoming the capital of a true "agro-pastoral empire."

The amazing prosperity and growth of Tiahuanaco was due to the rigorous exploitation of the agricultural and pastoral resources of the plateau. The territory around Lake Titicaca was transformed and made productive thanks to the construction of thousands of *waruwaru*, the artificial, elevated fields that made it possible to achieve intense productivity in the cultivation of quinoa, potatoes, and other tuber vegetables such as *ulluco* and *oca*. The grazing land of the Punas was home to thousands of herds of *camelidae* which, besides being a source of food and wool, were used as draft animals. The great llama caravans transported products such as corn, red peppers, and coca to Tiahuanaco from the exotic Andes valleys or the Amazon forest.

Tiahuanaco therefore became the hub of a trade network managed through colonial administrative centers such as Luqurmata. While the city probably had direct control only of the land around Lake Titicaca, a territory with a population of about 250,000, its economic sphere of influence extended from southern Peru (Urubamba, Moquegua) to the Chilean coast (Atacama) and the Bolivian Andes (Cochabamba). In more distant lands, in exchange

for agricultural products in great demand, the emissaries of Tiahuanaco offered textiles, tablets of hallucinatory substances (to be inhaled), *keros* (ceremonial glasses), and handmade wood, cooper, and gold products that enriched the local elites, thus attracting them into the cultural orbit of Tiahuanaco.

While Tiahuanaco was growing and flourishing, it enjoyed close relations with the important urban community of Wari in Peru, which since A.D. 600 had initiated an aggressive policy of expansion, establishing an empire of the same name. These relations have been subject to different interpretations. Once it was believed that Wari was a sort of military arm of the religious center of Tiahuanaco, whereas today there is a tendency to consider Wari and Tiahuanaco as two totally independent political entities that in some cases were also rivals, albeit linked by strong artistic, religious, economic, and administrative affinities.

Tiahuanaco's large economic-distribution network was probably run by an aristocratic class that, owing to its presumed sacred character and mythical origin, succeeded in collecting offerings and taxes and in mobilizing large numbers of laborers for the construction of the ma-

jor public works, which were the center of important collective rituals. The monumental district was thus the venue for these rites, which were held on the sacred ways that linked the various *wakas* (sacred grounds with temples) and that probably involved different "ceremonial passageways," hence the many monumental city gates that are one of the characteristic features of Tiahuanaco. The great collective rituals were most probably run by priests who, under the influence of hallucinatory substances (a great abundance of tablets, sniffing tubes, and spatulas was found here), achieved states of ecstasy which gave them divinatory and magic powers. The large, wide-open eyes so typical of the monumental sculpture pieces in the city may be an allusion to this very type of ritual.

The principal religious edifice in Tiahuanaco was the Akapana, the great half-cross Andean pyramid consisting of seven terraces that is 56 feet high and more than 656 feet long. On the top were residential structures made of stone and a large, sunken patio used to collect rainwater, which was then channeled down along the sides of the pyramids. Evidently this was a sort of "celestial moun-

296-297 View of the large courtyard in the Half-sunken Temple, with some stelae in the middle. The large Bennett monolith, now in La Paz, originally stood in this patio.

297 top The splendid walls of the Kalasasaya, whose large monolithic pillars, which alternate with stretches of wall made of perfectly square blocks of stone, clearly demonstrate the great building technique of the masons in Tiahuanaco.

297 bottom The Kalasasaya was a large ritual precinct used for astronomic ceremonies. In the middle is the famous Ponce Monolith.

tain," a source of water and the center of fertility cults. Akapana may have been dedicated to a supreme celestial god of water and lightning, known in a later period as Tunupa. The monuments found on the pyramid have art work that seems to allude to the dual character of this deity, who is represented by figures of pumas and condors that may have been sacred symbols of a political system that was also dual.

North of the Akapana pyramid is the Kalasasaya, a large rectangular platform (427 x 394 feet) with a stairway with a majestic portal giving access to a sunken court, in the middle of which is a sculpture known as the Ponce Monolith. The collective ceremonies that were held in this court were probably of an astronomic-calendarial character, since the Kalasasaya is oriented in such a way that during the solstice the sun would rise along the corners of the structure. Now the most famous monument in Tiahuanaco stands on the Kalasasaya platform, the Gateway of the Sun. This celebrated arch, which probably

comes from the edifice known as Pumapunku, is decorated with a marvelous bas-relief depicting the supreme god (known as the God of the Arch or God of the Staffs, who, as previously seen, is probably the antecedent of the Aymara deity Tunupa) surrounded by winged attendants.

East of the Kalasasaya is the smaller Semi-subterranean Temple, the walls of which are decorated with architectural nail-like elements in the shape of human heads with wide-open eyes. In the middle of the Temple were many sculptures, including the Bennett Monolith, a statue over 23 feet tall that now stands in a plaza in La Paz. According to certain experts, this sacred enclosure was a symbolic representation of the "world below" and many of the stelae in the middle may have been the booty from military conquests, much like what would occur in the future during the Inca period, when sacred images were "kidnapped" and taken to the center of the victorious city as "hostages."

Among the other monuments in Tiahuanaco, mention

298-299 The Pumapunka is a large T-shaped mound consisting of three terraces bordered by stone walls and with a large inner patio.

299 top The Ponce Monolith, inside the Kalasasaya. The figure, whose body is decorated with delicate carvings, is holding a *kero,* a drinking cup, and an object that seems to be a scepter.

299 bottom The Gateway of the Sun is now located near the Kalasasaya. It is thought that the central divinity may be an antecedent of Tunupa, the god of lightning, celestial fire, volcanoes, and rain for the Aymara, who existed during the period of the Spanish conquest.

should also be made of the Kanta Tayitu, a small building with a beautiful sculpted architrave, the Putuni. This was probably the residence of the city's political-religious ruling class, the Kerikala, which some scholars have interpreted as the site of ceremonial redistribution. Equally interesting, the Pumapunku is a large T-shaped platform with a central, half-subterranean court, stairways, and monolithic portals, one of which may have been the Gateway of the Sun. Around these edifices were minor monumental structures and residential complexes made of adobe, many of which have not resisted the ravages of time.

Starting in the year 700, Tiahuanaco went through its age of splendor, which was at the same time a period of great changes that seem to have been a prelude to the final crisis. The city population probably increased to 100,000 and most of the inhabitants were engaged in handicraft activity such as pottery, textiles, and metal production. It was this same period that witnessed the presumed military conflicts with the Wari armies in the Moquegua Valley, where around A.D. 800 Tiahuanaco lost the ancient administrative center of Omo. Some scholars say that political difficulties were accompanied by a serious drought that seems to have struck the Tiahuanaco area at the end of the first millennium A.D. Precisely in this period, dozens of bodies of men and llamas were placed on the Akapana, perhaps as sacrifices to avert disaster. Although the causes of the fall of Tiahuanaco are still partly unclear, we do know that the city was completely abandoned between 1000 and 1100, becoming a sacred site used for pilgrimages and offering rituals.

A few hundred years later, the Incas still considered Tiahuanaco the place where the creator god Viracocha had passed (it is no accident that this god has much in common with Tunupa) after being born on the sacred waters of Lake Titicaca. According to some versions of the myth, Manco Capac, the mythical founder of the Inca Empire, was also born at Tiahuanaco, which together with Lake Titicaca continued to be viewed as the most sacred site of creation in the Andean world.

CHAN CHAN

Text by DAVIDE DOMENICI

A veritable labyrinth of mud in the desert, the city of Chan Chan must have been one of the most impressive and sumptuous cities in pre-Columbian Peru. The seat of the rulers of the kingdom of Chimú, Chan Chan was the massive capital of a true empire which at its height extended for 800 miles along the northern coast of Peru. It has been calculated that the city had a maximum population of 25,000.

From the time of its foundation at the mouth of the Moche River Valley at the end of the ninth century, Chan Chan was probably planned as a political and administrative center, a function it maintained for the rest of its history. Although in the city and its environs there are several *wakas* in the shape of a pyramid such as the Huaca Esmeralda (Temple of the Emerald) or the Huaca del Dragón (or "of the Millipede"), most of the buildings in the city were either residential or administrative.

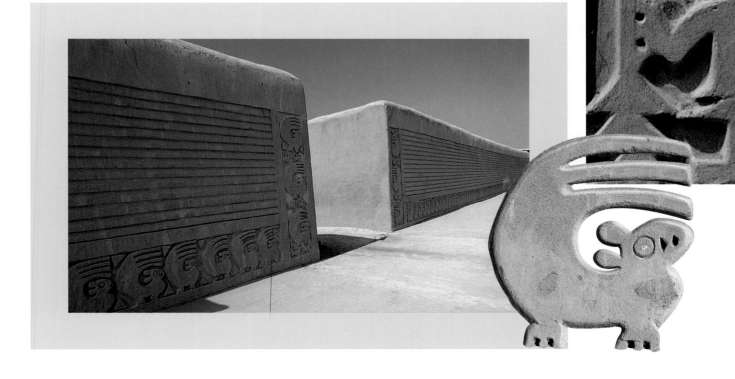

The architecture and town plan of Chan Chan have allowed archaeologists to understand the organizational configuration of the state of Chimú and its administrative hierarchy. Most of the eight square miles of the city area was occupied by lower class residential quarters consisting of houses made of reeds and mud where farmers and textile, pottery, and metallurgy artisans lived. In the mon-

300 bottom left The southern entrance to the large plaza in the Tschudi citadel (*ciudadela*), or palatial complex. These vast areas were most probably used to celebrate collective ceremonies in which such goods as *chichi*, the typical Andean alcoholic drink made from fermented corn, were distributed.

300-301 Detail of the decoration on the Huaca del Dragón, a temple at Chan Chan, the capital of the Chimú empire.

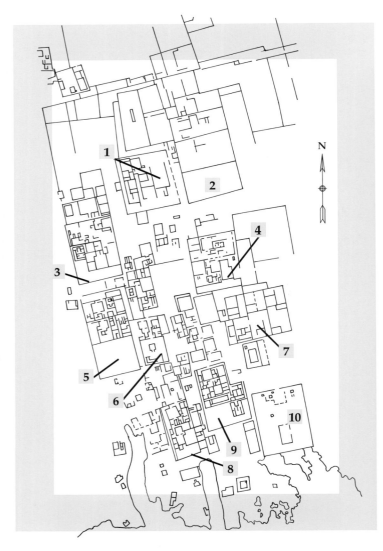

1) SQUIER
2) GRAN CHIMÚ
3) VELARDE
4) BANDELIER
5) LABYRINTH
6) TELLO
7) UHLE
8) RIVERO
9) TSCHUDI
   CITADEL
10) CHAYHUAC

302 center A row of cormorants in the lower register of a wall of the Tschudi citadel. In ancient times much of this decoration was painted with bright colors.

umental quarter, on the other hand, are the buildings where the upper class community lived and carried out its political-administrative duties. Thirty-four aristocratic complexes made of adobe included living quarters, storehouses, and *audiencias*, the typical U-shaped complexes used as administrative "offices" where taxes were collected and various kinds of goods were redistributed.

The true monumental quarter of Chan Chan, which covers a surface area of two and a half square miles, is almost completely occupied by a series (nine or eleven, depending on how they are counted) of "palatial complexes" known as *ciudadelas*. These are in fact actual walled citadels generally divided into three main sections. To the

north is a large public area surrounded by a series of benches, storehouses, and *audiencias*. In the middle section, besides the usual patios, storehouses, and *audiencias*, there is a large funerary mound, while the southern part of the *ciudadelas* usually has a large basin to collect rainwater and lower class houses probably used by servants.

It is thought that the *ciudadelas* were the residences of the Chimú kings and that their building sequence therefore should reflect the dynastic sequence, whether single or dual. Unfortunately, the difficulty in establishing the chronology of the various monumental complexes in Chan Chan has never allowed archaeologists to verify this theory with any certainty. If the Chimú rulers followed a

302-303 One of the portals of the large plaza in the Tschudi citadel. Thanks to extensive restoration work, the ancient wall decoration can now be seen. The entire city of Chan Chan was made of adobe.

custom similar to that of the later Inca rulers, when crowned the sovereign abandoned his father's palace in order to build a new one and begin his own family group (which the Incas called *panaca*). Even after the death of the king, his *panaca* continued to live in the royal palace, thus constituting an important power group from whose ranks would emerge the men destined to occupy the highest religious, political, and administrative positions. On the large main patios of the *ciudadelas*, whose walls are decorated with magnificent adobe bas-reliefs, important public ceremonies took place during which the mutual bonds between the king and his subjects were celebrated by means of distributing *chichi*, an alcoholic drink

303 top right A wooden anthropomorphic sculpture carved on the top of a cane or scepter.

303 bottom right A fish in a stepped cornice, an age-old Andean decorative motif.

made from fermented corn, and precious objects such as textiles, feather cloaks, jewels, and pottery. In the vicinity of the *ciudadelas* lived the more skilled artisans, whose products were made for the king, his family, and the most important nobles.

The importance of the cult of the ancestor who founded every royal family, which in the Inca world was reflected in the preservation of his mummy inside the Qorikancha, is manifested at Chan Chan in the large funerary mounds that dominate the *ciudadelas*. Unfortunately, intense plundering, which already began before the Spanish arrived and then continued during their dominion and into the modern age, has made it impossible to determine what was in some of the most sumptuous royal tombs in pre-Columbian Peru.

The great and complex administrative system that is reflected in the urban architecture of Chan Chan served to handle and sort the huge number of goods that arrived from the vast territory ruled by the capital. Most of the immediate subsistence was drawn from the products of the fields that extended south of the city. These plots of land were created by cutting out of the desert soil until the aquifer was reached. Other products came from the nearby valleys, as did water, which was channeled by means of prodigious hydraulic engineering. Such primary needs were handled during the

Chimú kingdom's first phase of military expansion, which from 1200 on led to the conquest of the entire coastline between the Zaña and Santa valleys. The raw materials from these valleys were transported to special administrative centers such as Farfán, in the Jequetepeque Valley, which had warehouses, *audiencias*, and other structures similar to *ciudadelas*. From Farfán, the products were taken to Chan Chan by means of llama caravans which stopped at the two caravanserais near the city, where there were kitchens, sleeping areas, stables, and even "llama cemeteries."

A second period of expansion, which began around 1350, brought about an enormous increase in the size of the Chimú kingdom, which now extended from Tumbes to the north, to Chillón to the south. In this period the Chimú kingdom conquered and incorporated the territory of the state of Sicán, situated in the northern valleys. The deportation of the highly skilled Sicán goldsmiths along with the influence they wielded seems

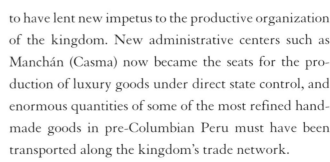

to have lent new impetus to the productive organization of the kingdom. New administrative centers such as Manchán (Casma) now became the seats for the production of luxury goods under direct state control, and enormous quantities of some of the most refined handmade goods in pre-Columbian Peru must have been transported along the kingdom's trade network.

Under the rule of Minchancamon, Chan Chan was in its golden age when, in the early 1460s, the city came into conflict with the expansionist policies of the

emerging Inca empire. Top Yupanqui, the Inca prince and future king, besieged the city for a long time and finally managed to conquer it by cutting off its water supply. Chan Chan was sacked, its tombs were desecrated, and most of its famous artisans were deported to Cuzco, where they worked for the new Inca sovereigns. Ironically, it was precisely the fine workmanship of these artisans in captivity that gave rise to the myth of the fabulous gold of the Incas, which in turn attracted the Spanish *conquistadores* a few decades later.

304 top Rooms and patios in the Tschudi citadel. The preservation of the adobe masonry in Chan Chan, which literally crumbles when it rains (which is fortunately rare here), is a problem that has not yet been solved.

304 bottom Birds carved on the walls of an *audiencia* of the Tschudi citadel. The geometric shape shows that this decorative motif originated in Andean textile production.

304-305 Wall decoration on the Huacan del Dragón. The central motif represents two supernatural beings crowned by a large two-headed serpent, which was probably a celestial deity.

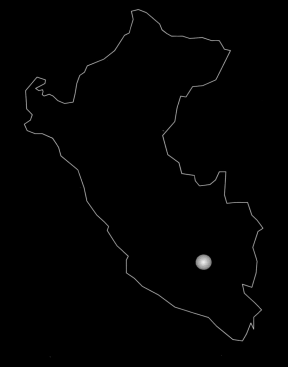

Machu
Picchu

306-307 Bingham, seen here with a sergeant of the Peruvian army, discovered Machu Picchu in 1911.

306 bottom This photograph taken by Hiram Bingham shows the city of Machu Picchu in the early 1900s, shortly after its discovery.

307 bottom Sergeant Carrasco poses for Bingham in front of an *intihatana*, or solar observatory, in Machu Picchu.

Text by DAVIDE DOMENICI

In a spectacular position on a saddle among the tall peaks of Machu Picchu and Huayna Picchu and overlooking the dizzying gorge of the Urubabma river 1,300 feet below, the most famous Inca city was so well protected and hidden by the tropical forest that even the Spanish *conquistadores* failed to see it.

Forgotten after it was abandoned, Machu Picchu was rediscovered only in 1911 when the archaeologist Hiram Bingham led an expedition promoted by Yale University in search of Vilcabamba, the locality where according to tradition the followers of the rebel Manco Inca took refuge from the Spanish soldiers.

The extraordinary scenery and the circumstances of the discovery have always sparked a number of fantastic and fascinating theories concerning the identity and role of Machu Picchu.

308 top left The original access way to the citadel of Machu Picchu was reached via a path that started off from Choquesuysuy, on which there was a checkpoint.

308 top right View of the Intellectuals' Quarter (Precinct of Mortars), one of the main areas in the civic sector of the city, which may have been dominated by textile production.

308 bottom The buildings in the "civic" sector of the city are distinguished by their masonry, which is less elegant than that of the religious edifices. The roof consisted of a wooden framework built on trusses that rested on the sidewalls; the roof itself waş placed on the framework, consisting of a layer of grass (*ichu*) that was tied to the stone pegs that stuck out of the masonry.

308-309 Machu Picchu in the natural setting of the eastern slopes of the Cordillera. It is obvious that the Incan architects were keenly aware of the surrounding countryside and sought to blend the city in with its environment, which is dominated by the Wayna Picchu peak.

MACHU PICCHU

The city was identified as Vilcabamba itself, the fortress of Vitco, the mythical Tamputoco (the place where the Incas originated), and lastly as the retreat of the Virgins of the Sun. In reality Machu Picchu was probably built at the end of the fifteenth century as an "estate" of Pachacuti's *panaca* and, even though its proximity to the Amazon forest made it an important site for the collection of luxury items such as coca and tropical bird feathers, the main activity of the city must have been the cultivation of corn. A vast network of terraces flanked the southern side of the city proper, which was divided by the central plaza into the traditional *hanan* and *hurin*.

310 bottom View of the farming area of the city with the typical terracing that allowed the inhabitants to grow corn on the steep slopes of the Cordillera. The cultivation of corn was probably the major activity of Machu Picchu's citizens.

310-311 View of the so-called Intellectuals' Quarter in Machu Picchu. In one of the parts of this quarter, the Precinct of Mortars, are stone mortars that were probably used to prepare pigments for dyeing fabrics.

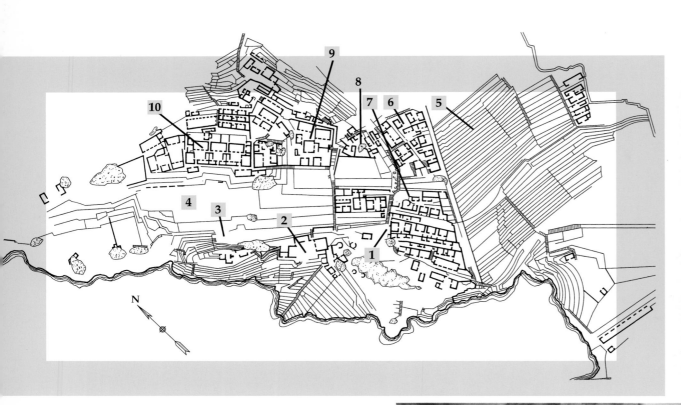

1) STAIRWAY OF THE FOUNTAINS
2) TEMPLE OF THE THREE WINDOWS
3) INTIHUATANA
4) MAIN PLAZA
5) SOUTHERN AGRICULTURAL TERRACES
6) WORKING CLASS QUARTER
7) TORRÉON QUARTER
8) PRISONS QUARTER
9) MORTARS QUARTER
10) THREE GATES QUARTER

The original access way to Machu Picchu was at its southern end, where a gate called Intipunku (Gate of the Sun) led one inside the walls that protected the city. From here, a street that skirted along the agricultural area led to the south side of the large central plaza.

To the west was the *hurin*, or lower city, with residential quarters for different social classes (which have been given rather fantastic names including Working Class Quarter, the Prisons, the Intellectuals' Quarter, and the Aqqlawasi, or House of the Virgins) where it is thought that most of the population lived and which was probably the site of the areas used to produce textiles and pottery.

The large stone mortars in the Aqqlawasi were probably used to prepare the pigments for wool dyeing.

At the northern border of the *hurin* is an important temple complex in the middle of which is a large natural rock, a *waka* dedicated to the cult of Pachamama, or Mother Earth.

But it is the *hanan* (upper) section of Machu Picchu that has the most beautiful and best preserved monuments. Proceeding from south to north, one sees a large complex of rooms at the front of which is a semicircular tower used for military purposes (the Sunturwasi, or Round House) and a network of small canals used by the water cult. Below the tower, the natural rock is magnificently sculpted with steps, niches, and an altar where offerings were placed; the function of this structure therefore had nothing to do with its common name, Royal Tomb.

Immediately north is the most important palace complex in Machu Picchu, the Royal Palace, most likely the residence of the political-religious ruling class. Past the so-called House of the Priest is the Temple of the Three Windows, built with large blocks of stone and decorated with the trapezoid windows typical of Incan architecture. Next to this temple is another temple structure known as the Great Central Temple, whose windows are decorated with niches that are also trapezoid.

In the uppermost part of the city, at the top of a 78-step stairway, is the most sacred edifice, the true focal point of religion and sacredness in Machu Picchu: the Intihuatana (Where the Sun Is Fastened), a monolithic solar observatory with a central pillar used as a gnomon for astronomical observation and as an altar.

Northeast of the plaza, between two craggy peaks, is the Temple of the Moon, made of large blocks of stone inserted into the natural rock to create grottoes with blind doors.

It is clear that the monuments in Machu Picchu comprise a variety of structures that are much more than buildings constructed to meet the needs of a community that produces corn. Like all the other Inca communities, Machu Picchu contains all the salient features of an Inca city and, though it was certainly not one of the most

important cities in the empire, the good state of preservation of its urban framework and its mythical aura make it one of the best examples of an ancient Inca city.

The city managed to avoid Spanish domination and was probably occupied by groups of natives who remained free until the end of the sixteenth century. After Machu Picchu was abandoned, more than 300 years passed before Bingham's expedition revealed to the world this "gem" set in the magnificent Urubamba Valley.

312 top right View of the Semicircular Tower or Sunturwasi, a structure that must have had a military purpose.

312 bottom right The Incan architects were true masters in combining natural rock formations and masonry.

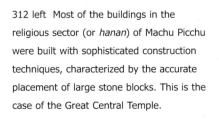

312 left Most of the buildings in the religious sector (or *hanan*) of Machu Picchu were built with sophisticated construction techniques, characterized by the accurate placement of large stone blocks. This is the case of the Great Central Temple.

313 The Great Central Temple is the starting point of the stairway that leads to the highest and most sacred point of Machu Picchu, where the Intihuatana Group stands.

INDEX

Note: c = *caption*
  nn = *dedicated chapter*

A

Abdu'r Razzaq, 215
Abu Kermal, 196
Achaemenids, 146, 166
Acropolis, 48c, 50, 51c, 52, 53, 55c, 56, 56c, 58, 59c, 60, 61
Acyutaraya, Temple of, 216c, 219
Aegistus, 45c, 47
Aeneas, 91
Aeschylus, 211
Africa, 10, 21, 25, 31, 43, 100, 101, 120, 130, 135, 138, 139
Afrodisia, 189
Agamemnon, 43, 44, 45c
Aglibal, 200c
Agora, Museum of, 57
Agrippa, 59, 77c, 79, 188
Ah Cacaw, 280
Ahpo Hel, 272c
Ahura Mazda, 177
Akapana, 297, 298, 299
Akkad, 159c, 161, 165, 168
Al-Malik Shirkuh, 197c
Alaungsithu, 237c, 239
Alcamene, 51c
Alexander Janneus, 191
Alexander The Great (Magnus), 20, 92, 147, 167, 173, 184, 187
Alexander Severus, 199
Algeria, 98
Allat, 198
Amar-Sîn, 154
Amarna, 100
Amazons, 182
Ambrosia, 118c
Amenhotep II, 110
Amenhotep III, 105, 105c, 107, 107c
America, 10, 21, 247, 249, 251, 252
Amman, 191
Amon, 104, 107, 108, 108c, 110
Amorites, 197
Anatolia, 25, 34, 182, 199
Ananda Pahto, 235c, 237
Anawratha, 213, 232c, 234, 235, 237
Andes, 251
Andrae, W., 164
Andronicus, 58
Angkor, 232
Angkor Thom, 224, 226
Angkor Wat, 211c, 226, 227, 228, 230
Angkor Wat, Temple of, 8c, 224, 224c
Annobal Tapapius Rufus, 113
Anti-lebanon, 205
Antioch, 147, 191
Antioch IV Epiphanes, 191

Antonine, 120
Antoninus Pio, 60, 64c, 116, 132, 132c
Antoninus Pio and Faustina, Temple of, 79
Antony, 187, 197
Apamea, 147, 193, 205
Apeyadana, 239
Apollo, 12c, 52c, 56, 201
Apollo, Temple of, 82c, 84, 86c
Appian, 197
Aqqlawasi, 311
Ara Pacis, 68, 70c, 77c
Arabs, 118, 120, 138, 160c
Arabia, 199
Aramaeans, 197
Arcadius, 187
Argos, 42
Arianna, 31, 128c
Artaxerxes I, 179, 180
Artaxerxes II, 168, 175
Artaxerxes III, 175
Artemis, 52c, 182, 183c, 184, 185, 188, 193, 195, 195c
Artemis Ephesias, 8c, 185
Asarhaddon, 161, 166
Asia, 31, 187, 241
Asia Minor, 147
Aspero, 250
Assurbanipal, 159, 161, 162, 166
Assurbanipal II, 162
Assyria, 145
Atacama, 296
Atargatis, 113c, 208c, 209
Ateban, 130, 131c
Atetelco, 259c
Athena, 48c, 50, 51, 52, 53, 56c, 57, 85, 203
Athenadoros, 80c
Athens, 10, 20, 25, 27, 30, **49-61**
Athens, National Museum of, 43c
Atlantic Ocean, 98
Atreus, 43c, 45c, 47
Attalids, 147, 187
Attalus, 56
Attalus II, 57
Attalus III, 187
Augustus, 25, 58, 63c, 68, 69, 69c, 77c, 79c, 88, 101, 113, 130, 187, 188
Augustus, Forum of, 67c, 70c, 76, 77, 91
Augustus, Mausoleum of, 70c
Aurelius, 80, 147, 199
Aurunci, 84
Austrian Archeological Institute, 184
Austurians, 118, 120
Avalokitesvara, 228c, 230, 230c
Ayasoluk, 189
Aymara, 299c
Ayutthaya, 212c, 213, 224, **240-245**

Ayutthaya, National Museum of, 244c
Azangara, 251
Aztecs, 252, 261

B

Baal Hammon, 134, 205, 207
Baalbek, 145c, **205-209**
Baalshamin, Temple of, 200c, 203
Babel, 168
Babylon, 163
Babylonia, 14, 146, 147c, 155, **164-168**
Bacchus, 84c, 92, 114, 208, 209
Bagan, 213. See also Pagan.
Bakong, 224
Bamar, 234
Bana, 228
Bangkok, 241
Banteay Srei, 226
Basilica Fulvia-Emilia, 67
Basilica Portius, 67
Basilica Sempronia, 67, 68. See also Basilica Julia.
Basilica Ulpia, 67c, 78
Basra, 150
Bawian, 156c
Bayinnaung, 244
Bayon, 221c, 228c, 230, 230c
Beauchamp, Abbot of, 164
Bel, Sanctuary of, 197c, 200c, 202
Belsor, Temple of, 200c
Benjamin da Tudela, 158, 164
Bentanta, 110c
Berkeley, 160
Bingham, Hiram, 294c, 307c, 308, 312
Black Sea, 26, 147
Blanton, Richard, 247
Bocco, 100, 101
Borom Rachathirat II, 244c, 245
Bosra, 193
Botta, P.E., 159
Bridge, H.J., 164
British Museum, 56c, 148c, 150, 150c, 154c, 155c, 159, 160, 165
Buddensieg, G., 165
Buddha, 211c, 237, 237c, 239, 239c, 241c, 242c, 244c
Budge, W., 164
Bukka, 215
Bulbul, 182
Burma, 232, 234, 235, 236
Burmese, 234, 245

C

C. Quinctius Valgus, 88
Caecilia Metella, Mausoleum of, 81c
Caecilius Iucundus, 97
Caelestis, 134

Cahuachi, 251
Caius Memmius, 189c
Calakmul, 267, 279, 280
Calicut, 212
Caligula, 90c, 101
Calvino, Italo, 213
Cambodia, 222, 226, 232
Campbell, Thompson, R., 150, 156c, 160
Campidoglio, 65, 67, 75c, 77, 79, 82c
Campus Martius, 67, 68, 70c, 75, 77, 79
Caracalla, 21, 80, 117, 118, 124, 125c, 139, 139c, 141c, 199, 207
Caracalla, temple of, 70c
Caracalla, Baths of, 80c
Caracol, 279, 280
Caryatids, 51c, 147
Carrasco, 307c
Casma, 304
Cassandra, 44
Castel Sant'Angelo, 78
Castor, temples of, 75
Catherwood, Frederick, 262c, 265c, 283c, 290c
Cato of Utica, 141
Celsus, 187c, 188
Celsus Polemeanus, 187, 189
Ceres Augusta, 114
Cerro Gordo, 257
Chak, 293c
Chak Toh Ich'ak, 278
Chak zutz', 272c
Chalchiuhtlicue, 254c, 257
Chan Bahlum, 267, 270, 270c, 271
Chan Chan, 248, 251, 252c, **300-305**
Chao Phraya, 241, 242
Chavin de Huantar, 250
Chiapas, 259, 267
Chicago, University of, 170c, 173
Chichén Itzá, 250, **282-293**
Chifflot, J.L., 82c, 193
Chillón, 304
Chimor, 300, 304
China, 199
Chinese, 242
Chiripa, 296
Choquesuysuy, 308c
Cholula, 248, 250, 289
Cipactli, 256c, 259c
Circus Flaminius, 67, 70c
Circus Maximus, 65, 70c
Claudius, 59, 101, 138
Clytemnestra, 47
Cloaca Maximus, 65
Cochabamba, 296
Column of Trajan, 67c
Colosseum, 63c, 70c, 75c, 76
Constantine, 69c, 75c, 80, 207
Conti, Niccolò, 215
Cooper, F.C., 156c

Copán, 249, 260, 267
Cordigliera, 308c, 310c
Corinth, 42
Crassus, 63c 62c
Cretans, 25
Crete, 25, 27, 30, 31, 34, 39, 139c
Cuzco, 248, 251, 305
Cyclops, 42, 44
Cyrus the Great, 147
Cyrus, 168

D

D. Octavius Quartio, 84c
Dacia, 67c
Darius, 92c, 147, 173, 173c, 176c, 177, 178c, 179, 180
Darius III, 175
Dedalus, 30
Deir el-Medina, 19, 100
Della Valle, Pietro, 158
Delaporte, Louis, 221c
Dhammayangy Pahto, 237, 237c
Diana, 143c
Diocletian, 80, 101, 199, 202, 203
Diocletian, Baths of, 70c
Dionysus, 56, 59c, 60, 136c, 143c
Doll, 28c
Domitian, 69c, 77, 187, 188
Domitian, Stadium of, 70c
Domus Augustana, 70c
Domus Aurea, 63c, 69, 76
Domus Flavia, 70c
Dougga, 101, **130-137**
Doura Europos, 147, 199
Durango, 284c

E

East, the 19, 21, 25, 26, 67, 193, 195, 199, 211, 212, 213
Ecole Francaise d'Extreme-Orient, 226
Edublamakh, 154, 155
Edzna, 290
Egypt, 10, 19, 25, 38, 98, 100, 104, 147, 199, 212
Egyptians, 100
Ekhursag, 154
Elamites, 154
Emesa, 199
Emporion, 26
E-nun-makh, 154, 155
Ephesus, 147, **182-189**
Erechtheion, 50
Ermodorus of Salamis, 67
Eros, 136c
Eruli, 60
E-sagila, 165, 168
Escuintla, 259
E-temenanki, 167, 168
Etruscans, 26, 196
Euphrates River, 146, 150, 164, 199

Eumachia, 82c, 86c, 91
Euripides, 211
Europe, 10, 25, 27, 31, 31c, 249
Evans, Arthur, Sir, 28c, 29c, 30,
   31c, 38

F
Farfán, 304
Fars, 173
Faustina, 64c
Fayyum, 100
Forum Boarium, 67, 70c, 75
Forum Holitorium, 67, 70c, 75
Forum Transitorium, 70c
Fox, Richard, 274
Fresnel, F., 164
Fyfe, Theodore, 29c

G
Gaius Julius Aquila, 187c, 189
Galindo, 251
Gallieno, 135
Gandhara, 178c
Ganesa, 219
Gaul, 26
Gautama, 242c
Gawdawpalin Pahto, 239, 239c
Gerasa, 147, **190-195**
Geta, 117
Gildone, 138
Gilgamesh, 160
Gipar, 154
Gismondi, Italo, 75c
Giuseppe Flavio, 205
Godard, A., 173
Grazie, 123
Greece, 25, 27, 42, 262c
Greeks, 26
Grotefend, G.F., 173
Guatemala, 259
Gubyaukgy, 239

H
Habuba Kebira, 145
Hadad, 205
Hadrian, 60, 61, 77c, 78, 79,
   183c, 191c, 199
Hadrian, Baths of, 12c, 114c,
   116, 117
Hadrian, Mausoleum of, 70c,
   79c
Hadriana Tadmor, 199
Hagesandros, 80c
Hairan, 202c
Hamilton, R.W, 160
Hammurapi, 146, 165, 166c,
   167c
Hampi, 213c
Hannibal, 100
Hardy, Osgood, 294c
Hasaw Chan K'awil, 278c, 280,
   281
Hatshepsut, 108c, 110
Hatun Jauja, 251
Hazara Rama, Temple of,
   216c, 219
Heliogabalus, 80
Heliopolis, 205

Helios, 76
Hellenistic, 26
Hellespont, 147
Hephaistos, 57
Hercules, 67, 85, 94, 95c, 114,
   116, 139c
Herodotus, 168, 211
Herzfeld, E., 170c, 173
Himalayas, 212, 234
Hittites, 107
Hogart, D.G., 182
Holy Land, the, 212
Homs, 196
Horemheb, 110, 110c
Horrea Galbana, 70c
Huaca del Dragon, 300, 301c,
   305c
Huaca Esmeralda, 300
Huánuco Viejo, 251
Hulagu, 207
Hunac Ceel, 290
Hutchinson, R.W., 160

I
Ibn Hawqal, 164
Iddibal Caphada Aemilius, 113
Ikitinos, 50
Ilissos, 60
Illimani, 294
Inca, 305
India, 199, 213, 215, 216, 232,
   234
Indian Ocean, 212
Indonesia, 224
Indrapura, 224
Indravarman I, 224
Indravarman III, 224
Intipunku, 311
Intiwatana, 307c, 312, 312c
Iol, 100
Iran, 173
Iraqi Department of
   Antiquities, 153c
Iraklion, Archeological
   Museum of, 37c
Iran, 145
Iran Archaeological Service,
   173
Irrawaddy River, 232
Ishme-Dagan, 154
Ishtar, 158, 159c, 161, 162c, 167,
   167c, 168
Islam, 215
Itzà, 290
Izamal, 290

J
Janiculum, Hill, 207
Jaussely, L., 82c
Jayavarman II, 224
Jayavarman VII, 213, 222, 224,
   228, 230
Jemdet Nasr, 146
Jincamocco, 251
Jonah, 159
Jones, J.F., 160
Jonuta, 271
Jordan, 191

Juba I, 101
Juba II, 101, 138
Judea, 191
Julia, 188
Julian the Apostate, 207
Julius Caesar, 59, 65c, 67, 68,
   69, 69c, 101, 130
Jupiter, 88, 120c, 202, 205, 206c
   207, 209
Julius Anthiocus, 59c
Jupiter Heliopolitan, 205
Jupiter Heliopolitanis, Temple
   of, 205c, 207, 208
Jupiter Maximus, Temple of,
   65, 70c, 86, 86c, 88
Jupiter Stator, Temple of, 67
Justinian, 189

K
Kabah, 284
Kadesh, 107
Kahun, 100
K'ak'Sih, 279
Kalasasaya, 297c, 298, 299c
Kallicrates, 50
Kallimachus, 53
Kaminaljuyù, 259
Kan Xul II, 271, 272c
Kandy, 235c
Kanta Taytu, 299
Karnak, 108c, 110, 110c
Karnak, Temple of, 102c, 105,
   107, 110
Kecrops, 51c, 53
Kerikala, 299
Khmer, 224
Khonsu, 108
Khrisna, 228
Khusur, 161
King, L., 150
K'inich Janahb'Pakal, 267
Knossos, 10, 21c, 27, **29-39**
Koldewey, R., 164, 166
Kolonos Agoraios, Hill of, 56
Koressus, 182
Kritios, 57
Krsnadevaraya, 218
Ksar Pharoun, 138
K'uk Bahlum, 267
Kukulkan, 289c
Kulen, 222, 224
Kurigalzu, 155
Kuruksetra, Battle of, 227,
   227c
Kuyunjik, 156c, 159, 159c, 160,
   160c, 161, 162, 162c
Kyansittha, 235c, 237

L
La Paz, 297c, 298
La Venta, 249
Lachish, 162
Lakamha, 267
Lanka, 228
Lanka, Battle of, 227c
Laocoön, 80c
Laodicea, 147
Larsa, 155, 166c

Latini, 26
Layard, A.H., 156c, 159, 164
Lebanon, 205, 207
Leptis Magna, 8c, 12c, 21c, 98c,
   101, **112-119**
Lhasa, 294
Libya, 98
Livia, 188
Lloyd Stephens, John, 262c,
   265c
Lobpuri, 213, 242
Loftus, W.K., 164
Lotus Mahal, 219, 219c
Louvre, 164, 168c
Lu-Nanna, 166c
Lucius Veros, 123, 189
Luigi XIV, 242
Luqurmata, 296
Lusimachus, 187
Luxor, 8c, 98c, 102c, 105, 105c,
   107, 107c, 110
Lycia, 147
Lycurgus, 56, 118c
Lydia, 147, 185

M
M. Minucio Rufo, 67
Machu Picchu, 248, **306-312**
Mackenzie, Duncan, 29c
Mallowan, M.E.L., 156c, 160,
   161
Manchan, 304
Manco Capac, 299
Manco Inca, 308
Mandalay, 232
Manishtushu, 159c, 161
Manhua, 234, 235, 239
Manhua Paya, 239
Marcellus, Theatre of, 79c
Marcus Aurelius, 77c, 116, 123,
   132, 189
Marcus Aurelius, Column of,
   77c
Marcus Portius Cato, 67, 88.
   See also Cato the Younger.
Marduk, 167c, 168
Marduk, Tempe of, 168c, 168
Marnas, 182
Marseille, 26
Marocco, 98, 138
Mars Ultors, Temple of, 67c
Massalia, 26 See also Marseille.
Maxentius, 63c, 80, 81c
Maxentius, Basilica of, 70c
Matacapan, 259
Maudslay, Alfred Percival,
   265c, 283c
Mauretania, 101, 138
Mayapán, 290
Mazeo, 187c, 188
Medes, 163
Mediterranean Sea, 26, 27, 39,
   122c, 147, 196, 199
Memphis, 98, 108, 160c
Menalaus, 43
Mercury, 134, 145
Merkès, 168
Meru, Mount, 227

Meskalamdug, 155c
Mesopotamia, 10, 146, 150
Messapians, 26, 255, 257, 259,
   260
Mexico, 249, 250, 253, 254,
   255, 257, 259, 260, 261, 284c,
   290
Mexico City, 250
Mexico, Gulf of, 255, 259, 267
Michalowski, K., 201
Middle East, 10
Miletus, 147
Milk'ashtart, 113, 114
Minchancamon, 304
Minerva, 88
Minnhathu, 232c
Minoan, 30, 34, 38
Minos, 30, 31, 39
Mirza, Farad, 173
Mithradates I, 168, 187, 188
Mnesikles, 53
Moche, 251, 300
Mochica, 251
Mongols, 235
Monte Albán, 248, 249, 260
Montu, 110
Moquegua, 296, 299
Mosul, 158, 159
Mostafavi, M.T., 173
Motul, 274
Mouhot, Henri, 226
Muse, 122
Mut, 108, 108c, 110
Mycenae, 10, 40c, **41-47**
Mycenaeans, 27, 39

N
N. Popidius Ampliatus, 88c, 97
Nabateans, 147
Nabonidus, 155, 164, 166, 167
Nabopolassar, 166, 167, 168
Nebuchadnezzar, 155, 165c,
   166, 167, 168, 168c
Nadaungmya, 237c, 239, 239c
Nahua, 254
Nandin, 219
Nanna, 154
Narai, 213, 242
Naram-Sin, 159c
Narapatisithu, 239, 239c
Narathu, 237c, 239
Nasq-i Rustam, 175
Neak Pean, 230c
Near East, 10
Nebi Yunus, 159, 161
Nebo, Temple of, 197c, 201
Nectanebo I, 107c
Nero, 59, 69, 76, 187c
Nerva, 77
Nesiotes, 57
Nieburh, 159
Nile River, 98, 100, 104, 105,
   105c, 110, 117
Ningal, 154, 155
Niniveh, 10, 156c, **157-163**
Niobes, 86c
Nong Sarai, Battle of, 244
Nubia, 104

Numidia, 101, 130
Nuniz, Fernão, 215

O
Oaxaca, 249, 257, 259
Oaxaca, Valley of, 255
Obeid, 145
Odenathus, 199
Odyssey, 137c
Oea, 120
Olympus, 51, 52c
Omo, 299
Oppert, J., 164
Orpheus, 117
Osci, 26
Osiris, 110c
Otter, J., 158

P
Pa Sak, 242
Pachacamac, 251
Pachamama, 311
Pacific Ocean, 212
Paes, Domingos, 215
Pagan, **232-239**
Pakal, 247c, 265c, 266c, 268, 269c, 270, 270c, 272c
Palatine, 62, 69c, 77, 79
Palenque, 247c, **262-273**
Palmyra, 147, 193, **196-203**
Pampa, 251
Pampapati, 219
Panayr, 182
Pantanios, 59
Paris, 122
Parthenon, 25c, 48c, 50, 51c, 52, 52c, 58, 60, 61
Pasiphae, 30
Patio, the White, 259c 261c
Pausanias, 19, 42, 43c, 44, 56
Peloponnesia, 39
Peninsula Chalcidian, 26
Pennsylvania, University of, 150
Pentheus, 95c
Pergamon, 147, 187
Pericles, 48c, 50, 52, 56
Persepolis, 10, 21c, 145c, 170c, **171-181**
Persian Gulf, 199
Persians, 51, 57, 147, 304
Petén, 279, 281
Petra, 147
Phaulkon, Constantine, 242, 242, 244
Phidias, 51, 51c, 52, 52c, 55c
Philopappos, 59c, 60
Phirmus, 138
Phnom Penh, 222
Phoenicia, 199
Phra Phetracha, 244
Phya U-Thong, 241, 242
Phrygia, 147
Pikillakta, 251
Piy, 232, 234
Polydoros, 80c
Polo, Marco, 213, 235
Pompeii, 8c, 27, **83-97**

Pompey, 67, 101, 114, 191, 205
Pompey, Theater of, 70c
Portico of Aemilia, 70c
Portico Metelli, 70c. See also Porticus Octavie.
Portunus, Temple of, 79c
Poseidon, 52, 52C, 53
Praxiteles, 185
Preah Khan, 226
Prytaneis, 57
Ptah, 108
Ptolemy, 101, 147
Puebla-Tlaxacala, 255
Pukara, 296
Pumapunku, 294c, 298, 299
Putuni, 299

Q
Quetzalcoatl, 252c, 289c
Quetzalpapáloti, 256c, 257
Quirinal, 77
Qorikancha, 251, 304

R
Rabirius, 69c
Rama, 227c, 228, 241
Ramses II, 98c, 105, 105c, 107, 107c, 108, 110, 110c
Ramses III, 110c
Ramesuan, 245
Rangoon, 232
Rassam, H., 160, 165
Ravana, 228
Reuter, O., 165
Rich, C. J., 159, 164
Rome, 8c, 10, 20, 26, 27, 27c, 58, 59, 61, **62-81**, 85, 86, 100, 101, 113, 114, 114c, 116, 117, 124, 125c, 187, 188, 207, 215
Rome, Forum of 8c, 62, 63c, 70c
Romulus, 62, 91
Roulos, 224, 226

S
Sabratha, 8c, 101, 101c, **120-129**
Saga Tigraxauda, 170c
Sais, 98
Sak Kuk, 268
Saladin, 207
Sami, A., 173
San Juan, 254, 257
Santa, 304
Sapa Inka, 251
Sardi, 147
Sargon, 159c, 161, 165
Sargon II, 165, 167
Sarno, 84, 86
Saturn, Temple of 63c, 75
Sayil, 284
Schliemann, Heinrich, 40c, 42, 45c
Schmidt, E.F., 173
Scopas, 185
Scythians, 163
Sechin Alto, 250
Seleucia, 168
Seleucids, 147, 166, 187

Sennacherib, 158, 159, 159c, 160, 161, 162, 162c, 163, 166
Serapis, 123
Servius Tullius, 65
Sestilius Pollione, 188
Seti I, 108, 110, 110c
Settimius Severus, 79, 113c, 116, 117, 118, 124, 125c, 132c, 168, 207
Settimius Severus, Arch of, 64c, 70c, 114c
Settimius Severus, Basilica of, 8c, 12c, 21c
Severans, 120, 199
Shadrapa, 113, 121
Shalamatt, 202c
Shamash, 167c
Shamshi-Adad, 161
Shulgi, 153, 154, 165
Shwegugy, 239
Shwesandaw, 232c
Shwezigon Paya, 235c, 237
Sican, 251
Sicani, 26
Sicily, 25, 26, 43, 100
Siculi, 26
Siem Reap, 226
Sile, 98
Silin, 118c
Silla, 57, 67, 86, 189c
Syracuse, 100
Sirens, 137c
Syria, 25, 43, 147, 191, 196, 199, 205
Sita, 227c
Shiva, 219
Siyah Chan K'awil, 278c, 279
Smith, G., 160
Sri Lanka, 224, 235c
Stronach, D., 160
Suez Canal, 98
Sulemani, 237c, 239
Sumer, 150, 155
Suphan Buri, 241
Suryavarman II, 224, 227

T
Ta Prohm, 226
Tabasco, 249
Tadmor, 196
Takht-i Jamshid, 173
Talikota, 215
Tamputoco, 310
Tangiers, 101
Tanit, 134
Tarquin, 75
Tarquinius Superbus, 65. (See also Tarquin the Proud)
Tarquinius Priscus, 65
Tartars, 236
Taylor, J.E., 150
Tayok Pye Paya, 232c
Taypikala, 294
Tell el-Muqayyar, 150, 150c
Tenan, 257
Tenochtitlan, 248, 250
Teotihuacán, 248, 249, 250, **252-261**, 279, 287, 289

Thai, 224
Thailandia, 242
Thamugadi, 101, 134
Thatbyinnyu, 237c, 239
Thaton, 234, 235
Thebes, 10, 19, 20, 95c, 98, 100, 101, **103-111**
Thugga, 130, 131c
Tiber River, 67, 68
Tiberius, 115, 207
Tigris River, 158, 159
Tikal, 249, 260, 267, 268, 269c, **274-281**
Tingis, 101
Tiryns, 42, 43c
Titicaca, 251, 294, 296, 299
Titus, 63c, 76, 80c
Titus, Arch of, 70c, 77
Tivoli, 67
Tiwanaku, 251, **294-299**
Tlahuizcalpantecuhtli, 288, 289c
Tláloc, 254, 257
Tollan, 261, 289, 290, 293c
Toltecs, 289
Toninà, 271
Tonle Sap, 222
Topa Yupanqui, 305
Tortuguero, 271
Trajan, 67c, 77, 78, 114c, 116, 168, 184c, 191
Trajan, Forum of, 70c, 77
Trajan, Baths of, 70c
Treto Pass, 42
Tripoli, Museum of, 12c, 98c
Tripolitania, 101, 112, 120
Troy, 42, 51
Tschudi, 301c, 302c, 303c, 305c
Tula, 248, 250, 284c, 287, 289
Tumbes, 304
Tungabhadra, 215
Tunupa, 298, 299, 299c
Tuthmosis I, 110
Tuthmosis II, 110

U
U-Thong, 241
Uadi Lebdah, 112, 116, 117
Uaxactun, 279
Ulysses, 137c
University of Pennsylvania, Museum of, 150
Ur, 10, 146, **149-155**, 165
Ur-Nammu, 150c, 153, 154
Urubamba, 296
Urubamba, Valley of, 312
Uruk, 145
Usumacinta, 267, 278
Utica, 100
Uxmal, 284

V
Vaballato, 199
Vandals, 118, 120
Vasco de Gama, 212
Vedius, Palaestra of, 184c
Vedius, Baths of, 189

Venus, 86, 89c, 93c, 97,140, 141, 206c, 208c, 288
Venus Genetrix, Temple of, 65c
Veracruz, 249, 259
Verulanus, Square of, 189
Vespasian, 63c, 76, 86c, 188
Vespasian, Temple of, 88
Vestal Virgins, 65c
Vesuvius, 84, 84c, 92, 94
Vettii, House of, 8c
Vijayanagara, 215, 217, 218, 219
Vilcabamba, 308, 310
Vilcaswaman, 251
Viracocha, 299
Viracochapampa, 251
Virupaksa, 217,
Vitcos, 310
Vithoba, 218
Vitthala, 218
Vitthalasvami, Temple of, 213c, 215c, 218
Volubilis, 101, **138-143**

W
Waldeck, 262c
Wari, 251, 296
Wat Na Phra Men, 245
Wat Phra Mahathat, 241c, 242c, 245
Wat Phra Si Sanphet, 241c, 245
Wat Ratchaburana, 242c, 244c, 245, 245c
Wayna Picchu, 308
West, the, 25, 27, 211, 212, 222
West Indies Company, 242
Wetzel, F., 164
Wood, J.T., 182
Woolley, C.L., 148c, 150

X
Xerxes I, 175, 175c, 179, 180
Xochicalco, 287

Y
Yale University, 308
Yama, 230
Yangon, 232
Yarhibal, 200c
Yasodharapura, 224
Yasovarman I, 224
Yax Ain I, 279
Yax Ain II, 278c
Yax Ch'aktel xoc, 275
Yaxchilan, 268, 269c
Yucatán, 284, 284c, 293c
Yunnan, 232, 235

Z
Zacatecas, 284c
Zaña, 304
Zapotechi, 254
Zenobia, 197c, 199
Zeus, 30, 51, 52c, 56, 59c, 60, 61, 192c, 195

PREFACE
Text by Maria Teresa Guaitoli

Maria Teresa Guaitoli, technical official at the Department of Archeology of the University of Bologna, Italy, graduated and specialized in archeology at the same institution. She has managed excavations for the Archeological Superintendent of the provinces of Emilia Romagna, Veneto, and Puglia in fields covering protohistory to the Medieval Era. With the University, she has participated as scientific director in the mission to the Celtic oppidum of Bibracte (Burgundy, France) and the investigation of the pre-convent phases of the monumental complex of San Giovanni in Monte (Bologna, Italy). She has held seminaries on the study of medieval wall structure and underwater archeology at the University of Parma's (Italy) Department of Cultural Heritage Conservation. Organizer of exhibits and conventions for the Department of Archeology, she is also a regular contributor to the magazine *Ocnus: Quaderni della Scuola di Specializzazione in Archeologia*. Her publications deal mainly with the relationship between ancient literary sources and archeological data and ancient decoration.

Photo Credits:
1 top Anne Conway/Archivio White Star;
2 bottom Marcello Bertinetti/Archivio White Star;
2 center Anne Conway/Archivio White Star;
3 Alfredo Foglia and Pio/ Foglia Ltd. Photografic Archives;
4-5 Marcello Bertinetti/Archivio White Star, Auth. S.M.A n. 316 of 8/18/95;
6-7 Marcello Bertinetti/Archivio White Star, Auth. S.M.A n. 316 of 8/18/95;
8 top Araldo De Luca;
8 bottom Araldo De Luca/Archivio White Star;
9 Livio Bourbon /Archivio White Star;
10 Araldo De Luca/Archivio White Star;
11 Araldo De Luca/Archivio White Star;
12-17 Araldo De Luca/Archivio White Star;
18 Araldo De Luca/Archivio White Star;
19 Araldo De Luca/Archivio White Star.

GENERAL INTRODUCTION
Text by Maria Teresa Guaitoli and Simone Rambaldi

Simone Rambaldi, received his diploma from the School of Archeology at the University of Bologna (Italy) where he wrote his thesis "Struttura e impiego del *monopteros* nell'architettura romana". A candidate for the Doctorate in Archeological Research (Roman, late ancient, and medieval archeology), he has actively participated in excavations sponsored by the University of Bologna's Archeology Department, including assignments in Albania at the Hellenistic Greek city of Phoinike and at the excavation of the so-called Palace of Theodoric in Galeata (FC). He also works as an instructor with the University of Bologna's Archeology Department in the field of classical archeology.

Photo Credits:
20 top Araldo De Luca/Archivio White Star;
21 Corbis;
22-23 Aisa.

EUROPE
Text by Marco Podini

Marco Podini received his degree from the School of Archeology at the University of Bologna. He has participated in several excavation campaigns lead by the University of Bologna's Archeology Department at locations such as the *domus* of the Coiedii in Suasa Senonum (Ancona, Italy) and the so-called Palace of Theodoric in Galeata and its late-Roman-era thermal bath system. He has also taken part in the Italian mission to the Hellenistic city of Phoinike (Albania). He dealt with the Roman mosaics of Suasa and Augustan VI's reign.

Bibliography
Greco E. and Torelli M., *Storia dell'urbanistica. Il mondo greco*, Rome-Bari 1983.
Gros P. and Torelli M. *Storia dell'urbanistica. Il mondo romano*, Rome-Bari 1988.
Mansuelli G.A., *Architettura e città. Problemi del mondo classico*, Bologna 1970.

Photo credits:
25 top Scala Archives;
25 bottom Araldo De Luca;
27 top Double's.

KNOSSOS
Text by Marco Podini

Bibliography:
Banti L., "Cnosso," *Enciclopedia dell'Arte Antica classica e orientale*, vol. II, Rome 1959.
Demargne P., *Arte egea*, Milan 1964.
Di Vita A. and La Rosa V., Rizzo M.A., ed. *Creta antica: Cento anni di archeologia italiana (1884-1984)*, Exhibit Catalog, Rome 1985.
Glotz G., *Civiltà egea*, Turin 1953.
Godart L., *I Minoici*, Archeo, n. 4 (86). April, 1992.
Greco E. and Torelli M., *Storia dell'urbanistica. Il mondo greco*, Rome-Bari 1983.
Palmer L.R., *Minoici e Micenei*, Turin 1969.

Photo credits:
28 top The Ashmolean Museum, Oxford;
28 bottom Alfio Garozzo/Archivio White Star;
28-29 The Ashmolean Museum, Oxford;
29 top right The Ashmolean Museum, Oxford;
29 bottom The Ashmolean Museum, Oxford;
30 left Antonio Attini/Archivio White Star;
30 center Alfio Garozzo/Archivio White Star;
30 right Antonio Attini/Archivio White Star;
30-31 Antonio Attini/Archivio White Star;
33 top Antonio Attini/Archivio White Star;
34-35 Antonio Attini/Archivio White Star;
34 top left Antonio Attini/Archivio White Star;
345 top right Antonio Attini/Archivio White Star;
34 bottom Alfio Garozzo/Archivio White Star;
36-37 Alfio Garozzo/Archivio White Star;
37 top Livio Bourbon/Archivio White Star;
37 center Alfio Garozzo/Archivio White Star;
37 bottom left Antonio Attini/Archivio White Star;
37 bottom right Giovanni Dagli Orti;
38-39 top Ricciarini Agency, Milan;
38-39 bottom Giovanni Dagli Orti.

MYCENAE
Text by Marco Podini

Bibliography
AA. VV. "Micene," *Enciclopedia dell'Arte Antica classica e orientale*, vol. IV, pp. 1105 ff.; pp. 486-487, Supplement I: 1970; pp. 650-653, Supplement II: 1971-1994.
Greco E. and Torelli M., *Storia dell'urbanistica:. Il mondo greco*. Rome-Bari 1983.
Gualandi G. "Il mondo egeo e la civiltà greca," *Archeologia*, pp. 215-250. Milan 1978.
Guglielmino R., "Micene," *Atlante di Archeologia*, pp. 378-381, Turin 1996.
Palmer L.R., *Minoici e Micenei*, Turin 1969.
Schliemann H., *Mycenae: A Narrative of Discoveries at Mycenae and Tiryns*, New York 1878.

Photo credits:
40 top Deutsche Archäologisches Institut, Athens;
40-41 top Deutsche Archäologisches Institut, Athens;
40-41 bottom Photo Nimatallah/ Ricciarini Agency;
41 top Bibliothèque Nationale de France;
41 center British Architectural Library, London;
41 bottom The Artarchive;
42-43 Livio Bourbon/Archivio White Star;
43 top Giulio Veggi/ Archivio White Star;
43 bottom left Livio Bourbon/Archivio White Star;
43 bottom right Giovanni Dagli Orti;
44-45 Giulio Veggi/Archivio White Star;
45 top AKG Photo;
45 bottom left Livio Bourbon/Archivio White Star;
45 bottom right Livio Bourbon/ Archivio White Star;
46 Aisa;
47 Henri Stierlin.

ATHENS
Text by Marco Podini

Bibliography
AA. VV. "Atene," *Enciclopedia dell'Arte Antica classica e orientale*, vol. I,

pp. 767-863; pp. 90-97, Supplement I: 1970; pp. 496-518, Supplement II: 1971-1994.

Bianchi Bandinelli R. and Paribeni E., *Grecia*, Turin 1976.

Charbonneaux J., Martin R., Villard F., *La Grecia arcaica; La Grecia classica; La Grecia ellenistica*, 3 vols., Milan 1970-71.

Greco E. and Torelli M., *Storia dell'urbanistica. Il mondo greco*, Rome-Bari 1983.

Gros P. and Torelli M., *Storia dell'urbanistica. Il mondo romano*, Rome-Bari 1988.

Lloyd S., Müller H.W., Martin R., *Architettura mediterranea preromana*, Venice 1972.

Mansuelli G.A., *Roma e il mondo romano*, 2 vols., Turin 1981.

Martin R., *La Grecia e il mondo greco*, 2 vols., Turin 1984.

Martin R., *Architettura greca*, Venice 1980.

Paletti M., *Atene: l'Acropoli in Atlante di Archeologia*, pp. 250-253, Turin 1996.

Paletti M., *Atene: l'Agorà in Atlante di Archeologia*, pp. 254-257, Turin 1996.

Rocchetti L., "Atene al tempo di Pericle," *Archeo*, n. 78, pp. 58-103, August 1991.

Ward Perkins J.B., *Architettura romana*, Venice 1974.

Photo credits:

ROME
Text by Marco Podini

Bibliography

AA.VV. "Roma," *Enciclopedia dell'Arte Antica classica e orientale*, vol. VI, p. 764 ff; p. 660 ff, Supplement I: 1970; pp. 784-996, Supplement II: 1971-1994.

Bianchi Bandinelli R., *Roma: L'arte romana nel centro del potere*, Milan 1969.

Bianchi Bandinelli R., *Roma. La fine dell'arte antica*, Milan 1970.

Bianchi Bandinelli R. and Torelli M., *Etruria*. Rome, Turin 1976.

Coarelli F., "Roma: Il Foro romano e il Palatino," *Atlante di Archeologia*, pp. 432-433, Turin 1996.

Ghedini F.E., "I Fori imperiali," *Atlante di Archeologia*, pp. 434-435, Turin 1996.

Gros P., *Architettura e società nell'Italia romana*, Rome 1987.

Ghedini F.E. and Torelli M., *Storia dell'urbanistica. Il mondo romano*, Rome-Bari 1994.

Mansuelli G.A., *Roma e il mondo romano*, 2 vols., Turin 1981.

Ward Perkins J.B., *Roman Imperial Architecture*, London 1994.

Photo credits:

POMPEII
Text by Antonella Coralini

Antonella Coralini received a research study grant from the University of Bologna's Department of Archeology and History of Roman Art. She is one of the scientific directors for the "Pompeii Project: Insula of the Centenary," in collaboration with the University of Bologna and the Superintendent of Pompeian Archeology's Office. She is a member of the Association Internationale pour la Peinture Murale Antique (A.I.P.M.A.) and the Association Internationale pour l'Etude de la Mosaïque Antique (A.I.E.M.A.). Her publications include *L'Alma Mater a Pompei*. She has supervised the didactic exhibits of "Le pitture dell'Insula del Centenario," together with D. Scagliarini Corlaita, in Bologna, Italy in 2001 and "Hercules Domesticus: Immagini di Ercole nelle case della regione vesuviana (first century B.C.- A.D. 79)," held in Naples in 2001.

Bibliography

AA. VV. *Un Piano per Pompei. Piano programma per la conservazione e la gestione del patrimonio storico-archeologico della città antica*, First Phase. Rome: Ministry for Cultural and Environmental Heritage, Superintendent of Pompeian Archeology, World Monuments Fund, 1997.

Cebeillac-Gervasoni M., ed. *Les élites municipales de l'Italie péninsulaire de la mort de César à la mort de Domitien entre continuité et rupture: Classes sociales dirigéantes et pouvoir central*, Rome 2000.

Allemandi U. and others, *Pompeii. Picta Fragmenta, Decorazioni parietali dalle città sepolte*. Turin-London 1997.

Varone A., *Pompéi*, Parigi, Terrail, 1995.

Borriello M. and others, eds. "Pompei: Abitare sotto il Vesuvio," *Exhibit Catalog*, Ferrara, Sept. 29, 1996 - Jan. 19, 1997. Ferrara 1996.

Cerulli Irelli G., ed. *La pittura di Pompei. Testimonianze dell'arte romana nella zona sepolta dal Vesuvio nel 79 d.C.* Milan 1991.

Ciarallo A. and De Carolis E., eds. "Homo Faber: Natura, scienza e tecnica nell'antica Pompei," *Exhibit Catalog*, Naples, National Archeology Museum, March 27 - July 18, 1999. Milan 1999.

Dobbins J.J., "Problems of Chronology, Decoration, and Urban Design in the Forum at Pompeii," *America Journal of Archaeology*, n. 98, pp. 629-694, 1994.

Guzzo P. G. and D'Ambrosio A. *Pompei*, Naples 1998.

Guzzo P. G. and Scarano Ussari V., *Figurae Veneris*, Naples 2000.

Guzzo P. G., ed. "Pompei: Scienza e Società," *Acts of the International Conference on the 250th Anniversary of the Excavations at Pompeii*, Naples, November 25-27, 1998, Milan 2001.

Pesando F,. *Domus: Edilizia privata e società pompeiana fra III e I secolo a.C.*, n.12. Rome: Ministry for Cultural and Environmental Heritage and the Superintendent of Pompeian Archeology Monographs, 1997.

Zanker P., *Pompei: Società, immagini*

urbane e forme dell'abitare, Turin 1993.
Zevi F., ed. *Pompei 79: Raccolta di studi per il decimonono centenario dell'eruzione vesuviana*, Naples 1979.
Zevi F., ed. *Pompei*, vol. I, Naples 1991.
Zevi F., ed. *Pompei*, vol. II, Naples 1992.

Photo credits
82-83 top Ècole Nationale Supérieure des Beaux Arts, Paris;
82-83 bottom Ècole Nationale Supérieure des Beaux Arts, Paris;
83 center Mary Evans Picture Library;
83 bottom Roger Viollet/Contrasto;
84 top Erich Lessing/Contrasto;
84 bottom left Erich Lessing/Contrasto;
84 bottom right Alfredo e Pio Foglia/ Foglia Photographic Archives;
84-85 Guido Cozzi/Atlantide;
86 left Giulio Veggi/Archivio White Star;
86 right Giulio Veggi/Archivio White Star;
87 Anne Conway/Archivio White Star;
88-89 Anne Conway/Archivio White Star;
89 top Anne Conway/Archivio White Star;
89 right Erich Lessing/Contrasto;
89 bottom Anne Conway/Archivio White Star;
90 top Anne Conway/Archivio White Star;
90 center Anne Conway/Archivio White Star;
90 bottom Giulio Veggi/Archivio White Star;
90-91 Giulio Veggi/Archivio White Star;
92 top Erich Lessing/Contrasto;
92 center Alfredo e Pio Foglia/Foglia Photographic Archives;
92-93 Alfredo e Pio Foglia/Foglia Photographic Archives;
93 top Alfredo e Pio Foglia/Foglia Photographic Archives;
94 top Giulio Veggi/ Archivio White Star;
94 bottom Giulio Veggi/Archivio White Star;
95 top Anne Conway/Archivio White Star;
95 bottom Giulio Veggi/Archivio White Star;
96 top Alfredo e Pio Foglia /Foglia Photographic Archives;
96 center Anne Conway/Archivio White Star;
96-97 Scala Archives;
97 top Giulio Veggi/Archivio White Star.

AFRICA
Text by Simone Rambaldi and Marco Zecchi

Marco Zecchi, doctor of Ancient African History, also obtained an M.Phil. in Egyptology from the School of Archeology and Oriental Studies at the University of Liverpool as well as a scholarship from Brown University in Providence, Rhode Island (USA). He is involved with the excavations at Kom Umm el-Atl in Bakhias (Fayyum, Egypt) sponsored by the universities of Bologna and Lecce (Italy). He teaches a course of Coptic Language and Literature at the Department of Egyptology at the University of Bologna. His publications deal with the Egyptian civilization until the Hellenistic-Roman era with particular emphasis on the role of religion.

Bibliography
Decret F. and Fantar M., *L'Afrique du Nord dans l'Antiquité: histoire et civilisation des origines au Ve siècle*, Paris 1981.
Di Vita A., "Gli Emporia di Tripolitania dall'età di Massinissa a Diocleziano: Un profilo storico-istituzionale,"*Aufstieg und Niedergang der römischen Welt*, vol. II.10.2, pp. 515-595. Berlin, New York 1982.
Lepelley C., *Les cités de l'Afrique romaine au Bas-Empire*, 2 vols., Paris 1979-1981.
Février P.A., "Urbanisation et urbanisme de l'Afrique romaine," *Aufstieg und Niedergang der römischen Welt*, vol. II.10.2, pp. 321-396, Berlin-New York 1982.
Picard Ch. G., *La civilisation de l'Afrique antique*, Paris 1990.
Romanelli P., *Storia delle province romane dell'Africa*, Rome 1959.
Romanelli P., "Topografia e archeologia dell'Africa romana," *Enciclopedia Classica*, section III, vol. X, tome VII. Turin 1970.

Photo credits
98 top Alfio Garozzo/Archivio White Star;
98 bottom Araldo De Luca/Archivio White Star;
101 top Araldo De Luca/Archivio White Star.

THEBES
Text by Marco Zecchi

Bibliography
Baines J. and Malek J., *Atlas of Ancient Egypt.*, Oxford 1980.
Davoli P,. *Città e villaggi dell'antico Egitto*, Imola 1994.
Donadoni S., *Tebe*, Milan 1999.
Kemp B.J., *Ancient Egypt. Anatomy of a Civilization*, London 1989.

Photo credits
102 top Archivio White Star;
102 bottom Roger Viollet/Contrasto;
103 top Harlingue-Viollet/Contrasto;
103 bottom left Archivio White Star;
103 bottom right P. Lacau Archives;
104 left Alfio Garozzo/Archivio White Star;
104 bottom left Marcello Bertinetti/ Archivio White Star;
104 right Giulio Veggi/Archivio White Star;
104-105 Marcello Bertinetti/Archivio White Star;
106-107 Alfio Garozzo/Archivio White Star;
106 bottom Giulio Veggi/Archivio White Star;
107 Antonio Attini/Archivio White Star;
108 left Marcello Bertinetti/Archivio White Star;
108 top right Alfio Garozzo/Archivio White Star;
108 bottom right Marcello Bertinetti/ Archivio White Star;
108-109 Marcello Bertinetti/Archivio White Star;
110 top Alfio Garozzo/Archivio White Star;
110 bottom left Antonio Attini/ Archivio White Star;
110 bottom right Alfio Garozzo/ Archivio White Star;
111 Marcello Bertinetti/Archivio White Star.

LEPTIS MAGNA
Text by Simone Rambaldi

Bibliography
Bacchielli L., *Libya. The lost cities of the Roman Empire*, Colonia 1999.
Bianchi Bandinelli R., Caputo G., Vergara Caffarelli E., *Leptis Magna*. Milan 1964.
Di Vita A., "Il progetto originario del forum novum Severianum a Leptis Magna," *150-Jahr-Feier Deutsches Archäologisches Institut Rom* (Mitteilungen des Deutschen Archäologischen Instituts, Römische Abteilung, suppl. 25), pp. 84-106. Rome 1982.
Di Vita A., Evrard G., Floriani Squarciapino M., *Le sculture del Foro Severiano di Leptis Magna*, Rome 1974.
Ward Perkins J.B., Kenrick P., ed. *The Severan Buildings of Leptis Magna: An Archaeological Survey*, Tripoli-London 1993.
Ward Perkins J.B., "Town Planning in North Africa during the first two centuries of the Empire, with special reference to Leptis and Sabratha: Character and Sources," *150-Jahr-Feier Deutsches Archäologisches Institut Rom* (Mitteilungen des Deutschen Archäologischen Instituts, Römische Abteilung, suppl. 25), pp. 29-49, Rome 1982.

Photo credits:
112 bottom left Marcello Bertinetti/ Archivio White Star;
112 bottom right Marcello Bertinetti/ Archivio White Star;
112-113 Araldo De Luca/Archivio White Star;
114 top left Marcello Bertinetti/ Archivio White Star;
114 top right Araldo De Luca/Archivio White Star;
114-115 Marcello Bertinetti/Archivio White Star;
115 Araldo De Luca/Archivio White Star;
116-117 Araldo De Luca/Archivio White Star;
117 top left Araldo De Luca/Archivio White Star;
117 bottom left Araldo De Luca/ Archivio White Star;
117 right Araldo De Luca/Archivio White Star;
118 top left Marcello Bertinetti/ Archivio White Star;
118 top right Araldo De Luca/Archivio White Star;
118 bottom Araldo De Luca/Archivio White Star;
119 Araldo De Luca/Archivio White Star.

SABRATHA
Text by Simone Rambaldi

Bibiliography
Caputo G., *Il teatro di Sabratha e l'architettura teatrale africana*, Rome 1959.
Pesce G., *Il tempio di Iside in Sabratha*, Rome 1953.

Photo credits:
120 left Araldo De Luca/Archivio White Star;
120 right Araldo De Luca/Archivio White Star;
120-121 Araldo De Luca/Archivio White Star;

THUGGA
Text by Simone Rambaldi

Bibliography

Poinssot C., *Les ruines de Dougga*, Tunis 1983.

Golfetto A., *Dougga: Die Geschichte einer Stadt im Schatten Karthagos*, Basel 1961.

VOLUBILIS
Text by Simone Rambaldi

Bibliography

Etienne R., *Le quartier nord-est de Volubilis*, Paris 1960

Jodin A., *Volubilis regia Iubaeù: Contribution à l'étude des civilisations du Maroc antique préclaudien*, Paris 1987.

Lenoir M., Lenoir E., Akerraz A., "Le forum de Volubilis: Eléments du dossier archéologique," *Los foros romanos de las provincias occidentales. Actas de la Mesa redonda*, pp. 203-219. Valencia 1986, Madrid 1987.

MIDDLE EAST
Text by Antonella Mezzolani
and Riccardo Villicich

Antonella Mezzolani, doctor in African and Ancient Near Eastern Archeology, has taught both Punic-Phoenician Archeology and Ancient Near Eastern Art History at the Department of Cultural Heritage Conservation at the Ravenna Branch of the University of Bologna. She has excavated at Tharros and is currently working in Carthage with a joint mission sponsored by the universities of Amsterdam and Cambridge. She works with the iconography of the sea in Roman-era and North African mosaics. Her many publications have dealt with city planning in Punic cities and ceramic materials of the Greek and Roman eras.

Riccardo Villicich, doctor of Roman Archeology, holds seminars at the Department of the Archeology of the Roman Provinces within the departments of Humanities and Cultural Heritage Conservation at the University of Bologna. He shares the scientific directorship of the excavations of the Roman cities of Suasa, Galeata (the so-called Palace of Theodoric and the late-Roman-era baths), and the Italian mission in the Hellenistic city of Phoinike (Albania), all sponsored by the Department of Archeology of the University of Bologna. He has also handled the difficulties of dealing with ancient numismatics in his supervision of the study of coins discovered at Suasa, urban systems and the architecture of the Roman provinces, and the restoration of ancient metal artifacts.

Bibliography

Jones H.M., *The Cities of the Eastern Roman Provinces*, Oxford 1971.

Giuliano A., *Le città dell'Apocalisse*, Rome 1978.

Macro D., "The Cities of Asia Minor under the Roman Imperium," *Aufstieg und Niedergang der Römischen*, Welt II, 7, 2, pp. 658-697, 1980.

Rinaldi Tufi S., *Archeologia delle province romane*, Rome 2000.

UR
Text by Antonella Mezzolani

Bibliography

Brinkman J.A., "Ur: The Kassite Period and the Period of the Assyrian Kings," *Orientalia*, n. 38, pp. 310-348, 1969.

Moorey P.R.S., "Where did they bury the kings of the IIIrd Dynasty of Ur?," *Iraq*, 46/1, pp. 1-18, 1984.

Pollock S., "Chronology of the Royal Cemetery of Ur," *Iraq*, 47, pp. 128-58, 1985.

Pollock S., "Of Priestesses, Princes, and Poor Relation: The Dead in the Royal Cemetery of Ur," *Cambridge Archaeological Journal*, n. 1, pp. 171-89, 1991.

Weadock P., "The Giparu at Ur," *Iraq*, 37, pp. 101-28, 1975.

Woolley C. L., *Ur of the Chaldees*, New York 1982.

NINIVEH
Text by Antonella Mezzolani

Bibliography

Barnett R. D., *Sculptures from the North Palace of Ashurbanipal at Nineveh, 668-627 B.C.*, London 1976.

Bleibtreu E. and others, *The Southwest Palace of Sennacherib at Nineveh*, London 1996.

Campbell Thompson R. and Hutchinson R.W., *A Century of Exploration at Nineveh*, London 1929.

Mallowan M.L.E., "The Prehistoric Sondage of Nineveh, 1931-32," *Annals of Archaeology and Anthropology,* 20, pp. 127-186. Liverpool, University of Liverpool, 1933.

Matthiae P., *Ninive*, Milan 1998.

Russel J.H., *Sennacherib's Palace without Rival at Nineveh*, Chicago 1991.

Scott M.L. and Macginnis J., "Notes on Nineveh," *Iraq*, 52, pp. 63-73, 1990.

159 bottom The British Museum, London;
160 top The British Museum, London;
160 bottom Erich Lessing/Contrasto;
160-161 Erich Lessing/Contrasto;
162 bottom Erich Lessing/Contrasto;
162-163 Giovanni Dagli Orti;
163 bottom The British Museum, London.

BABYLON
Text by Antonella Mezzolani

Bibliography
Bergamini G., "Levels of Babylon Reconsidered," *Mesopotamia*, n. 12, pp. 111-52, 1977.
George A.R., "The Topography of Babylon Reconsidered," *Sumer*, n. 44, pp. 7-24, 1986.
George A.R., "Babylon Revisited: Archaeology and Philology in Harness," *Antiquity*, n. 67, pp. 734-46, 1993.
Koldewey R., *Das Ischtar-Tor in Babylon*, Leipzig 1918.
Koldewey R., *Die Königsburgen von Babylon*, 2 vols., Leipzig 1931.
Matthiae P., *La storia dell'arte dell'Oriente Antico. I grandi imperi, 1000-330 a.C.*, pp.150-160, Milan 1996.
Wetzel F., and Weissbach F.H., *Das Hauptheiligtum des Marduk in Babylon: Esagila und Etemenanki*. Leipzig 1938.

Photo credits:
164 left Thouvenin/Farabolafoto;
164 right Erich Lessing/Contrasto;
165 top Giovanni Dagli Orti;
164-165 Giovanni Dagli Orti;
166-167 Francoise De Mulder/Viollet Roger/Contrasto;
166 bottom Erich Lessing/Contrasto;
167 bottom Erich Lessing/Contrasto;
168 left Thouvenin/Farabolafoto;
168 right Giovanni Dagli Orti;
169 G. Mereghetti/Marka.

PERSEPOLIS
Text by Antonella Mezzolani

Bibliography
Cahill N., "The Treasury at Persepolis," *American Journal of Archaeology*, n. 89, pp. 373-89, 1985.
Calmeyer P., "Textual Sources for Interpretation of Achaemenian Palace Decoration," *Iran*, n. 18, pp. 55-63, 1980.
De Francovich G., "Problems of Achaemenid Architecture," *East and West*, n. 16, pp. 201-60, 1966.
Ghirshman R., *Arte persiana: Protoiranici, Medi e Achemenidi*, pp. 154-223. Milan: 1982.
Matthiae P., *La storia dell'arte dell'Oriente Antico: I grandi imperi, 1000-330 a.C.*, pp. 225-240, Milan 1996.
Porada E., "Classical Achaemenian Architecture and Sculpture," *The Cambridge History of Iran*, vol. 2, pp. 793-827, Cambridge 1985.

Photo credits:
170 top left Oriental Institute, University of Chicago;
170 top right Oriental Institute, University of Chicago;
170-171 Henri Stierlin;
171 Oriental Institute, University of Chicago;
172-173 Double's;
172 bottom Henri Stierlin;
173 bottom Henri Stierlin;
174 top J. Fuste Raga/Marka;
174-175 Aisa;
175 top right Double's;
176 top Aisa;
176 bottom Christophe Boisvieux;
176-177 Aisa;
178 top Henri Stierlin;
178 bottom Henri Stierlin;
178/179 Henri Stierlin;
179 Henri Stierlin;
180 top Henri Stierlin;
180 center Henri Stierlin;
180 bottom Henri Stierlin;
181 Henri Stierlin.

EPHESUS
Text by Riccardo Villicich

Bibliography
AA. VV. *Forschungen in Ephesos*, vols. 1-12. Vienna 1906-1989.
Alzinger W., "Augusteische Arkitektur in Ephesos," *Sondnummer der Österreichisches Archäologisches Institut*, XIV, Wien 1974.
Oberleitner W. ed. *Funde aus Ephesos und Samothrake*, Vienna 1978.

Photo credits:
182 top Erich Lessing/Contrasto;
182 bottom Livio Bourbon/Archivio White Star;
182-183 Livio Bourbon/Archivio White Star;
184 center Livio Bourbon/Archivio White Star;
184/185 J. Fuste Raga/Marka;
185 top Erich Lessing/Contrasto;
186 Livio Bourbon/Archivio White Star;
186-187 Livio Bourbon/Archivio White Star;
187 top Livio Bourbon/Archivio White Star;
187 bottom Livio Bourbon/Archivio White Star;
188-189 Livio Bourbon/Archivio White Star;
189 top Livio Bourbon/Archivio White Star;
189 bottom Livio Bourbon/Archivio White Star.

GERASA
Text by Riccardo Villicich

Bibliography
Kraeling C.H., *Gerasa: City of the Decapolis*, New Haven 1938.
Browning I., *Jerash and the Decapolis*, London 1982.

Photo credits:
191-191 Massimo Borchi/Archivio White Star;
191 top Massimo Borchi/Archivio White Star;
191 bottom Massimo Borchi/Archivio White Star;
192 bottom Henri Stierlin;
192 center Massimo Borchi/Archivio White Star;
192-193 Massimo Borchi/Archivio White Star;
194-195 Massimo Borchi/Archivio White Star;
194 bottom Massimo Borchi/Archivio White Star;
194 left Massimo Borchi/Archivio White Star;
194 right Massimo Borchi/Archivio White Star.

PALMYRA
Text by Riccardo Villicich

Bibliography
Amy R., Seyrig E., Will E., *Le Temple de Bel à Palmyre*, 2 vols. Paris 1975.
Colledge M.A.R., *The Art of Palmyra*, London 1976.
Starcky J. and Gawlikowski M., *Palmare*, Paris 1985.
Wiegand T., *Palmyra*, 2 vols., Berlin 1932.

Photo credits:
196-197 Giovanni Rinaldi/Il Dagherrotipo;
197 top Felipe Alcoceba;
197 bottom left Giovanni Rinaldi/Il Dagherrotipo;
197 bottom right Aisa;
198-199 Franck Lechenet/Hemispheres;
199 top Felipe Alcoceba;
199 bottom Giovanni Rinaldi/Il Dagherrotipo;
200 top Double's;
200 bottom Erich Lessing/Contrasto;
200-201 Henri Stierlin;
202 top Giovanni Rinaldi/Il Dagherrotipo;
202 bottom left Charles Lénars;
202 bottom right Erich Lessing/Contrasto;
202-203 Henri Stierlin.

BAALBEK
Text by Riccardo Villicich

Bibliography
Coupel P., *L'autel monumental de Baalbek*, Paris 1951.
Dussaud R., "Temples et cultes de la triade héliopolitaine à Baalbek," *Syria*, XXIII-XXIV, pp. 33-77, 1942-1943.
Seyrig H., "Questions héliopolitaines," Syria, XXXI, pp. 80-98, 1954.
Wiegand T., *Baalbek*, 3 vols. Berlin 1921-1925.

Photo credits:
204 Double's;
205 top Antonio Attini/Archivio White Star;
205 bottom Cozzi, G./Atlantide/Agence ANA;
206 bottom Diaf/Marka;
207 Henri Stierlin;
206-207 Aisa;
208 left Antonio Attini/Archivio White Star;
208 right Antonio Attini/Archivio White Star;
208-209 Henri Stierlin;
209 Henri Stierlin.

FAR EAST
Text by Marco Ceresa

Marco Ceresa, born in Lodi (Italy) in 1959, graduated from the University Ca' Foscari of Venice in 1984 with a degree in Chinese Language and Literature. In 1992, he received his doctorate in Oriental Studies from the Oriental Institute of the University of Naples. Between 1986 and 1991, he lived in Taiwan and Japan while he conducted research at the Center for Chinese Studies of the National Central Library of Taipei and at the Research Institute for Humanistic Studies at the University of Kyoto. He is currently an associate professor of Chinese Literature at the Department of East Asian Studies at the University Ca' Foscari in Venice. He has also held conferences and seminars at the University of Marburg (Germany), the

University Eotwos Lorand of Budapest (Hungary), the University of Lund (Sweden), and the University of Munich (Germany). His work mainly deals with the literature and culture of China and Southeast Asian countries with particular emphasis on Cambodia. He lives and works in Venice.

Bibliography

Benevolo L., *Storia della città orientale*, Rome 1988.
Calvino I., *Le città invisibili*, Turin 1980.
Polo M., *Il libro di Marco Polo detto Milione, nella versione trecentesca dell'Ottimo*, Turin 1962.

HAMPI
Text by Cinzia Pieruccini

Cinzia Pieruccini graduated with a degree in Classical Humanities and wrote her thesis on the Sanskrit language at the University of Milan (1981). She has been a doctor of Indian and Far East Asian Art since 1994 and has spent much time studying and conducting research in India. Her many scientific publications deal with classical Indian literature and the iconography and architecture of India. She has translated several important works from Sanskrit and Prakrit such as the *Dasakumarakarita* of Dandin (Dandin, *The Ten Princes.* Brescia: Paideia, 1986) and the *Kamasutra* of Vatsyayana (Vatsyayana, *Kamasutra.* Venezia: 1990, 6th ed., 2001). She has held the position of tenured professor at the universities of Trento and Milan for several years and is currently the recipient of a research grant in Indology at the University of Milan.

Bibliography

Dallapiccola A. L. and Verghese A., *Sculpture at Vijayanagara: Iconography and Style*, New Delhi 1998.
Fritz J.M. and Michell G., eds. *New Light on Hampi: Recent Research at Vijayanagara*, Mumbay 2001.
Michell G., *Architecture and Art of Southern India: Vijayanagara and the Successor States, 1350-1750.* The New Cambridge History of India, VI.1. Cambridge 1995.
Michell G. and Fritz J., *City of Victory: Vijayanagara, The Medieval Hindu Capital of Southern India*, New York 1991.
Michell G. and Wagoner P. B., *Vijayanagara: Architectural Inventory of the Sacred Center*, 3 vols., New Delhi 2001.
Paes D. and Nuniz F. *The Vijayanagar Empire,* ed. Filliozat, V. and trans. Sewell, R. New Delhi 1977.
Sewell R., *A Forgotten Empire (Vijayanagar): A Contribution to the History of India*, London 1900; reprint, Shannon, Ireland 1972.
Stein B., *Vijayanagara.* The New Cambridge History of India, I. 2. Cambridge 1989.

ANGKOR
Text by Marco Ceresa

Bibliography

Boisselier J., *Le Cambodge. Manuel d'archéologie d'Extrême-Orient,* vol. I, Paris 1966.
Chandler D., *A History of Cambodia*, Boulder 1983.
Coedès G., *Angkor: an introduction*, trans. Gardiner, F.E. New York, Hong Kong 1963
Coedès G., *Histoire des États hindouisés d'Indochine et d'Indonésie*, Paris 1964.
Dagens B., *Angkor: la forêt de pierre*, Paris 1989.
Delaporte L., *Voyage au Cambodge: L'architecture khmère*, Paris 1880.
Finot L., Goloubew V., Coedès G. *Le Temple d'Angkor Vat*, 5 vols. Paris 1929-1932.
Freeman M. and Warner R., *Angkor: The Hidden Glories*, Boston 1990.
Giteau M., *Histoire du Cambodge*, Paris 1957.
Giteau M., *Khmer Sculpture and the Angkor Civilization*, New York-London 1965.
Glaize M., *Les monuments du groupe d'Angkor*, Paris, Guide, 1963.
Groslier P. and Arthaud J., *Angkor: Art and Civilization*, New York-London 1966.
Jacques C., *Angkor*, Paris 1990.
Mouhot M. H., *Travels in the Central Parts of Indochina (Siam), Cambodia, and Laos During the Years 1858, 1859, and 1860*, London 1864.
Rawson P., *The Art of Southeast Asia: Cambodia, Vietnam, Thailand, Laos, Burma, Java, and Bali*, London 1967.
Zhoi D., *The Customs of Cambodia*, Bangkok 1992.

PAGAN
Text by Marco Ceresa

Bibliography

Luce G. H., *Old Burma-Early Pagan.* New York: 1970.
Pichard P., *Inventory of Monuments at Pagan*, vols. I-IV. Paris, and others: 1992-1994.
Strachan, P. *Pagan: Art & Architecture of Old Burma*. Whiting Bay, Arran (Scotland) 1989.
Taylor K. W., "The Early Kingdoms," *Early Times to c. 1800.* The Cambridge History of Southeast Asia, vol. 1, pp. 137-82, Cambridge 1992.

AYUTTHAYA
Text by Marco Ceresa

Bibliography

Kasetsiri C., *The Rise of Ayudhya: A History of Siam in the Fourteenth and Fifteenth Centuries*, Kuala Lumpur 1976.
Coedès G., *The Indianized States of Southeast Asia.* Honolulu 1968.
Coedès G., *The Making of Southeast Asia.* Berkeley, Los Angeles 1969.
Smyth D., *Thailand*, revised ed. Oxford, Santa Barbara, (CA) 1998.
Vincent F., *The Land of the White Elephant: Sights and Scenes in Southeast Asia, 1871-1872*, Bangkok 1988.
Wyatt D. K., *Thailand: A Short History.* New Haven 1986.

AMERICA
Text by Davide Domenici

Davide Domenici, born in Rome in 1968, he received his degree in Modern Humanities and wrote his thesis on the pre-Columbian history and civilization of America, graduating with the highest of grades and honors, while his thesis was published. He has conducted and directed several academic seminars about the ancient peoples of Mesoamerica and currently holds a research grant from the Department of Paleography and Medieval Studies at the University of Bologna. Since 1997, he has participated in archeological expeditions in Chiapas, Mexico, and since 1998, he has been co-edited the Rio La Venta Archeological Project. Editorial consultant for Sperling & Kupfer and Jaca Book Publishing, he has also written numerous articles for specialized archeological magazines on pre-Columbian Mesoamerican archeology and has completed several books, including *I naufragi del pacifico* (in *Rapa Nui, gli ultimi argonauti*, 1995), *Rio La Venta, Tesoro of Chiapas* (1999), and *Guida archeologica del Mediterraneo* (2000). He is the author of *Mexico: Guida ai siti archeologici*, published by White Star in 2001.

Bibliography
Adams McC. R., *The Evolution of Urban Society. Early Mesopotamia and Prehispanic Mexico*. Chicago: 1966. Italian trans., *La rivoluzione urbana. Mesopotamia antica e Messico preispanico*. Turin: 1982.
Blanton, Richard E. "The Rise of Cities," Sabloff, J., ed. *Handbook of Middle American Indians: Archaeology*, suppl. 1, pp. 392-400. Austin 1981.
Braidwood R.J. and Willey G., eds. *Courses Toward Urban Life*. Chicago 1962.
Craig M. and Von Hagen A., *The Inka Empire and its Andean Origins*, New York 1993.
Fox R., *Urban Anthropology*, Englewood Cliffs 1977.
Hardoy J.and E., *Pre-Columbian Cities*, New York 1964.
López A. A. and López L. L., *El pasado indígena*, México 1997. Davide Domenici, italian trans. *Il passato indigeno. Per una nuova storia del Messico precolombiano*, Milan 1998.
Lumbreras L. G., "Childe y la tésis de la revolución urbana: la experiencia central andina," Manzanilla L., ed. *Coloquio V. Gordon Childe: Estudios sobre las revoluciones neolítica y urbana*, pp. 349-366, México 1988.

Manzanilla L., "El surgimiento de la sociedad urbana y la formación del Estado: consideraciones," Manzanilla L., ed. *Coloquio V. Gordon Childe. Estudios sobre las revoluciones neolítica y urbana*, pp. 293-308, México 1988.
Joyce M., "On the Nature of the Mesoamerican City," Vogt E. and Leventhal R., eds. *Prehistoric Settlement Patterns*, pp. 195-242, Albuquerque 1983.
Moseley M. E., *The Incas and Their Ancestors: The Archaeology of Perú*, London, New York 1992.
Nalda E., "La città maya," Schmidt P., De la Garza M., Nalda E., eds. *I Maya*, pp. 102-129, Milan 1998.
Rowe J. H., "Urban Settlements in Ancient Perú," *Ñawpa Pacha*, n. 1. 1963.
Sanders W. T. and Price B. J., *Mesoamerica: The Evolution of a Civilization*, New York 1968.
Sanders W. T. and Webster D. "The Mesoamerican Urban Tradition," *American Anthropologist*, vol. 90, pp. 521-546, 1988.
Scarduelli P., "La città nell'America pre-colombiana," Rossi, P., ed. *Modelli di città: Strutture e funzioni politiche*, pp. 273-295, Turin 1987.
Schaedel and others. *Urbanization in the Americas from the Beginnings to the Present*, Chicago 1978.
Von Hagen A. and Craig M. *The Cities of the Ancient Andes*, London 1998.
Wheatley P. "The Concept of Urbanism," Ucko P.J., Tringham R., Dimbleby G.W., eds. *Man, Settlement and Urbanism*, pp. 601-637, London 1972.
Willey G., "Precolumbian Urbanism: The Central Mexican Highlands and the Lowland Maya," Lamberg-Karlowsky, C.C. and Sabloff, J., eds. *The Rise and Fall of Civilizations: Modern Archaeological Approaches to Ancient Cultures, Selected Readings*, pp. 134-156, Menlo Park 1974.

Photo credits:
247 top Antonio Attini/Archivio White Star;
247 bottom Massimo Borchi/Archivio White Star;
251 Henri Stierlin.

TEOTIHUACÁN
Text by Davide Domenici

Bibliography
Berrin K. and Pasztory E., eds. *Teotihuacán. Art from the City of the Gods*, London 1993.

Evans S. and Berlo J. C., "Teotihuacán: An Introduction," Berlo, J. C., ed. *Art, Ideology, and the City of Teotihuacán*, pp. 1-26, Washington, D.C. 1992.
López A. A., "La historia de Teotihuacán," *Teotihuacán*, pp. 13-35 México D.F. 1989.
Manzanilla L., "The Economic Organization of the Teotihuacán Priesthood: Hypothesis and Considerations," Berlo J. C., ed. *Art, Ideology, and the City of Teotihuacán*, pp. 321-338. Washington, D.C. 1992.
Manzanilla L., "La zona del Altiplano Central en el Clásico," Manzanilla L. and López L. L., eds. *Historia Antigua de México*, vol. II, *El horizonte clásico*, pp. 203-239, México D.F. 2001.
Millon R. "Teotihuacán: City, State, and Civilization," Sabloff, J., ed. Suppl. to *Handbook of Middle American Indians*, vol. I, *Archaeology*, pp. 198-243, Austin 1981.

Photo credits:
252 top Antonio Attini/Archivio White Star;
252/253 Antonio Attini/Archivio White Star;
254 left Antonio Attini/Archivio White Star;
254 right Antonio Attini/Archivio White Star;
254/255 Antonio Attini/Archivio White Star;
255 center Jorge Perez de Lara;
255 bottom Antonio Attini/Archivio White Star;
256/257 Antonio Attini/Archivio White Star;
256 bottom Antonio Attini/Archivio White Star;
257 bottom left Antonio Attini/Archivio White Star;
257 bottom right Antonio Attini/Archivio White Star;
258 Charles Lénars;
259 top Charles Lénars;
259 bottom Charles Lénars;
260 Giovanni Dagli Orti;
261 top Archivio Scala;
261 bottom Henri Stierlin.

PALENQUE
Text by Davide Domenici

Bibliography
AA.VV. "Palenque: Trabajos recientes, nuevas interpretaciones," *Arqueología Mexicana*, vol. VIII, num. 45, México 2000.
Schele L. and Freidel D., *A Forest of Kings. The Untold Story of the Ancient*

Maya, New York 1990. Italian trans., *Una foresta di re*, Milan 2000.
Schele L. and Mathews P., *The Code of Kings. The Language of Seven Sacred Maya Temples and Tombs*, New York 1998.
Sharer R. J., *The Ancient Maya*. Stanford 1994. Spanish trans., *La civilización maya*, México 1998.

Photo credits:
262 bottom Archivio White Star;
262/263 Archivio White Star;
263 top Bibliotèque Nazionale de France, Paris;
263 bottom Bibliotèque Nazionale de France, Paris;
264 Bibliotèque de l'Homme/BNP;
265 top left Bibliotèque de l'Homme/BNP;
265 top center Bibliotèque de l'Homme/BNP;
265 top right Bibliotèque de l'Homme/BNP;
265 bottom Giovanni Dagli Orti;
266-267 Massimo Borchi/Archivio White Star;
267 top Laura Accomazzo/Archivio White Star;
267 center Massimo Borchi/Archivio White Star;
267 bottom Massimo Borchi/Archivio White Star;
268-269 Massimo Borchi/Archivio White Star;
269 top Massimo Borchi/Archivio White Star;
269 center Massimo Borchi/Archivio White Star;
270 top Massimo Borchi/Archivio White Star;
270 center Massimo Borchi/Archivio White Star;
270 bottom Massimo Borchi/Archivio White Star;
270-271 Massimo Borchi/Archivio White Star;
272 top Henri Stierlin;
272 center Henri Stierlin;
272 bottom Henri Stierlin;
273 Henri Stierlin.

TIKAL
Text by Davide Domenici

Bibliography
Coe W. R., *Tikal. A Handbook of the Ancient Maya Ruins*, Philadelphia 1988.
Coe W. R., "Excavations in the Great Plaza, North Terrace, and North Acropolis of Tikal," *Tikal Report*, n. 14. Philadelphia: Monographs of the University of

Pennsylvania Museum, 1990.
Harrison P. D., The Lords of Tikal. Rulers of an Ancient Maya City, Londra 1999.
Schele L. and Freidel D., *A Forest of Kings. The Untold Story of the Ancient Maya*. New York 1990. Italian trans. *Una foresta di re*. Milan 2000.
Sharer R. J., *The Ancient Maya*. Stanford 1994. Spanish trans. *La civilización maya*, México 1998.

Photo credits:
274 left Massimo Borchi/Archivio White Star;
274 right Giovanni Dagli Orti;
275 Massimo Borchi/Archivio White Star;
278 top Massimo Borchi/Archivio White Star;
278 bottom left Massimo Borchi/Archivio White Star;
278 bottom right Massimo Borchi/Archivio White Star;
278-279 Massimo Borchi/Archivio White Star;
280 top left Laura Accomazzo/Archivio White Star;
280 top right Massimo Borchi/Archivio White Star;
280 bottom Massimo Borchi/Archivio White Star;
280-281 Massimo Borchi/Archivio White Star.

CHICHÉN ITZÁ
Text by Davide Domenici

Bibliography
López A. A. and López L. L., *Mito y realidad de Zuyuá*. México 1999.
Nalda E. and others. *Gli ultimi regni maya, Corpus Precolombiano*, Milan 1998.
Piña Chan R., *Chichén Itzá: La ciudad de los brujos del agua*, México 1993.
Schele L. and Freidel D., *A Forest of Kings. The Untold Story of the Ancient Maya*, New York 1990. Italian trans. *Una foresta di re*. Milan 2000.
Sharer R. J., *The Ancient Maya*. Stanford 1994. Spanish trans. *La civilización maya*, México 1998.

Photo credits:
282 top Archivio White Star;
282-283 Archivio White Star;
283 top Archivio White Star;
283 left Archivio White Star;
283 right Bibliotèque De L'Homme/Bibliotèque Nazionale de Paris;
283 bottom Bibliotèque Nazionale De Paris;

284 left Massimo Borchi/Archivio White Star;
284 top right Henri Stierlin;
284 bottom right Henri Stierlin;
285 Massimo Borchi/Archivio White Star;
286 Massimo Borchi/Archivio White Star;
287 left Massimo Borchi/Archivio White Star;
287 top right Henri Stierlin;
287 bottom right Massimo Borchi/Archivio White Star;
288-289 Massimo Borchi/Archivio White Star;
289 left Massimo Borchi/Archivio White Star;
289 top right Massimo Borchi/Archivio White Star;
289 bottom right Massimo Borchi/Archivio White Star;
290 top left Massimo Borchi/Archivio White Star;
290 top right Massimo Borchi/Archivio White Star;
290 bottom J. Huber/Simephoto;
290-291 J. Huber/Simephoto;
292-293 Massimo Borchi/Archivio White Star;
293 top Massimo Borchi/Archivio White Star;
293 center Massimo Borchi/Archivio White Star;
293 bottom Massimo Borchi/Archivio White Star.

TIWANAKU
Text by Davide Domenici

Bibliography
Arellano J. L., "The New Cultural Contexts of Tiahuanaco," Isbell W. H. and McEwan G., eds. *Huari Administrative Structure: Prehistoric Monumental Architecture and State Government*, pp. 259-280, Washington 1991.
Browman D., "New Light on Andean Tiwanaku," *American Scientist*, n. 69, pp. 408-419, 1980.
Craig M. and Von Hagen A., *The Inka Empire and its Andean Origins*, New York 1993.
Kolata A. L., *The Tiwanaku: Portrait of an Andean Civilization*, Cambridge-Oxford 1993.
Ponce Sanginés C., *Tiwanaku: Espacio, tiempo y cultura*. La Paz: Academia Nacional de Ciéncias de Bolivia, 1972.
Von Hagen A. and Craig M., *The Cities of the Ancient Andes*, London 1998.

Photo credits:
294 top National Geographic;
294 bottom Henri Stierlin;
295 Antonio Attini/Archivio White Star;
296-297 Antonio Attini/Archivio White Star;
297 top Antonio Attini/Archivio White Star;
297 bottom Antonio Attini/Archivio White Star;
298-299 Antonio Attini/Archivio White Star;
299 top Antonio Attini/Archivio White Star;
299 bottom Antonio Attini/Archivio White Star.

CHAN CHAN
Text by Davide Domenici

Bibliography
Day K. C., "Urban Planning at Chan Chan, Perú," Ucko, P.J., Tringham, R., Dimbleby G.W., eds. *Man, Settlement and Urbanism*, pp. 927-930, London 1972.
Klymyshyn A. M. U., "The Development of Chimú Administration in Chan Chan," Haas, J., Pozorsky, S., Pozorsky, T., eds. *The Origins and Development of the Andean State*, pp. 97-110. Cambridge 1987.
Moseley M. E. and Day K. C., *Chan Chan, Andean Desert City*, Albuquerque 1982.
Moseley M. E. and Cordy-Collins A. *The Northern Dynasties: Kingship and Statecraft in Chimor*, Washington, D.C. 1990.
Ravines R., ed. *Chan Chan metrópoli chimú*, Lima 1980.

Photo credits
300 bottom left Massimo Borchi/Archivio White Star;
300 bottom right Massimo Borchi/Archivio White Star;
300-301 Henri Stierlin;
302 center Massimo Borchi/Archivio White Star;
302-303 Massimo Borchi/Archivio White Star;
303 top right Henri Stierlin;
303 bottom right Massimo Borchi/Archivio White Star;
304 top ICP;
304 bottom Henri Stierlin;
304-305 Charles Lénars.

MACHU PICCHU
Text by Davide Domenici

Bibliography
Angles Vargas V., *Machupijchu*, Lima 1972.
Bingham H., *Machu Picchu*, Yale-Oxford 1930.
Craig M. and Von Hagen A., *The Inka Empire and its Andean Origins*, New York 1993.
Gasparini G. and Margolies L., *Inca Architecture*, Bloomington 1980.
Hyslop J., *Inka Settlement Planning*, Austin 1990.
Kauffmann Doig F., *Manual de arqueología peruana*, Lima 1983.
Ligabue G., ed. *Perú*, 2 vols. (Italian trans.) Venice 1993.
Protzen J., "Architettura Inca," Laurencich Minelli L., ed. *I regni preincaici e il mondo inca, Corpus Precolombiano*, pp. 193-218, Milan 1992.
Von Hagen A. and Craig M., *The Cities of the Ancient Andes*, London 1998.

Photo credits:
306/307 National Geographic;
306 bottom National Geographic;
307 bottom National Geographic;
308 top left Antonio Attini/Archivio White Star;
308 top right Antonio Attini/Archivio White Star;
308 bottom Antonio Attini/Archivio White Star;
308-309 Antonio Attini/Archivio White Star;
310 bottom Antonio Attini/Archivio White Star;
310-311 Antonio Attini/Archivio White Star;
312 top right Antonio Attini/Archivio White Star;
312 bottom right Antonio Attini/Archivio White Star;
312 left Antonio Attini/Archivio White Star;
313 Antonio Attini/Archivio White Star.

The maps on pages 24, 99, 144, 210, and 246 are by Elisabetta Ferrero/Archivio White Star.
The drawings on pages 32-33, 54-55, 71-74, and 276-277 are by Monica Falcone and Roberta Vigone/Archivio White Star.
The maps on pages 70, 107, 109, 153, 159, 166, 207, 217, 223, 235, 242, 254, 269, 277, 287, 296 are by Michela Auricchio/Archivio White Star.
The maps on pages 33, 45, 52, 114, 122, 132, 140, 175, 184, 192, 198, 302, 310 are by Archivio White Star.